The Seeking

OTHER TITLES IN

The Northeastern Library of Black Literature

EDITED BY RICHARD YARBOROUGH

Erin Aubry Kaplan	*The Accidental Populist: Dispatches of a Black Journalista*
Albery Allson Whitman Ivy G. Wilson, ed.	*At the Dusk of Dawn: Selected Poetry and Prose of Albery Allson Whitman*
Frances Smith Foster, ed.	*Love and Marriage in Early African America*
Frank London Brown	*Trumbull Park*
Trey Ellis	*Platitudes*
Joanna Brooks and John Saillant, eds.	*"Face Zion Forward": First Writers of the Black Atlantic, 1785–1798*
John Edward Bruce	*The Black Sleuth*
Fran Ross	*Oreo*
Richard Wright	*The Long Dream* *Lawd Today* [unexpurgated]
John A. Williams	*Sons of Darkness, Sons of Light*
Clarence Major	*All-Night Visitors*
Ann Allan Shockley	*Loving Her*
Sterling A. Brown	*A Son's Return: Selected Essays*
Jessie Redmon Fauset	*The Chinaberry Tree*
Lloyd L. Brown	*Iron City*
Wallace Thurman	*Infants of the Spring*
Andrea Lee	*Sarah Phillips*
Claude McKay	*Home to Harlem*

For a complete list of books that are available in the series,
visit www.upne.com

WILL THOMAS

The Seeking

Introduction *by* DOROTHY CANFIELD FISHER

Edited, and with a New Introduction and Afterword,
by MARK J. MADIGAN *and* DAN GEDIMAN

Northeastern University Press
BOSTON

NORTHEASTERN UNIVERSITY PRESS

An imprint of University Press of New England

www.upne.com

Northeastern University Press edition © 2013
by the Estate of William Thomas
Originally published in 1953 by A. A. Wyn, Inc., New York
First Northeastern University Press edition 2013
Manufactured in the United States of America

For permission to reproduce any of the material in this book,
contact Permissions, University Press of New England,
One Court Street, Suite 250, Lebanon NH 03766;
or visit www.upne.com

Library of Congress Control Number: 2013941809
ISBN 978-1-55553-827-9

5 4 3 2 1

to Helen

CONTENTS

Introduction to the New Edition   ix

Introduction *by Dorothy Canfield Fisher*   xxxiii

THE SEEKING   1

Afterword to the New Edition   291

Acknowledgments   299

Appendix   301

Bibliography of Will Thomas   303

INTRODUCTION TO THE NEW EDITION

Mark J. Madigan

Sᴏᴍᴇ ᴡʀɪᴛᴇʀs, ᴀs ᴛʜᴇ sᴀʏɪɴɢ ɢᴏᴇs, need no introduction. Will Thomas is not one of those writers. Unless you are a specialist in African American or Vermont literature, you have probably never heard of him. The author of one novel, *God Is for White Folks* (1947), and an autobiography, *The Seeking* (1953), Thomas faded into obscurity soon after their publication. In this introduction you will find information on the life and literary career of an unduly forgotten writer. For the lifeblood of his story, I invite you to read *The Seeking*.

Born on November 19, 1900, in Kansas City, Missouri, the author's full name was William Madison Thomas, Jr.[1] His father was William Madison Thomas, Sr., a white man who is identified as an artist in *The Seeking*.[2] His mother was Anna Hopkins, an African American from New Orleans. When Thomas was an infant, his father died and his mother moved them to Chicago, where she was remarried to Howard B. Smith, a medical doctor. Her reason for moving, Thomas writes, was so that he could be raised in a city that was less racially prejudiced.[3] According to Thomas, his mother's assumption about the lack of racism in the city proved true, as he did not suffer racial discrimination in Chicago. Nonetheless, when he was twelve the family returned to Kansas City, where his stepfather opened a medical practice.[4]

Confirming his mother's fears, Thomas experienced the implications of racial difference in Kansas City. As racial epithets were directed at him by his white peers, he quickly learned his own racist retorts and eventually participated in a racial gang fight. Upon the latter, he reflected, "When that day began, I was but a boy. At its end I had become a *Negro* boy, and as such, for the first time, troubledly glimpsed walls which, like morning mists, arose between people different in something called race."[5] Little did he know the extent to which the "walls" of race would preoccupy his mind and trouble his soul from that day forward.

Thomas stayed in Kansas City until age eighteen, when he left to attend Lincoln University of Pennsylvania (his stepfather's alma mater). After his first year, he dropped out, claiming the historically African American institution seemed like an exercise in "self-chosen segregation."[6] For the next three years, Thomas lived an itinerant existence. He boxed professionally on the West Coast, worked on a salmon boat in Alaska, rode freight trains from Mexico City to San Francisco, and traveled the world seas as a merchant sailor. Upon returning to the United States, he attended the University of Kansas for two years, but quit one year shy of earning a diploma for reasons similar to why he left Lincoln University: he could not abide the racial segregation on campus and in Lawrence. His next move was to Kansas City to write for the *Kansas City Call,* an African American newspaper. Though he would spend over a decade working as a journalist for African American publications in Atlanta, Chicago, Houston, Memphis, New York, and elsewhere, his goal was to be a creative writer. As he explains, "newspaper work was supposed to be good training for one with ambitions as a writer of fiction; and regardless of what else I did, to be a writer, a novelist, was my real ambition. I considered that everything which happened to me was grist for that mill."[7]

Tiring of journalism, the peripatetic Thomas moved to Los Angeles in the late thirties, where he worked in advertising. He completed a novel manuscript during this period, but was unsuccessful selling it to a publisher. He was sure the reason was that the plot centered on an interracial love affair. Discouraged, he moved on to other literary projects, including writing for pulp magazines, ghostwriting a biography, and scriptwriting.[8] In Los Angeles, he met his future wife Helen Chappel, a reporter for the *California Eagle,* with whom he would have three children: Anne, William, and Bradley.

It was also in Los Angeles that Thomas met Chester Himes, the celebrated detective novelist. As Thomas recounts, the two writers became acquainted soon after their wives met in the early 1940s.[9] Thomas was encouraged to learn that Himes's racially-charged "protest novel," *If He Hollers Let Him Go,* was under contract to Doubleday Doran, a major publisher. Himes read Thomas's novel manuscript and liked it enough to give to an editor he knew, but no sale developed. Nevertheless, Himes's enthusiasm prompted Thomas to put his manuscript back into editorial circulation. It was eventually accepted by Creative Age Press, a small New York house that specialized in books on spiritual and psychic subjects, but also published general titles.

Thomas's contract called for his manuscript to be developed into a three-novel trilogy.[10] The first in the proposed series, provocatively titled *God Is for White Folks,* was published on September 23, 1947. The plot focuses on Beau Beauchamp, whose father is a white Louisiana plantation owner and deceased mother is an "octoroon" (a person of one-eighth African ancestry). Because he is of mixed race, Beauchamp is rejected by his father and disliked by the

darker-skinned workers on the plantation. He considers
suicide, but instead leaves with a well-meaning Yankee mill
owner, who gives him a job and convinces him to "pass" for
white in his new town. There, he falls in love with Elisse
Leseur, a young woman also identified as an "octoroon,"
who is aggressively pursued by a villainous white man,
Gaynor Brackens. Upon learning Beauchamp's true racial
heritage, Leseur requites his love. The remaining action of
the novel concerns the conflict between Beauchamp and
Brackens and the subsequent return of the protagonist
to his father's plantation with Leseur, to whom he is be-
trothed. Although the familial background of Beauchamp's
mother bears some resemblance to that of Thomas's own
mother (she, too, was from New Orleans and of one-eighth
African ancestry), he claimed the novel was based on "real
incidents" reported in the Louisiana press.[11]

God Is for White Folks received mixed reviews, and sales
appear to have been modest at best. Thomas thought the
book might have done better had it not been for the publication of Sinclair Lewis's *Kingsblood Royal,* another novel
on the theme of "passing" and racial identity, earlier in
1947.[12] The remainder of Thomas's contracted trilogy with
Creative Age was never realized, and by 1952 the publisher
was defunct. In 1950, *God Is for White Folks* was published
as a Signet paperback with a revised ending and new title,
Love Knows No Barriers. According to Thomas, this edition
sold over 400,000 copies in its first year.[13]

Prior to Creative Age's acceptance of *God Is for White
Folks,* a reader's report from another publisher nearly sent
Thomas into exile from the United States. The reader wrote,
"With proper revisions this would make a quite satisfactory
novel. It is certainly publishable. I would not press for our
doing it, however, because . . . I do not see a very promising
future for a writer who would probably continue to base
his writings upon Negro more than human situations and

problems."[14] Thomas found the differentiation between "Negro" situations and problems and "human" ones abhorrent. As he explains in *The Seeking,*

> Looking back, this episode probably marked the point at which I really gave up on my native land, for it occurred to me that my every major contact with life had been in one way or another spoiled by the poison of race prejudice of a kind against which it was impossible to defend.
>
> And I wondered sadly if *that* was a Negro situation, a purely Negro problem, completely unrelated to those who had created it, and therefore not a matter of interest to them or anyone else.[15]

Thomas thereafter resolved to move his family to Haiti, which was touted as a "paradise" in the popular press in the mid-forties. In 1946, the year he planned to emigrate, a *Time* magazine article presented an alluring view of life for American expatriates on the island republic: "On porches overlooking the improbable blue harbor of Port-au-Prince, the 200 or more members of the American colony in Haiti basked in a New World Majorca, living like nabobs on $300 a month, and comfortably on $150."[16] As enticingly as Haiti was portrayed, leaving his native soil did not prove to be easy. For all its faults, the United States was still his homeland, which when faced with abandoning, he realized he loved.[17] Consequently, instead of Haiti, he moved to Vermont.

Thomas could not entirely explain why he chose Vermont, but his decision to relocate there was informed by the state's historical opposition to slavery and its proximity to Canada.[18] He wanted to see if he could be "accepted or rejected according to how [he] proved up as an individual, a human being" in the Green Mountain State.[19] But acceptance by others was not all he sought. In the opening scene of *The Seeking*, Thomas, the one-time prizefighter, verbally spars with a group of men assembled on the steps of the Westford general store.[20] He is challenged by their questions about why he, an African American, chose to leave Los Angeles for "chilly ole Vermont."[21] The scene effectively dramatizes the profound internal conflict posed by the "double consciousness" that W. E. B. Du Bois famously described in *The Souls of Black Folk:* "One ever feels his two-ness,—an American, a Negro; two souls, two thoughts, two unreconciled strivings; two warring ideals in one dark body, whose dogged strength alone keeps it from being torn asunder."[22] Thomas wonders if he has made a mistake in moving to Vermont. Are his new neighbors' queries based on the racist assumption that African Americans prefer warm climates? Are they expressing a tacit animosity toward him for daring to move his family to their all-white community? Would his Vermont sojourn prove true the assertion in James Weldon Johnson's *The Autobiography of an Ex-Colored Man* that "Northern white people love the Negro in a sort of abstract way, as a race. . . . Yet, generally speaking they have no particular liking for individuals of the race"?[23] Or are the men merely curious and well-intentioned? The process of answering these questions is the main substance of Thomas's autobiography.

The genesis of *The Seeking* began with a letter Thomas wrote to the editor of the *Chicago Defender* in late 1948. Responding to a derogatory comment about Vermont by actress Faye Emerson Roosevelt, Thomas defended the state and its citizens. Because it adumbrates *The Seeking*'s main currents, his letter is quoted here in full:

> I read with interest Lillian Scott's fine story on Faye Emerson Roosevelt in your Nov. 27 issue. And while I applaud Miss Emerson's recognition of the dangers of racial bigotry, I deplore her little back-handed slap at Vermont.

My reference is to this paragraph:

Speaking of her early southern background, Miss Emerson said with a touch of irony, "I know the problem from that hand. I do not speak idly from Vermont."

No, Miss Emerson did not "speak idly from Vermont"—she spoke from Dixie and her implication was typical of Dixie double-talk which hotly insists that everything would be all right if the meddlesome, busybody damyankees would keep their big mouths shut, because they don't know what they are talking about, not having lived in the South. Let me remind Miss Emerson that one does not need live with a skunk to unfailingly recognize its powerful stench. Further, if as Miss Emerson was quoted as saying, "the greatest cancer in America is its race situation," then everybody, damyankees and damcrackers, too, had better shout loudly about it from all points, lest the lot of us perish.

I should also like to remind Miss Emerson that she has hardly earned the right to in any way impugn Vermont or Vermonters. This tiny state was born out of its indomitable will to freedom. It is one of the few Northern states where slavery was never permitted. Its underground railway convoyed thousands of escaped slaves to freedom. Countless of its sons fought and died in the Civil War because of their loathing of human slavery. And to this day many Vermonters, notably the famous and much loved author, Mrs. Dorothy Canfield Fisher, actively fight the good fight on our side. And the tradition of freedom still has vital meaning in Vermont, for here one is permitted to live without restriction because of race, a fact of which I do not speak idly since I am a Negro and I live here; and I have also lived in the South.

Let's have more of those who, according to lovely Faye Emerson, do "speak idly from Vermont."[24]

Thomas would indeed continue to speak—but not idly—from Vermont. The scourge of racism and his entreaty for American citizens to unite against it would be central to his autobiography. The integral role of individual liberty in the history and ethos of Vermont would be presented in the same spirited, colloquial prose as his letter, and the state's "much loved" author Dorothy Canfield Fisher would play an important part in the book's making. What there would not be is "double-talk" from Dixie, with which Thomas was well-familiar from his time in the South.

Thomas's first explicit reference to *The Seeking* is in an October 30, 1949, letter to Fisher. He wrote, "If I should get a contract to write this Vermont story, I know I can do an acceptable job, but it is going to be a most difficult thing, for, as you, better than many, can realize, its inherent complexities add to the problems intrinsic to any piece of serious writing."[25] The "inherent complexities" to which Thomas refers become clear as his narrative unfolds. Although *The Seeking* is an affirmation of Vermont, it is not an unblemished one. He calls attention to instances of anti-Semitism, bias against French Canadian Catholics, and racist behavior (born of ignorance, not malice), even as he enumerates the virtues of Vermonters.

In the same letter to Fisher, Thomas discloses that he initially considered co-authoring *The Seeking* with his wife. The idea was dropped, however, because she had "so much else to do." Thomas wrote, "I'm quite sorry about that, for I had hoped that we might do the thing together, just as we do practically everything else. But I am going to try to use as closely as possible her thinking and feeling about our experiences here."[26] Thomas fulfilled his pledge, as Helen Smith is a prominent figure in the autobiography. For her, the move to Vermont presented a formidable challenge. Having endured racial injustices in high school in Pennsylvania, she chose to attend Wilberforce University in Ohio, a historically African American school, and as Thomas writes, "Her dearest wish was to pursue a career in a solidly Negro community, with as little contact as possible with white people."[27] In her early days in Westford, she is skeptical of her new neighbors, and Thomas gives voice to her doubts about them. The salient question for Helen, like her husband, is whether the wounds inflicted by racism will be healed and suspicion of white people overcome against all odds in an all-white village in Vermont.

Thomas's rejection of racism and his work on *The Seeking* came in the wake of a major event in American literary history: the publication of Richard Wright's autobiography *Black Boy*. Aside from the narratives of former slaves, no text by an African American had presented such graphic first-person testimony of the effects of racial prejudice. A 1945 bestseller and Book-of-the Month Club main selection owing in large part to Dorothy Canfield Fisher's advocacy on the Committee of Selection, it confronted readers with the specter of American racism, just as Wright's novel *Native Son* did five years earlier. A comment by Helen Smith to her husband underscores the impact of Wright's novel: "You yourself have remarked that certain publishing taboos have been fading since Richard Wright's *Native Son* made such a big success."[28] Wright broke ground for Thomas and other writers who wanted to address racism candidly in their work. In *The Seeking,* Thomas does precisely that. From Kansas City to Chicago to Los Angeles and points in between, he documents the epithets, segregation, and sundry forms of discrimination to which he was subject. As he writes,

Eventually, inevitably, I learned that for me there would never be a maiden fair nor even the kinds of adventure which had so stirred my childish fancies.

I did not really understand why for a long, long time,

but only that all I read and dreamed was of another world into which I would not be allowed to enter.

Gradually the reason emerged: I was one of Uncle Tom's children, one of the dark ones, born to serve and to suffer, and to ever walk with head bowed and eyes cast down, in the shadows, forever doomed to humbly speak and forever to genuflect.[29]

In his autobiography, *The Quality of Hurt,* Chester Himes tells several provocative, if unverifiable, anecdotes that illustrate how anguished his friend Thomas was by racism. For example, in contrast to the rather subdued description of Thomas's daughter Anne's birth in *The Seeking,*[30] Himes asserts that Thomas was upset to the point of threatening the nurses with a gun: "Helen was in the public hospital when she gave birth to a white, blue-eyed, tow-headed baby girl, which amused the members of the staff so much, to Helen's great annoyance, that Bill went over to the hospital with his pistol and threatened to shoot the next person who made a snide crack about the baby's parentage."[31] Likewise, Himes's description of Thomas's relationship with his white neighbors is fraught with racial acrimony: "He knocked down a couple of white men on the street and the police came around to give him a warning. Some neighbors threw some milk bottles and trash onto his front porch one night, and if it hadn't been for Helen's pleas he would have shot up the neighborhood."[32] Lastly, as told by Himes, Thomas's exodus from Los Angeles is characterized by a distrust of white institutional authority and a flair for the absurd: "Bill got twenty-three thousand dollars in cash for his property, and there was some unpleasantness about the check given in payment. Bill wanted it cashed and the cashier of his bank said they didn't have that much cash on hand on Friday afternoon. Bill got the cashier of the bank on which it was drawn to intercede and his bank grudgingly paid him the twenty-three thousand dollars in old five-dollar bills, taking until eleven o'clock that night to count it, and he had to take it home in a Campbell's Soup carton. He kept it in that carton in the boot of his car all the way across the U.S.A."[33]

Thomas's inner-torment over racism is further illuminated by the memory of Lawrence Christon, a classmate of Thomas's daughter Anne at Brentwood High School on Long Island in the late 1950s. He recalls that on the night before he took Anne to her senior prom, Thomas drove to his house in a white neighborhood, parked in front of the house, and gave him twenty dollars for the date. Thomas then put the car in reverse and sped backwards down the street in the direction from which he came. At the time, Christon attributed the act to Thomas's "impetuous" temperament. However, he later surmised that Thomas's haste was due to his being an African American man driving in a white neighborhood after dark. According to Christon, "race was Bill's ulcer."[34]

It was not only racism that Thomas contended with as a writer. He also struggled to use writing as a means to help support his family.[35] As a result, he engaged in two alternative money-making activities: raising chickens, which he seems not to have minded very much, and writing pulp fiction, which he detested. The chickens he sold to the A&P supermarket in Burlington, the stories to magazines such as *True Romance* and *Argosy*.[36] He found the production of those formulaic tales, published under pseudonyms, to be demoralizing. To fellow Vermont author Bradford Smith, he complained of "the unbearably painful boil of having to scribble pulp against my desires."[37] To Dorothy Canfield Fisher, he wrote, "however trite the yarn, I have never been able to cease trying to put something good in them. . . . But even so, I can only do so much pulp before the mental gagging throws me."[38]

Lawrence Christon, again, provides insight into what Thomas hoped to accomplish as a writer, as opposed to the hack work he felt financially pressured to produce. As an aspiring writer in his teens, Christon sought advice from Thomas, whose "seriousness and intensity" about literature impressed him. Thomas emphasized that writing was difficult and said he would rather be in a fistfight than have to sit down and write. He also cautioned Christon that if he was to pursue a literary career, he would need "a camera running in his head full-time irrespective of experience, or even choice, which meant he had to accept a certain unscrupulousness in himself."[39] The writer's primary responsibility, Thomas posited, was to the work, regardless of whom it might upset.

Thomas illustrated his point about how a writer must pay close attention to detail with a memorable anecdote. While in a brothel in Seattle, he heard two prostitutes bet on which could make the other orgasm first, and then he watched as the two women performed oral sex on each other in a room lit by a single blue lightbulb. He told Christon he would never forget that one of the women was wearing a comb in her hair and, for just a moment, the comb was illuminated by the blue light in such a way that it became strikingly beautiful. For young Christon, this anecdote showed the way a writer sees things. He was impressed that what struck Thomas was the fleeting image of the comb in the blue light.[40] Such was the beauty Thomas sought to capture in his writing.

While he was never able to leave pulp work behind, writing *The Seeking* provided a respite. Nearing the end of the project, Thomas was assisted by Chester Himes, who visited him in Westford in late 1952.[41] Himes recalls, "He was rewriting his Vermont story of that time; he had finished it and the publisher had rejected it and he was trying to revise it as suggested, but he didn't agree with the editors. I settled down to help him, typing and proofreading simultaneously a couple of hours each morning before taking my hour's walk along the frozen country roads."[42] Thomas expressed his appreciation for Himes's help in a presentation copy of *The Seeking*, which bore this inscription: "In inscribing this copy of my book to you, I'd like to express my deep and sincere gratitude for your expert and generous help in its production. I hope you will not always have to be coming to my rescue as you did with my first book, and now, with this one. But anyway, thanks a million." That Himes was the godfather of Thomas's son Bradley is further evidence of their close friendship.[43]

The Seeking was published on May 29, 1953, by A. A. Wyn, the hardback book imprint of Aaron A. Wyn, owner of Ace Books, which specialized in genre paperbacks, and Ace Comics. On the front cover of the first edition is an artist's rendering of a New England village set in a landscape of rolling hills;[44] on the back is a photograph of the author at his writing desk with a picture of Franklin D. Roosevelt visible on the wall. Advertisements for the book featured a blurb from Nobel Prize-winning author Pearl Buck: "What a relief and a pleasure to read about one place in our country where an American Negro family can live as all Americans should live . . . We need Americans like these, people who in spite of bitter experience will try again, and then will share with us the joyful news that even in America they can live happily among white folks . . . I would like to see this book find many readers." The advertising copy emphasized the book's democratic theme in the midst of the Cold War: "An American Negro's moving and personal story of a search for democracy in his own land—and how he and his family found it in a small Vermont town." For his part, Thomas promoted *The Seeking* by reading an essay based upon his time in Vermont and the theme of "the birthright of human dignity" on Edward R. Murrow's popular *This I Believe* radio program.[45]

Thomas's autobiography was introduced by Dorothy Canfield Fisher. Their friendship dated to Thomas's early days in Vermont when he wrote to her for guidance on how to properly object to editorial revisions to *God Is for White Folks*. Fisher told him he might contest some of the changes, but that above all he should not jeopardize the publication of his first book. He took her advice, and friendly relations between the two ensued, as described in *The Seeking*.[46] While it is impossible to quantify her influence in number of books sold, having her imprimatur on *The Seeking* no doubt served Thomas well. As a best-selling author and a member of the Book-of-the-Month Club Committee of Selection from 1926–1951, Fisher was a well-known literary figure. She had already entered the discourse on African American civil rights in her introductions to Wright's *Native Son* and *Black Boy* and further asserted her credentials by noting her work on the Howard University Board of Trustees in her introduction to *The Seeking*. Known as "The First Lady of Vermont," Fisher's assurances that Thomas's book told the "multicolored truth of human life, with all its complex shadings" and made a "contribution of real value to American life" would have been trustworthy to both regional and national readers.[47]

Thomas hoped Fisher's association with the Book-of-the-Month Club would increase sales of his autobiography. On March 18, 1953, he wrote to fellow Vermont author Bradford Smith that Fisher was going to ask to review his forthcoming book for the *Book-of-the-Month Club News*.[48] Although she did not write the review, *The Seeking* was featured in that publication in the "Other New Books to Know About" section. Book-of-the-Month Club preliminary reader Jennifer Graham wrote, "If the injustices suffered by Americans of colored skin make you uneasy (and they should), read this account of what happened to a Negro family when they moved from California to Vermont to see if they could live free of discrimination. It's not a simple open-and-shut story with a Hollywood happy ending."[49]

Another potential way to sell books was through the U.S. Department of State. On October 2, 1950, Thomas wrote to Fisher, "I'm so glad you told me how *Black Boy* is being used. I'll manage somehow to escape that trap."[50] A letter to Bradford Smith dated April 7, 1951, explains the earlier reference. The "commies," Thomas wrote, had printed and distributed many copies of Wright's work in Europe in a campaign to discredit the United States. Fisher believed *The Seeking* could serve as an "antidote," he continued, and the State Department might be interested in having "a lot of copies" distributed abroad.[51] Unfortunately for Thomas, this State Department marketing gambit did not materialize. Even so, sales were strong enough to warrant a second printing in 1953.

Most reviews of *The Seeking* were positive. Bradford Smith delivered an unqualified endorsement in the *New York Herald Tribune Book Review.* He began, "Will Thomas has written a heartening and heart-warming book about his experience in Vermont, a narrative so skillfully ordered that it has the suspense and drama of a good novel." The tone, he wrote, was that of "good talk—informal, but disciplined with the random order of memory at work." He found Thomas's narrative flashbacks, in which "past and present support each other like themes in counterpoint," especially skillful. In closing, he alluded to how the issue of racism was being used against the United States in Cold War propaganda: "No one can read this book without feeling shame for the illogical and outmoded notions about race which still plague this nation and daily endanger our position of world leadership."[52] Elizabeth Yates, too, gave *The Seeking* an unequivocally positive review in the *Christian Science Monitor,* after reading it upon the recommendation of Dorothy Canfield Fisher. Yates emphasized the image of Vermont as a place where personal freedom was honored regardless of one's race: "Vermont has much to be proud of—its Constitution and its cows; its mountains and its maple sirup [sic]; but the tale that is told in 'The Seeking' is one of its proudest achievements. Proved by the people in one small community is the fact that democracy can be made to work for the good of all."[53] On the West Coast, a reviewer for the *San Francisco Chronicle* praised *The Seeking* as "a sharp commentary on the times we live in and the corrosion prejudice brings into the lives it touches" and "a vivid story of human relations." Fisher's call for Americans to contemplate the "dark shadow" of racism in the introduction was quoted as well. The review concluded that *The Seeking* "should help us understand ourselves better."[54]

The most notable negative review was Owen Dodson's in the *New Republic*. He praised Thomas for his "camera eye" and allowed that his Vermont sojourn was a story "well worth telling." Dodson faulted Thomas, though, for using clichés and stilted dialogue, and failing to exploit the dramatic potential of the incidents he describes. "These are hard things to say," he submitted, "about an autobiography that is obviously sincere."[55]

While *The Seeking* may not be a literary masterpiece, it is better than Dodson maintained. Thomas's bipartite autobiography is at turns endearing, prickly, humorous, poignant—and consistently engaging. Whether writing about the neighborhoods of his youth in Chicago and Kansas City, his career in the boxing ring, reporting for African American newspapers, the births of his three children, or daily life in Los Angeles during World War II (including a trenchant condemnation of the "relocation" of his Japanese American neighbors), Thomas brings an analytical mind, an appreciation for irony, and a novelist's eye for detail to his subject matter. In the second half of the book, he delivers a compelling account of his family's experience as the only nonwhite residents of a New England town at the middle of the twentieth century. In addition to its textual attributes, *The Seeking* occupies an important position in New England literary history: it is arguably the first long-form book written by an African American resident of Vermont.[56]

In a broader literary context, *The Seeking* claims a place in the mainstream African American autobiographical tradition. The text's primary concerns are the standards of the genre. Chief among them are the creation of identity and assertion of selfhood, the establishment of familial and community bonds, the pursuit of educational and vocational opportunities, and the development of strategies of resistance to both individual and institutional racial discrimination ranging from the act of writing to expatriation. Its form is that of the quest narrative, a structure central to African American autobiography since its inception in the mid-nineteenth century when former slaves wrote their life stories to aid the cause of abolition. Like those literary forebears, Thomas undertakes a journey in search of autonomy and the answer to an existential conundrum: how to live in a nation that espouses democratic principles in its constitution, yet denies civil rights to individuals based on race. Confronted with that puzzle, he poses the same disjunctive argument Frederick Douglass made so eloquently in his *The Narrative of the Life of Frederick Douglass, an American Slave* (1845): that one simply cannot hold racist beliefs that betray the nation's founding documents and be an honorable American at the same time.

While rhetorically aligned with Douglass, Thomas's conduct of daily of life shows him to have been pragmatically attuned to Booker T. Washington. In his autobiography *Up from Slavery* (1901), Washington argued that African Americans would attain civil rights and social integration as white people gradually came to recognize the benefits of their practical skills in the industrial and domestic arts.

He counseled patience and economic self-sufficiency in his program to uplift the race. In Westford, Thomas put Washington's advice into practice. Initially suspicious of racist intent when the white tradespeople of the village declined to help him rebuild a porch on his first home, he earned their respect when he completed the project on his own. When work needed to be done soon after he moved into his second house, those same people were eager to help as friends, not hired hands. For Thomas, their assistance was a revelation that integration into the community was not dependent upon race, but rather patience and an understanding of his neighbors' values.

With the ascendancy of the Black Power movement in the 1960s, moderate integrationist views like Thomas's fell out of favor. Autobiographies such as Malcolm X's *The Autobiography of Malcolm X* (1965) and Eldridge Cleaver's *Soul on Ice* (1968), which advocated black nationalism, Pan-Africanism, and Marxist political revolution, became bestsellers. With no political ideology to espouse other than an adherence to democratic principles, a bucolic setting, and an emphasis on the domestic sphere, *The Seeking* was rendered quaint in a turbulent era. Out of print and commercially nonviable as a candidate for literary resuscitation, Thomas's autobiography began its protracted descent into obscurity.

In March 1948, Will Thomas was profiled in an *Ebony* magazine article titled "Shangri-La in Vermont."[57] He could not have known then that his time in "Shangri-La" would come to an end shortly after the publication of *The Seeking*. Nor could he have known that that book would be his last. (For an account of Thomas's life in the years following *The Seeking,* see Dan Gediman's afterword.) Without a major publisher and with looming personal travails, Thomas never rose through the literary ranks. Yet in *The Seeking* he made a significant contribution to African American autobiography and the mid-twentieth century discussion of race in the United States. Now back in print sixty years after its first publication, *The Seeking* is positioned to contribute to that discussion once more. The problem of racism which frames Will Thomas's narrative is obviously not outdated. Nor is the work of those who struggle against such injustices. The "seeking"—for autonomy, fellowship, equal opportunity, freedom of expression, and self-identity—is not bound to any one historical moment. The simple title of Will Thomas's autobiography aptly describes not only his quest, but that of all people who refuse to accept less than the "birthright of human dignity."[58]

NOTES

1. In the 1910 U.S. Census, Anna Hopkins's son is listed as William Thomas. He subsequently adopted his stepfather's surname and in adult life was known as Bill Smith. The name Will Thomas is used in this essay, as is customary in scholarship on a literary work published under a pseudonym. For example, criticism of *The Adventures of Huckleberry Finn* generally uses the author's pseudonym Mark Twain, not his given name Samuel Clemens. Thomas is said to have published pulp fiction under a variety of as yet unidentified pseudonyms. He published articles in the *Chicago Defender* under the names Bill Smith, Billy Smith and Billy "K.C." Smith, William Smith, William T. Smith, and William Thomas Smith (see Bibliography).

2. Will Thomas, *The Seeking* (New York: A. A. Wyn, 1953), 38.

3. Ibid., 34.

4. Ibid.

5. Ibid., 51.

6. Ibid., 66.

7. Ibid., 73.

8. Ibid., 129–130.

9. Ibid., 121.

10. Ibid., 136.

11. Ibid., 138.

12. Will Thomas to Bradford Smith, [late August 1948], Bradford Smith Papers, Special Collections, Bailey/Howe Library, University of Vermont, Burlington.

13. Thomas, *The Seeking*, 287.

14. Ibid., 130.

15. Ibid., 131.

16. Anonymous, "Paradise 1946," *Time* 48, no.19 (November 4, 1946): 44.

17. Thomas, *The Seeking*, 142.

18. Ibid., 56–57.

19. Ibid., 10.

20. Thomas discusses his boxing career in *The Seeking*, 67–68. According to Lawrence Christon, Thomas fought on the West Coast as a welterweight under the name Stuff Smith. Lawrence Christon, in discussion with the author, January 21, 2011.

21. Thomas, *The Seeking*, 10.

22. W. E. B. Du Bois. *The Souls of Black Folk*. Introduction by John Edgar Wideman. (New York: Vintage Books/Library of America, 1990), 8–9.

23. James Weldon Johnson, "The Autobiography of an Ex-Colored Man," In *Writings*, Notes by William L. Andrews (New York: Library of America, 2004), 103–104.

24. Will Thomas, Letter to the Editor. *Chicago Defender* (December 18, 1948), 6.

25. Will Thomas to Dorothy Canfield Fisher, October 30, 1949, Dorothy Canfield Fisher Collection, Bailey/Howe Library, Special Collections, University of Vermont, Burlington.

26. Ibid.

27. Thomas, *The Seeking*, 135.

28. Ibid., 120. During one of his visits to Westford, Chester Himes house-hunted for Wright. Thomas's Westford neighbor Irene Allen wrote in a March 23, 1947 letter that Wright might come "next week." Irene Allen to Family, Irene Allen Papers, Special Collections, Bailey/Howe Library, University of Vermont, Burlington. In *The Several Lives of Chester Himes*, Edward Margolies and Michel Fabre provide these details about the proposed visit: "Himes knew that Wright in Greenwich Village was subject to neighborhood prejudice similar to what Smith had experienced in Los Angeles. In a note to Wright, Himes said that a fine house could be had north of Burlington for $7,000. He and a friend would even drive him there, if he were inter-

ested. Wright did consider it but then decided to move to France instead." Edward Margolies and Michel Fabre, eds., *The Several Lives of Chester Himes* (Jackson: University Press of Mississippi, 1997), 63.

29. Thomas, *The Seeking,* 19.

30. Ibid., 102–103.

31. Chester Himes, *The Quality of Hurt: The Early Years* (New York: Paragon House, 1972), 126.

32. Ibid., 127.

33. Ibid., 128.

34. Lawrence Christon, in discussion with the author, January 21, 2011. Christon was a staff writer for the *Los Angeles Times* from 1972 to 1995, specializing in theater and comedy criticism.

35. Thomas's wife Helen Smith also contributed to the family's income by working as a schoolteacher in Westford.

36. Bradley Smith, in discussion with the author, January 18, 2011.

37. Will Thomas to Bradford Smith, June 6, 1948, Bradford Smith Papers, Special Collections, Bailey/Howe Library, University of Vermont, Burlington.

38. Will Thomas to Dorothy Canfield Fisher, July 9, 1950, Dorothy Canfield Fisher Collection, Special Collections, Bailey/Howe Library, University of Vermont.

39. Lawrence Christon, in discussion with the author, January 21, 2011.

40. Ibid.

41. Other notable visitors to Thomas's Westford home included diplomat Ralph Bunche and sociologist Horace Cayton, Jr. Thomas writes with admiration for both in *The Seeking* (263–264, 235–239). According to Anne Smith, author Ralph Ellison also stayed with the family in Westford. Anne Smith, in discussion with the author, January 17, 2011.

42. Himes, *The Quality of Hurt,* 138–139.

43. Anne Smith, too, had a famous literary godparent: Zora Neale Hurston. In October 1941, Hurston inscribed a copy of her novel *Their Eyes Were Watching God* to Anne's paternal grandmother, Anna Hopkins, "a ray from the flame eternal." The book was apparently signed at a Zeta Phi Beta sorority event in honor of Hurston in New York City. Both Anne Smith's mother, Helen, and her grandmother belonged to the sorority.

44. The artwork is signed "Bruder." I have been unable to otherwise identify the artist.

45. Will Thomas, "The Birthright of Human Dignity," *This I Believe*, CBS, July 30, 1953.

46. Thomas, *The Seeking*, 184–187, 242–244.

47. Dorothy Canfield Fisher, "Introduction," *The Seeking*, xi.

48. Will Thomas to Bradford Smith, March 18, 1953, Bradford Smith Papers, Special Collections, Bailey/Howe Library, University of Vermont, Burlington. Smith was director of the Vermont Forums, which sponsored speakers to discuss controversial issues in communities across the state. Thomas describes his participation in a Vermont Forum on the topic of "Race Relations" in *The Seeking*, 227–228.

49. Jennifer Graham, "The Seeking," *Book-of-the-Month Club News* (July 1953): 10–11.

50. Will Thomas to Dorothy Canfield Fisher, October 2, 1950, Dorothy Canfield Fisher Papers, Special Collections, Bailey/Howe Library, University of Vermont, Burlington.

51. Will Thomas to Bradford Smith, April 7, 1951, Bradford Smith Papers, Special Collections, Bailey/Howe Library, University of Vermont, Burlington.

52. Bradford Smith, "Experiment in Democracy in a Northern Vermont Town," *New York Herald Tribune Book Review* (June 7, 1953): 3.

53. Elizabeth Yates, "To the Honor of Vermont," *Christian Science Monitor* (June 11, 1953): 11.

54. E. B., *San Francisco Chronicle* (August 23, 1953): 17.

55. Owen Dodson, "But Not Transformed," *The New Republic* 129 no.12 (July 27, 1953): 21.

56. My claim for *The Seeking* is based on its being a work of substantial length written by an African American residing in Vermont at the time of its publication. Lemuel Haynes, an African American minister, who lived in Rutland, Vermont, published many of his sermons and a narrative, *Mystery Developed; Or, Russell Colvin, (supposed to be Murdered,) in Full Life*, in 1820; the latter is his longest work at forty-eight pages. Thomas's admiration for Haynes is evident in his article "Vermont Man of God," published in the *Negro Digest* (July 1950): 14–18. The life of Jeffrey Brace, a former slave who lived in Poultney, Vermont, was first published in 1810, but he did not write it. Due to blindness, he narrated his story to an amanuensis. For further information on Brace, see *The Blind African Slave: Or Memoirs of Boyrereau Brinch, Nicknamed Jeffrey Brace*, edited and with an introduction by Kari J. Winter, Madison: University of Wisconsin Press, 2005.

57. [Era Bell Thompson,] "Shangri-La in Vermont," *Ebony* (March 1948): 48–51.

58. The phrase is taken from Thomas's essay for Edward R. Murrow's *This I Believe* radio program, in which he wrote, "I think the core of my earlier bitterness had been the conviction that I had been denied my birthright of human dignity." "The Birthright of Human Dignity," *This I Believe,* CBS, July 30, 1953. Published in *Edward R. Murrow's This I Believe: Selections from the 1950s Radio Series,* ed. Dan Gediman with John Gregory and Mary Jo Gediman, BookSurge Publishing, 2009: 156–158.

INTRODUCTION

Dorothy Canfield Fisher

Vermonters all proudly learn, as school children in their class-rooms, that our Constitution (adopted in 1777) was the first to forbid human slavery. Our primitive, eighteenth-century Vermont flag, with the seal of the state—the mountains, the shocks of grain, the pine tree and that oddly drawn cow—was the first to proclaim that wherever it was flown, no man, woman or child could be held as a slave. Because of this, most Vermonters have a special feeling about doing their share to help widen the freedom of Negroes. When a chance for such service falls into our personal lives, few of us can turn our backs on it.

So I was only following the example of earlier generations of my family from my great-grandmother on, when, rather late in my life, I accepted the honor of being one of the trustees of Howard University, the great national Negro university. I went regularly to trustees' meetings, till too many birthdays made these recurrent trips from Vermont to Washington physically impossible. From them, I always returned to Vermont, stimulated, inspired, downcast, uplifted, and thoroughly ashamed.

It was not the situation of the undergraduates which made me hang my head. To begin with, there were seven or eight

thousand of them, and such a number of vigorous, intelligent, vital youth rushing forward into life, enjoying each other
as only youth can, is a spectacle which quickens to cheer-
fulness the pulse of any older generationer, no matter what
the circumstances. Nor did the trustees' meetings arouse any
special feelings. They were wearyingly long, concerned with
the same old details of university administration which had
been familiar to me from my childhood, "faculty child" that
I am. It all sounded like what I had been brought up to in
a professor's family.

Mrs. Roosevelt, the great Mrs. F.D.R., was the other
woman among the trustees. Comparing notes once, we found
that we had the same impression:—during the first ten minutes of the meeting of a committee or of the trustees, or of a
faculty dinner-party, we were vaguely aware that it felt a
little odd to be the only white people present. But after that,
because the people with us were so entirely like others we
had worked with, we completely forgot any difference of
race, and when something reminded us of it, we were quite
startled and surprised.

I can never forget one occasion when this unawareness of
color let me into making a casual remark which, to the people around me, must have seemed of the most doltish un-
perceptiveness. It came vividly to mind as I took up this book
by Will Thomas, my fellow Vermonter.

Mrs. Roosevelt and I were not ignorant of the absurd,
ignominious (to white people) discriminations made in Washington—and everywhere else—against Howard University
faculty and students—and all other colored people. We knew
well enough that the most distinguished M.D. on the faculty
of the university medical school could not step into a Washington drugstore soda-fountain to get a drink of lemonade on
a hot day, but was obliged to tip any young white child hang-
ing around the door to go in and bring out the cool glass for
him to drink, standing on the sidewalk. Those were the days

when Marian Anderson was not permitted to sing in the
D.A.R. auditorium. Oh yes, we knew, well enough. And yet
we could forget—as my Vermont neighbors, Mr. and Mrs.
Thomas, say that here in Vermont they forget sometimes, the
surface item that they have darker complexions than their
friends and neighbors. We forgot at trustees' meetings, because the proceedings were so precisely like those at any trustees' meeting. And we forgot even more at genial social gath-
erings such as joint dinners of faculty and trustees.

Most of all it was impossible not to forget in the to-and-fro
personal talk of groups waiting in one of the handsome reception rooms of the university for a meal to be served; or in
front of the noble façade of the main building, waiting for
a taxi to appear. The unforgettable occasion which left me
so shamed and startled was one evening after dinner with
the faculty, as I stood with a group of professors having after-
dinner coffee. The talk turned on summer vacations. One of
the educators in the group asked another casually, "Dr. Lane,
where are you and your wife going this summer?"

"We've got our tickets to Jamaica, sailing June 23rd—same
place where we always go."

Somebody else said, "It's going to be Mexico for us this
summer, an inexpensive place that Professor Morris told us
about. We are saving up for our sabbatical, to spend it in
France."

Stirring the sugar in my coffee cup, I looked about me at
the group of distinguished professors so like the faculty folk
I had been brought up with—Ph.D.'s from Harvard and the
Sorbonne; M.D. specialists with international reputations in
the medical profession; chemists just back from a year's leave
of absence to serve their nation—our nation—in laboratory
atomic research; sociologists talking of a recent erudite book;
a dean back from a year's work with the Quakers in India.
Their very speech was like that of the professors I had always
known, with a careful choice of words; with the pleasantly

cosmopolitan, cultivated accent and intonation of much-travelled professional men. How could I incessantly bear in mind that they were of a different race?

I didn't. One of the deans remarked, "My wife and I think we'll try Brazil this vacation. My brother has a position in a bank there, and he'll find us a place to live."

I said—for the instant the words were passing my lips it seemed a natural remark, "Good gracious! What travellers you all are! Don't you ever spend a vacation in the United States?"

Silence fell on the group, so cold, so total, that all the cheerful talk and stir around us was blotted out. The dean to whom I had by chance addressed my remark looked straight at me. The others, silent, motionless, were looking down at their hands, or up at the ceiling. The dean said one word, said it in an equable, restrained, neutral voice. He said, "No."

I did not burst into tears of shame and sorrow. I was past sixty then, too old to weep in public. But still echoing in my ears I often hear in memory that "No" from a fellow American.

It echoed like a warning of danger when, some years ago—this book will tell you how many—I had a well-turned letter from a young woman of evident good breeding and education, who told me that she and her husband and their three little children had come to settle in a small town in the north of Vermont because they were Negroes. She wrote quietly that they wanted to make one last try to see if anywhere in their native land—my native land, too—they could bring up their American children without having their early years embittered by the incessant social discrimination made against all dark-skinned races by their fellow Americans. Put yourself in my place and you can see why I heard again that tragic "No," and why the cold sweat came out on my forehead. Would a small rural community in Vermont rise to this challenge? Would they recognize it as a challenge? Who could know beforehand? My hands were shaking in hope and fear as I laid the letter down.

You who read this book will know the answer to that question.

Mr. Thomas has managed the extremely difficult task of writing the story of his family's life in Vermont by the simple expedient of telling the truth. Not the black-and-white book-truth, but the multicolored truth of human life, with all its complex shadings. I like nothing about it more (and that is saying a good deal) than his unsparing criticism of occasional instances of anti-Semitism in Vermont. That is a brave, a fine, a disinterested act for a Negro to make, and it lifts the touching, simply and vividly told, intimate story of his personal life here, to a widely universal meaning, which is an inspiration to all those who profess and call themselves Americans.

With literary skill, honesty and intelligence, he has made this book a contribution of real value to American life, has given us all reason to feel intensely, both sorrow and comforted reassurance, and to think with all our brains about a dark shadow which now—as our nation is watched by all the world—hangs threateningly over that effort for human solidarity which is the one hope for survival we have—we men and women and our children and our grandchildren.

Part One

CHAPTER *one*

W HEN I SAW THE GROUP IDLING IN
front of the village store I began to wish I had chosen another time to make my purchases. Perhaps a dozen men were
there, some sitting on the store steps, some clustered nearby.
I was sure they were watching my approach, certain that I
was being discussed. My heart sank, for this could be a kind
of test, an unwelcome one.

Later I was going to start the three-hundred mile drive
down to New York, where on the morrow I would meet my
wife, Helen, and our children who were arriving by train
after a visit with my mother in Kansas City; and I knew my
wife's first question would be: "Well, how is it up there in
Vermont?"

I didn't know—yet. But I hoped I could reply, "It's a bit
too soon to really know. These things take a little time."

My wife would know I was stalling. I could foresee the
quizzical look which would come into her brown eyes and I
so much wanted to be able to honestly add, "But I'm sure
things are going to work out; I've no reason to believe otherwise."

But when I'd run the gantlet of those men in front of the
store, I feared I might.

Was I anticipating the worst? Old familiar tensions awak-

3

ened and I thought, "Oh Lord! Will it be like that even here?"

Perhaps that was not so much a thought as a prayer. But now there was no time for either, because I had rounded the Common and was nearing the store.

Although I managed a casual gait there certainly was nothing casual about my feelings, for I sensed the air of waiting about that Saturday morning knot of loungers, and was acutely aware of the abrupt silence which fell as I neared.

Even when I came within a few feet, they were but a blurred mass, those men, those strangers with white skins. I suppose I stared back, but I saw them not as individuals, perhaps because I might find in their faces confirmation of what I feared.

"Hi, Will," a voice greeted.

It was a blessedly familiar voice and made me feel less tense, for it belonged to the only villager I knew. We had become acquainted during the past week while arrangements were being made for me to buy his house.

"Hello, Wilse," I replied as I started up the store steps.

Another voice halted me. "Hey, Mister," it demanded, "how come you left sunny California for chilly ole Vermont?"

The speaker was elderly, his face tanned and seamed, his eyes shrewd, gray, and although his tone was not unfriendly, it was disturbing.

Pausing, I looked down to where he sat on the bottom step.

"Maybe," I told him, trying to match his unwavering glance, "maybe California isn't quite so sunny as it is cracked up to be."

"Well," another voice drawled, "Vermont sure as hell is as chilly as *she's* cracked up to be."

My glance shifted to the tall, spare, denim-clad man who had spoken in that dust-dry tone. His unsmiling blue eyes lanced into mine.

"So I've heard," I replied.

The bushy brows over the steely blue eyes lifted the merest trifle. "She drops down to thirty, thirty-five around here sometimes."

"Hell," announced a bearded little man in a slow, deep bass, "I've seen her forty below up on Bald Hill." As he spoke he eyed me closely, expectantly; and so, I was sure, did the others.

I got the idea, believed I knew what was in their minds: Negroes were supposed to be warm-weather creatures. They couldn't stand real cold. Therefore, what made me think I could?

"I've worked in better than forty-below weather," I remarked. "When I was a kid I worked in Maine lumber camps. Northern Maine, high in the mountains, near Rockwood."

A tingling scrap of silence, then:

"Reckon you like cold weather, hey?"

"Well," I said, "I sure missed it after living in California for so long."

"First time I remember hearing of anybody leavin' California for Vermont," a snow-thatched oldster twanged, peering up at me. "Usual, it's t'other way around. Only Vermonters, they mostly go down Floridy way to get thawed out."

An appreciative chuckle met this sally, but I failed to grasp its humor. So Vermonters went to Florida?

Florida: The South! . . . The South: Mobs, lynchings, raw, naked prejudice, violence, evil!

I glanced at the speaker. He was blue-eyed, too. My impression was that all these men had light eyes. I felt myself surrounded by them, and it was disturbing.

I dared not verify that impression. Instead I gazed up the middle of the Common to the rock-ledged slope, and beyond to the high-spired Congregational Church, gracious, sun-dappled and pale against the autumnal gold and scarlet of massed maples.

"California is beautiful," I said, "but I never saw anything like *that*, out there."

For a few seconds nobody said anything. It was the oldster who finally spoke. "It is," he admitted grudgingly, "right sightly."

"Kind of pretty after a snow, too," said another.

" 'Tain't too dern bad come spring, neither," somebody else remarked.

The oldster's brightened gaze came back to me. "Wuth comin' all th' way from California for?"

Beneath his mild tone I sensed dry frost. It was in the depths of his eyes, too.

I took a step or two toward the store door, pushed it half open, turned back and allowed my glance to drift over the group, meeting the eyes of its members squarely for the first time.

"Some things," I said slowly, deliberately, "are worth coming a long way for." I was aware of the note of challenge in my voice and I did not soften it as I added, "at least that is what I thought."

In the ensuing silence I entered the store and closed the door behind me.

Later, when grocery-laden, I emerged, the crowd was gone. I was glad, relieved, felt free to stand briefly on the store porch regarding the dozen or so houses of the village proper. A few lined the black-topped state highway which led into it. Several ringed the Common, among them the flat-faced, buff dwelling to which I now held title.

"I'm committed now," I thought. "I've bought that ugly little house. Oh, Lord!"

Slowly I walked back around the Common. I felt as if I was in enemy territory. The window panes of every house had a cold, hostile look. Behind them the enemy lurked, watching me. I shuddered. What a fool I'd been to believe, or even hope, that even in Vermont would I find what I sought.

I saw our brave dream fade, and I sickened with the conviction of having made a most serious blunder. We should have stuck to our original plan to emigrate, to seek a freer land, such as Haiti, Brazil, or Mexico, where race and color were not the inevitable and final determinants of status and opportunity. A number of people we knew had done that. Others planned to, and for the same general reasons as ours.

Sadly I wondered where now was the bright aura of hope with which Vermont had seemed endowed when we lived in Los Angeles; and I could not help thinking of the comfortable home we had enjoyed there. I remembered with a stab of regret the small cabin cruiser which, along with our home, we had sold to make possible our hegira. It seemed impossible that this sere countryside, rimmed by dark, dour hills and mountains, could ever replace the sparkling blue ocean we had so loved out West. We had traded that, and a pleasant life in a sunny land, for what?

That was something I didn't know on that cheerless October morning in 1946, but I feared it was not good.

When I turned into the graveled driveway of the house I'd bought the previous day, my heart sank. For one thing, my wife was not going to like it. The real estate catalogues over which we'd pored out West had given us definite ideas of the kind of property we meant to acquire: a country place, with some wooded land, and perhaps a brook. A house with a Colonial look—and a fireplace.

But what I had got was in the country all right, but was not even remotely Colonial. Instead of even a small, wooded area, it had one scrawny tree, and no fireplace. Nor did I then appreciate such virtues as it did have: modern plumbing, electricity, telephone and furnace.

The house originally had been square, like a box. Now dormers pouted sullenly from what had been the attic and formed two small bedrooms upstairs. An addition had been built onto the back, providing two more rooms downstairs, one the kitchen. Yet it was a sturdy house, in good repair, but not the kind of which we had dreamed.

Along with this house I'd bought enough of its furnishings to make do until ours arrived. So there was a kitchen table on which I could dump my groceries, a chair into which I could dispiritedly drop, dismally certain we'd torn up our lives to chase a chimera. Like the Children of Israel, we'd set forth to seek the Promised Land, only to find old Pharaoh there before us.

Later I found myself clumping restlessly through the nigh-empty rooms, wondering, as though just awakened from a dream, what I was doing in them, in this village, this state. I stared out of a window at the browning Common, a dreary sight. A tractor racketed down the hill, choosing the unpaved road on my side of the Common rather than the smooth macadam of the state highway, which curved around the other. The choice seemed deliberate, the reason obvious: the driver wanted a good look at the house "those people" had bought.

He certainly had a look, gaping so long he apparently forgot he was on a moving vehicle, and righted it only after its front wheels slammed into a culvert, almost unseating him. Even after he regained the road he glanced back several times.

I resented such raw curiosity, for I had noted how others, passing in cars, trucks, or afoot, also had slowed down to stare. I had read on their faces the same expression of morbid shock as gapers at the scene of a murder, an expression well remembered from my newspaper years. Had I not already suspected that our settling in the community was a kind of calamity to its residents, that bemused tractor driver would have made me believe that it was.

I tried to charge myself with prejudgment. But that did not help. I'd seen houses which had been fired or dynamited

to intimidate Negroes who had moved into white neighborhoods and I knew of many other incidents in Northern cities
in which unpleasant methods had been used to warn off
Negroes and others who had bought property in sections occupied by white Christians.

Thinking over such violent reactions, I wondered how I
could possibly have come to believe that in any state in America the situation would greatly differ. There would be no
violence here, I was sure. But there very probably would be
something, under present circumstances, almost as bad: the
"deep-freeze" treatment.

I kept remembering the oldster on the store steps who had
asked, "How come you left sunny California for chilly ole
Vermont?" And I was sure he meant, instead, "Why did you
come here?"

Why? "Well, Old Man, I'll try to tell you:

"I came here looking for something. I didn't just swap
climates. I was trying to swap people. In a swap, a man tries
to get something better, doesn't he? Well, I was trying to find
better people, such as the history of your state had led me to
believe I might find here. For on the record you are of a
fighting breed, Old Man. In the books you sounded great because what you fought for right from the start was Freedom.

"You see, I got a fine picture in my mind of your huge,
swaggering Ethan Allen and his doughty Green Mountain
Boys, and of the Underground Railroad by which Vermonters
helped hundreds of escaped slaves to Canada and freedom,
and of how you Vermonters had scrapped with redskins, red-
coats, New York State, the South, and anybody or anything
that stood between you and what you considered a man's nat-
ural-born rights to be.

"So, Old Man, I figured those are the kind of people I
would like to live among. I thought maybe their idea of the
natural rights of man was big and strong enough to include

*me and my family, or anyone at all who came seeking a brave,
free land.*

"*So, what about it, Old Man? Was I wrong?*"

And I fancied his reply:

"*Well, can't say as I rightly know. It's just that in these
here kind of things, it's maybe better, ain't it, for us all to
stay where we belong? To herd with our own kind? Now,
we are one kind of people, and you, another. So why do you
want to come barging in on us? Me, I wouldn't push in where
I wasn't wanted. Got too dern much pride. You don't want
me, I sure as hell don't want you. Leastways, that's how it ap-
pears to me. So why did you come?*"

To this I would say:

"*I tried to tell you why, Mister. But listen—I wouldn't have
come had I not believed there was at least a chance I'd be
accepted or rejected according to how I proved up as an individual, a fellow human being. Because I, too, have pride,
Old Man, too much pride to go where I am unwanted, and
especially if it is because of my race. As you put it, Mister, if
you don't want me, I don't want you. It is like that with me,
also.*"

That wasn't any good. Anger, resentment, they altered
nothing, damaged none but me. Besides, it was not my wish
to change things from what they were to what I had hoped,
or dreamed they might be. For if even in this supposedly lib-
eral state I was required to prove my mere humanity as a
prerequisite to residence, I might as well have remained in
California.

At that moment I wished I had, for I was sure I'd erred
seriously in thinking that in Vermont I would find what I
was seeking, which is something impossible to capture in one
word or a hundred, for it has many names and none conveys
exactly the same meaning to different people. Some call it

"brotherly love," which at least is of its essence. Others refer to it as "tolerance," which is not.

And I thought, "Oh, forget it. The thing is done. Make the best of it."

But—the thing was not done, not finished! At least it did not have to be. Because it was still possible to go to Haiti, as my wife and I had first planned.

CHAPTER *two*

I STARTED THINKING ABOUT HOW IT HAD happened. Certainly our decision to try Vermont was no impulsive act. My wife and I had agreed we no longer wished to remain in our own country. To implement our decision, we had sold our Los Angeles property. But instead of leaving the country as we had planned, here I was in a Vermont village I wished I'd never seen.

Being responsible for this, I was disgusted with myself. Because I was a Negro, and I was still in the United States of America, and I had but to add the two facts to get the answer —which had not changed and probably would not—not in my time. Yet, that is what most concerned me—my time, me, the flesh and blood creature which bore my lineaments, was alive, as capable of joy and suffering and love and hate as was any man.

Any *man?*

No! Because so long as I was on American soil, I would be a Negro male, not a man.

I'd come to believe that long ago, had dimly sensed where, as a Negro, I stood in the ranks of American citizens: at some distance behind the rear one.

Was that in childhood, in those first dozen years when I had lived in Chicago?

Chicago . . . Lake Michigan . . . The great stone lions which flanked the entrance to the Art Institute . . . The lofty tree which each Christmas appeared, as though by magic, in the fountain on Grand Boulevard, at Thirty-fifth Street, whose multicolored lights shone through the sheath of ice it wore. And my Aunt Dode and Uncle Frank, who lived on Dearborn Street, a shabby street forever filled with noise and movement whose poverty my child's eyes did not see. Instead, our block seemed quite wonderful.

Gramma Ravin, who lived next door, thought so too, and often said so.

I didn't know it then, but Gramma Ravin was saying one thing, but meaning much more. Her English wasn't up to making that clear, so what I gathered from her over-the-fence confabs with my Aunt Dode or Mrs. Manelli, her immediate neighbor, was that ours was a wonderful country, wonderful city, wonderful street. Only it came out "vunderfil." Vunderfil c-t. Vunderfil strit. *Vunderfil!*

I still think it was. Vividly alive, often raucous, and sometimes violent, it had undertones quite different. And there were always lots of exciting things to be heard and done and seen, like one morning, Gig Manelli, who was sixteen, hammering a chisel on the blade of a table knife, and you asked what he was making, and he laughed and said, "I'm making me a stiletto, Willy."

You wondered what a stiletto was until later you saw Gig whetting it, and saw it was only a table knife with a sharp point. But after Gig wrapped its handle in red and green raffia, it looked like a real dagger. And when you asked Gig what he was going to do with it, stab somebody? he said, "Sure, kid, that's what it's for, ain't it?" and you said, "Sure, stab 'em to death."

Later, he did: his sweetheart, Rosie, his rival, Pat. Their wriggling in the high weeds of a vacant lot betrayed them to Gig.

My mother, Anne, and I lived on the first floor of a narrow, three-storied red-brick house in the middle of the block. It was really Uncle Frank and Aunt Dode's apartment, but Aunt Dode and mother were sisters, so it was ours, too.

There was a large kitchen whose oak floor Aunt Dode scrubbed to spotless whiteness every day. And in the front room, the parlor, there was a small fireplace where, belly flat, I spent endless, spangled hours dreaming and where, before I was eight, I had read *Robinson Crusoe,* adventured in Sherwood Forest and, on the Hispaniola, sailed tropic seas to Treasure Island.

On our right, in a two-storied wooden house frizzy with scaling paint, lived the Goldfarbs: fat, blond Mr. Goldfarb, who owned the delicatessen on State Street and sold the wonderful dill pickles for a penny and long sweet, peppermint sticks to cram into the soft pickle hearts for another penny; and Mrs. Goldfarb, a thin, dark woman with lovely, sad eyes. At least they seemed sad whenever she looked at Gramma Ravin, her mother, who had come from somewhere away over the ocean because of something terrible called a *po-grom.* And of course there were Phil and Sauli. Phil was dark, like his mother, and Sauli, the younger, bright-haired and blue-eyed like his old man.

The Manellis lived on our left on the first floor of another two-storied frame house exactly like the Goldfarbs', except there was hardly any paint on it at all. Mr. Manelli made wine in the basement, and you could always smell it, and you could smell Mr. Manelli, too, if you got anywhere near him before he washed and changed clothes after he came home from working in the stockyards.

Mr. Manelli's sister, Gina, a chunky little bright-eyed woman, who couldn't speak much English, ran the Manelli household. She was very good to us kids and we didn't mind that she couldn't speak English, because we understood her all right, especially when she passed out richly spiced cookies, or wonderful little cakes which tasted as perfume smells.

On the second floor of that house dwelled the Donegans. Old Man Donegan dug sewers for the city, and Mrs. Done-. gan, a fat, red-faced, jolly woman, forever coming and going from and to early Mass, took care of the house and their children, Oliver and Mae.

Oliver and Phil Goldfarb were in my grade at school, and we three usually stood together on matters of mutual defense. Mae was twelve, much older than we; she had red-gold hair, dancing gray-green eyes, ravishing dimples, and I thought nobody, not even Elaine The Fair, could possibly be as pretty as she. She was my first love, but she never knew it.

Sometimes Mr. Goldfarb and Mr. Donegan, or Mr. Sam Johnson from across the street, would come and sit in our kitchen and drink beer from the square bucket filled at Domenick's saloon on State Street. In winter they would heat a poker and plunge it into the beer before they drank it.

That exciting rite made the foaming drink seem nectar and I begged so hard to taste it that one evening, when Aunt Dode and Mother were out, Uncle Frank gave me a sip. It was bitter and I spat it out. Uncle Frank and the others laughed. I couldn't imagine why they liked that nasty stuff so well. Not then.

My Uncle Frank was looked up to because he was a "Government Man" and went to work in his dress clothes. He was a clerk in the Dearborn Street Post Office. His was regarded as a good job, especially because post office workers, "Government Men," were never laid off when business got bad.

Uncle Frank, a light brown, quiet, slow-moving man, always good-humored, was a great one for lodges. He was quite splendid when he donned his *Knights of Pythias* regalia, which included a plumed hat and a sword in a scabbard which looked like gold.

My Aunt Dode, plump, motherly, with wise, smiling eyes, had a personality so warm and understanding that she attracted the troubled and beset of the neighborhood. She and my mother were hairdressers and regularly went, with their little black satchels, to attend the rich ladies of the "Gold Coast."

Among their regular clients were the girls of an exclusive French school. My Aunt Dode spoke fluent French, painfully learned through study at home and practice with these patronesses. She was also a pianist of some skill and often our apartment came alive with the music she made and with that which came out of the big horn of the phonograph. Her piano choices were mostly Beethoven and Chopin, but she liked opera best, particularly when sung by somebody named Caruso.

Some evenings she would play for us and relate the story of each piece, or about its composer. Beethoven she liked best, because, she said, he was a man of "color."

I didn't quite know how to visualize a man of color. I pictured him as a strange creature who was sometimes red, green, yellow, purple, or whatever.

Uncle Albert could never accept Beethoven as a man of color. "I've seen lots of pictures of Beethoven," he would say, "and he sure doesn't look like a man of color to *me*."

And Aunt Dode would reply, "But, Albert, Will, my father, often told me that in Germany everyone knew he was. And Will saw pictures and paintings of him, and over there in Beethoven's own country they were different from those we see here. They showed plainly his bushy hair and brown skin, Will said. And in the German books nobody made a secret of his ancestry."

But Uncle Albert would shake his head and grudgingly say, "Well, maybe so. Will sure wandered around over there in Europe enough to know what he was talking about. But just the same . . ."

Uncle Albert wasn't really a relative, but I liked him even better than I did Uncle Frank, my real uncle, because whenever he returned from his trips on the dining cars he always had something fine for me. He, my aunt and uncle were close friends and he had made his home with them for years.

Mother and Aunt Dode often discussed him. He was a dining car waiter. He'd never had a day's schooling, but he could quote practically anything Shakespeare ever wrote and he was an avid patron of light opera—the tenor, Chauncey Olcott, being his favorite star. His tastes, Aunt Dode said, were those of a rich, cultivated man. He wore expensive, conservative clothes and kept his person meticulously.

"The cleanest man I ever saw," my Aunt Dode said.

And she and Mother soberly agreed that he was in every respect a gentleman, even when he had drunk too much. That was Uncle Albert's one failing; "The Demon Rum," Aunt Dode called it.

Aunt Dode had the clear Indian color and features of my maternal grandmother and the large, expressive eyes of my pale-skinned grandfather, except her eyes were dark and his were light. I never saw him, only faded pictures of him.

My mother was milky-skinned, her hair soft, waving, brown with a reddish sheen. Aunt Molly, the other and eldest sister, who lived on the West Side with ruddy, plump Uncle Si, had a foreign look with her high coloring, shining black hair and slanting black eyes. Both she and Mother were fairer than many of our neighbors. Even Aunt Dode's clear brown color was no darker than that of some of them.

That may be why color variance did not impress me as creating differences between people. So it seemed perfectly natural that Pud Johnson, who lived across from us, should be pitch-black, and that Mae Donegan, my beloved, should have the coloring of a white rose, for we all played together and Pud was the best fighter and most popular boy in our block.

Nor did I find it strange that Ollie and Mae Donegan were always munching raw potatoes, or that Sauli and Phil often chewed slivers of dried salt herring between meals, or that Pud Johnson's ma, a large, dark woman with a big, booming laugh, frequently cooked chitterlings in her steamy kitchen, the only food I could not abide. But of Mrs. Johnson's fried yam pies I never got enough. So food, to me, was not an index to race, nor an indicator of nationality or religion or any other difference.

Because my widowed mother had to work and Aunt Dode chose to, since she and Uncle Frank were saving to buy their own home, I was often alone; and sometimes when dusk fell before my mother or aunt got home, I would be afraid; and lots of times when they did arrive, they'd find me next door, usually on the Goldfarbs' front porch, in the circle of one of Gramma Ravin's arms, my head cushioned on her capacious bosom, with Phil on the other side and Sauli, who was the littlest, snuggled on her wide lap, all of us lulled to delicious drowsiness by the lullaby she crooned. And I can still remember the strange, soothing melody of it, and some of its words:

> *Sluf, mine kind, mine trayst,*
> *mine shayner, sluf-zhe-ne-new . . .*

Sleep, my child. . . .

Truly ours *was* a wonderful street, and it was a street for dreaming the golden dreams such as sustain the lowly like a glimmer of heaven fleetingly glimpsed, a beacon of hope toward which we all groped and which we believed we could one day reach. And it was our common dream, the dream which had drawn some of us from places far away across the sea; from Malta, and Poland and Germany and Russia, and from Erin; and this dream had brought the Johnsons from the American Southland, just as it had drawn the fair-skinned widow, Anne Thomas, and her baby from Kansas City to the greater freedom of Chicago.

What was this great dream? For all of us, in one way or another, it was a vision of freedom—freedom from the most hurting things of life, of which mere poverty, the lack of enough bread and such things, was not always the most important. The most wanted freedom was that which would enable the achievement of our human birthright.

I had my part in the dreaming too, mayhap, but daydreams fired by the books I read so very early: *Treasure Island, Robinson Crusoe, The Swiss Family Robinson,* the Horatio Alger Series, and *The Three Musketeers.* Images of high adventure in faraway, exotic places, of golden treasure and of the clash of rapier and cutlass most often quickened my imagination.

Later I dreamed of knighthood, of bright armor and charging steeds and, of course, the fair maiden whom I always rescued and with whom I always lived happily forever and ever after.

Eventually, inevitably, I learned that for me there would never be a maiden fair, nor even the kinds of adventure which had so stirred my childish fancies.

I did not really understand why for a long, long time, but only that all I read and dreamed was of another world into which I would not be allowed to enter.

Gradually the reason emerged: I was one of Uncle Tom's children, one of the dark ones, born to serve and to suffer, and to ever walk with head bowed and eyes cast down, in the shadows, forever doomed to humbly speak and forever to genuflect.

Never for me the Lily Maid, nor jeweled nights in Samarkand, nor red-sailed barques on emerald seas—not even, any longer, in imagination.

But, I did not know that, then.

CHAPTER *three*

DELVING BACK INTO THOSE YESTERYEARS
was a pleasant excursion, and it required an effort to return
to reality. I was still in Vermont, no nearer to a decision
whether to remain or to give up the United States and go to
Haiti.

A large part of what worried me was the suspicion I'd paid
too much for our new house. Who would buy it? Would I
get anywhere near as much as I had put into it? I doubted it.

Then, too, selling the property might take a great deal of
time.

It was as if I heard the sly, vindictive laughter, the venge-
ful remarks which would be voiced once my plight became
known:

"That feller (probably an uglier word than *feller*) wants to
sell that house he just bought. Reckon he saw he wasn't
wanted."

"E-yah, so. I hear. Well, he might just have a mite of trouble selling her, hey! Leastways, at the price *he* paid."

"Naturally. But somebody'll take her off his hands. At the
right price, of course."

Well, I thought tiredly, somebody might come along who
would be willing to pay almost as much as I had. But meanwhile, Helen and our children were speeding East. Where

would they stay until I had sold the house? I certainly wouldn't want them around in such a hostile atmosphere while I tried to find a buyer. And what of our truckload of goods which was due to arrive soon?

When first we decided on Haiti, we had planned to sell most of our household goods. Now, wishing we had done so, I wondered how still we might without too much financial loss, too much inconvenience to my family.

Sudden remembrance of the long drive down to New York made me glance quickly at my watch. I was relieved to find it was only three-thirty. I did not plan to start until about eight or nine that night, but the day had so darkened that I had a strong feeling of late afternoon, despite what my watch told me.

That impression was strengthened when I glanced out of a window into a grayness which shrouded the hills, veiled the mountains above them. But I felt them there, those grim, dark peaks that were the flinty spine of this rock-cold land. What in the world had ever drawn me to it, anyway?

Inwardly I flinched, for there it was again, that tormenting question, still demanding an answer I had not found, mantling me in a despair I seemed unable to exorcise.

As though to break some spell, I shoved up stiffly from the chair where I'd slumped for hours, conscious now of how chill it was. Unbidden thought strayed across my mind, evoking pictures of palm trees, blue skies, sunshine over California. And I felt again the sad regret of parting from the little craft I'd so loved out there which I had christened *The Amazon* because she was strong, of welded steel throughout her thirty broad-beamed feet. What times we'd had together on the so-often unpeaceful waters of the great and warm Pacific!

Yet I had sold her, as I had our home, beset by some fevered dream now akin to a nightmare.

Again I became aware of how cold it was in this cheerless

Vermont house—my house. I shivered, thinking that here soon, icy winds would scream out of the North; and for endless, dreary months there would be only snow and cold. Morosely I decided that alone would be sufficient penalty for exile in this barren clime. Where now were my brave morning words of liking for the harsh New England winter?

I thought of making a fire in the furnace, but dismissed the idea. I would do nothing like that which implied my acceptance of this house or intention to keep it. I might have lighted the big cookstove in the kitchen, but it was an oil burner and I was in no mood to figure out how it worked.

So I shaved with cold water, ate cheerless cheese and crackers, drank a couple of glasses of sherry, then, hoping to sleep, I lay upon the living room divan beneath a couple of heavy car robes. But I was not to escape that easily, for sleep did not come. I kept thinking of Chicago and realized that the solution to our problem would not now be so elusive had I absorbed certain understandings about race as a part of my childhood learning; but until I was past twelve, I could not recall having the slightest notion of its real implications.

Living in Chicago at that time, in a neighborhood mainly of immigrants who had not yet learned prejudice toward Negroes from the white American-born, there was little to enlighten me.

In those days, the South Side was not bursting at its ghetto seams with Negroes as it did after World War I when thousands of them flooded up from the South.

Hence there was not yet a "Negro Problem," and our native-born showed more prejudice toward the "foreigners," meaning the immigrants, than toward Negroes.

Actually I cannot remember a single incident of those formative years which indicated that my race was regarded as inferior. Possibly one reason was that I was not made aware of the subject even at home.

Because my father had been an artist, my mother and my

aunt read into my childish drawings what was not really
there, and when I was eight I went each Saturday morning
to a beginner class at the Chicago Institute of Art.

That was always an enjoyable adventure, especially after
I was permitted to make the trip downtown alone. Soon I
learned where to get off the trolley car on lower Wabash
Avenue beneath the fearsome thunder of the "el" overhead.

There was an awesome thrill in the clangor and confusion
of the district, an even greater one in darting through the
heavy traffic of Michigan Boulevard.

Once safely across, there was the great gray bulk of the
Institute. I was always secretly proud that in my small way
I was a part of its life, and that, like the father I had not
known, I would become an artist and travel in strange, foreign lands and paint pictures of what I saw.

I don't think I learned very much in all the months I attended classes at the Institute. Perhaps had I gone longer I
might have. But once I revealed that I saw naked ladies
all the time in the life classes (where I had no business
being) my mother withdrew me.

However great my regret at not to be going to art classes
any longer, it vanished when Uncle Albert, just in from one
of his trips on the railroad, brought me a pair of real-looking
toy pistols.

Later that day, when he was going out for groceries,
Mother asked him to take me to the barber. He left me there
while he went "shopping." But he did not go to the grocery
store across the street as I had expected, but to Domenick's
saloon at the corner. I saw him enter the saloon as I climbed
up on the board across the arms of the barber's chair.

I had been constantly teased by the other boys because my
mother made me wear my hair in curls. So when Mr. Slocum
asked if it was to be the usual trim, on impulse I said no, I
wanted a real haircut, "Take off lots of hair." Mr. Slocum
laughed and his breath smelled like Uncle Albert's after he

had been to Domenick's. He asked whether that was what
my mother wanted and I told a big, fat lie and said sure it
was. He began to hum and snip at my hair and he did cut
off lots of it.

I knew my mother was going to give me why-for when I
got home with my cropped head and wanted to delay that
moment of reckoning; I hoped Uncle Albert wouldn't come
for me right away, and he didn't.

Mr. Slocum, a big, bald, tawny man, gave me some funny
papers to read while he shaved a customer and afterwards
said, "Willie, I'm going across the street to get your Uncle
Al. You take care of the shop until I come back, hey?"

"Sure," I said, pleased to be entrusted with such a responsibility.

At the door, Mr. Slocum called back, "If anybody comes,
tell them to stick around, I'll be back in a couple of minutes."

Several customers did come, and they stuck around much
longer than a couple of minutes, but Mr. Slocum didn't come
back, and after a while they left.

I read more funnies I found among the crumpled newspapers strewn around the place and soon it grew dark and
I began to get scared because I didn't know how to turn on
the lights. I wanted to go across to Domenick's to get Mr.
Slocum and make Uncle Albert leave before he got sick as
he always did when he stayed there too long. But I didn't
quite dare, for Mother and Aunt Dode were very strict about
my even going near such a place. Besides, I'd promised Mr.
Slocum I'd mind his shop.

Street lights blinked on and I saw Uncle Frank get off
a trolley at the corner and I yelled at him from the door, but
he didn't hear me because the trolley began moving again.
When it passed Uncle Frank was out of sight.

However, in a little while he came back, walking very fast,
which was strange for him. I ran to the curb and hollered
at him again but he didn't hear me that time either because

he hurried into Domenick's and I wondered whether he too was going to stay in there like Uncle Albert and Mr. Slocum.

I began to cry and I couldn't stop even when Mr. Gilligan strolled out of the police station at the corner a few doors away. He was a huge, red-faced man in a blue uniform with a long nightstick swinging from his right hand. He was striding toward me, his big shoes squeaking, and when he reached me I didn't dare say a word because he was a cop and I was afraid of cops; they arrested you and put you in jail.

Even so I was glad when he stopped and said in his rumbling, burry voice, "Well, if it isn't Willie O'Thomas, and what would you be doin' here, lad?"

I blubbered unintelligibly and Mr. Gilligan looked past me into the dark barbershop and asked, "Where's Slocum, lad?"

I pointed toward Domenick's, now aglow behind its curtained windows, and managed to tell him that my Uncle Albert was over there too.

"For how long?" he asked.

"A long time," I sobbed. "Almost all afternoon, I guess."

"Oh, hell!" he exclaimed, then banged the barbershop door shut and scooped me up in one terrible arm and my heart almost stopped. "We'll go get 'em out of there, hey, Willie?" he said, and somehow his voice made me stop being scared. All the way across the street I felt important to be up there so high in the arms of "the law."

Mr. Gilligan pushed right through the swinging doors of the saloon and we saw at once that Uncle Albert wasn't ready to leave, even though I could tell that he was very, very sick because his face had a funny look and his eyes were shut tight and he was gritting his teeth. On one side of him Mr. Slocum was laughing in a kind of silly way, and on the other Uncle Frank was tugging at his arm. But Uncle Albert was clinging to the bar and wouldn't let go.

Still holding me in one arm, Mr. Gilligan went up to the bar and took hold of Uncle Albert's shoulder and said in a tired voice, "All right, Al, you got enough; come on with me."

Uncle Albert tried to stand straight but if Mr. Gilligan and Uncle Frank hadn't held him he would have fallen flat on his face.

"Now you leave me alone, Officer," he said in a funny, blurry voice, "'cause I'm not in th' least 'tox-tox-*in*-tossicated, unnerstan'?"

"'Course you're not," Mr. Gilligan said, at the same time impelling Uncle Albert toward the door. "But you'll feel better for a bit of th' fresh air outdoors." As he left he said, "Slocum—go home. Or when I get back . . ."

Mr. Slocum said effusively, "Going, Mr. Gilligan! Going, going, gone. Yes sir!" And Domenick, the big, fat bartender, said, "I'll see he goes, Mike," and as the doors swung behind us, Mr. Gilligan said, like he was angry, "You'd damnsight better."

They had almost to carry Uncle Albert home and a familiar scene followed in which Aunt Dode, tears in her eyes, thanked Mr. Gilligan, then turned on Uncle Albert and rode him hard with sharp words, and Mother wept and said, "Poor Albert. Dode—don't fuss at him. Poor man, he can't help himself."

"Well, I'll help him!" Aunt Dode said fiercely. But all she ever did was fuss and shush Uncle Albert every time he mumbled, "'Pol'gize, Dode. Mos' humbly 'pol'gize," and with Uncle Frank's help, disrobe him and put him to bed and lock the door of his room so he couldn't get out and go back to the saloon.

So my haircut wasn't noticed until my bedtime, and then my mother didn't, as I had expected, punish me, but wept and said, "My baby, my baby!" and stuff like that and I felt very bad, very guilty, although I didn't in the least understand what made my mother act like that just because I'd had my hair cut short.

CHAPTER *four*

ALL THAT CAME BACK TO ME, BUT NO matter how deeply I probed into those childhood years, there was nothing which told me I had been liked, or disliked, because of my race; nor that I had liked, or not, for the same reason.

Gramma Ravin and the Goldfarbs, the Manellis, the Donegans, and the dark-brown Johnsons across the street—they were, so far as I could remember, the same in my eyes. Indeed the differences in their appearances, their customs, the manner in which they spoke, were what made them interesting and had no bearing on how I felt about them. All that had mattered was how they treated me, which in the case of the adults was invariably with kindness.

The kids didn't. We had block gangs and sometimes these merged into neighborhood gangs, and if you went past the boundaries of your block, or of your neighborhood, members of other gangs would paste you good and shag you back to your own borders.

But even in my own precincts the way was seldom smooth. My mother dressed me expensively, and certainly in a style not consonant with our neighborhood: white-linen shirts with flaring, starched collars, jackets with velveteen facings, kid or patent-leather pumps or sandals, and other such items which had upon kids the effect red is popularly believed to have on bulls.

My sweet mother hadn't understood why, when so garbed, I had hung around the house. At least not until she finally realized that each time she shooed me outdoors when I was "dressed up" I'd soon come tearing back, my fine clothes torn and dirty, and ofttimes with a bloody nose.

Even with my sartorial emancipation, there was but slight compromise in the matter of those darned curls, and they continued to embroil me with my fellows who jeered and yanked them and called me that most deadly of insults, "sissy."

But my dear Ma just could not seem to understand and alternated between believing the other kids were all bully-brutes, or that I deliberately got into fights.

Uncle Albert understood though, and one day, as he often did, took me with him to the railroad yards where he, as pantryman on his dining car, was in charge of stocking it for the trip that night.

But this time his purpose was more than to give me and perhaps himself the pleasure we found on such excursions, for he turned me over to a chunky dark young waiter, called "Killer," who was a former pugilist.

That day he wore a cotton singlet on his upper body—which revealed an astoundingly muscular torso—and I remained much too enchanted by its bulging sinews to pay really close attention to his attempts to instruct me in the art of fistic mayhem.

Killer got down on his knees to show me how it was done, but I kept making him flex his biceps so that they balled enormously. About all I remembered of his teaching was that if you stuck out your left when a guy came charging at you, he ran into it with his face, then you whopped him with your right. He illustrated this several times while doing a strange hopping, shuffling sort of jig, shooting out his left hand fearsomely indeed, then throwing his right in a short, terrible arc.

And he showed me how to make a proper fighting fist, how to keep the thumbs tucked down against the fingers so they wouldn't get hurt.

The very next morning came the chance to try that left-hand business, for, en route to the grocery, a nickel clutched in my palm for a half pint of coffee cream, Hymie and Ricky, a couple of my consistent tormentors, waylaid me at the alley and started yanking on my hair and teasing me about pulling down my britches to see if I was really a boy instead of a girl in boy's clothes.

In the scuffle I dropped my nickel and Hymie, an older, larger boy, scooped it up and ran. I chased him and leaped on his back and we went down. We both jumped up and Hymie ran at me and I stuck out my left as Killer had instructed and sure enough, Hymie ran into it with his nose and the blood spurted, and he howled like he had been killed. I picked up my five-cent piece which he had dropped and flew.

But even such a potent blow as the straight left could not protect me, and until the day when I deceived Mr. Slocum into shearing me nigh to baldness, my curly locks were forever getting me into trouble.

But it was curls, not race, which brought all that upon me.

Later, when Mother narrowed down the field of her numerous suitors to an Indian-looking young doctor from Baltimore, and married him, we lived with Aunt Molly in her fine big brownstone house on Prairie Avenue. The street had only recently been opened to others than Caucasians. For whatever reason, Aunt Molly and Uncle Si had left the West Side, and I was glad, for the Polish kids of that district were strictly tough and when I used to visit my foreign-looking aunt I kept within her backyard, or out front.

My stepfather, a handsome man of middle height, copper-skinned, with intensely black, deeply waving hair, was a graduate of Lincoln University in Pennsylvania, and of the Medical School of the University of Pennsylvania. The summer after he completed his internship he had worked as a dining car waiter to earn enough money to open an office.

I guess he didn't make enough, or else he spent too much of it on the honeymoon with my mother, for he went back to the dining cars after their return and continued that work for more than a year. Mother worked too, at her hairdressing, helping him save enough money for a start.

His being away on the road so much pleased me, because I didn't like him very well and I guess I showed it, for he was a stranger and I was becoming a big boy and understood things better. One of those understandings was that this man was replacing my real father, whose image my mother had implanted so vividly in my mind and in my heart.

We didn't live with Aunt Molly long, for soon my stepfather got an apartment on Rhodes Avenue, near Forty-Seventh Street. It too was several cuts above our old Dearborn Street neighborhood, but not half so much fun.

The new locality had advantages, though, the best being its proximity to Lake Michigan. What with my mother going out daily to her work, and my stepfather away most of the time on the dining cars, I could do just about as I pleased and summers I mostly pleased to go to the lake at every possible opportunity.

The Forty-Seventh Street beach, if it could be called that, was immediately behind the breakwater, a double row of deep-driven pilings chained together to contain the high-piled rocks which kept the waves from flooding back over the streets.

It wasn't much of a beach—bottle-strewn and untended— and the water behind the pilings was shallow. But with dozens of other youngsters I splashed in it and learned to swim by making the motions vigorously with my arms and one leg while I propelled myself with one foot against the sandy bottom.

When I stopped "mud paddling" and swam without the re-

assuring touch of the solid sand beneath that one foot, I graduated into the gang of the bigger boys who inhabited the
rocks atop the breakwater.

They were boys of every kind, including a few of dark
skin, and we swam and played and sometimes fought, but not
because of race or religion. In the summer we came to the
beach daily, and I learned to swim well, to dive deep, and
soon made my first long swim with the older boys to a light-
house perhaps a quarter mile offshore.

One day we were all indolently sprawled on the breakwater beneath a warm, bright sun when we saw a girl with
jet-black skin being carefully assisted over the jagged rocks
by a blond young giant who wore only torn dungarees, and
from whose hip pocket protruded the neck of a whisky bottle.

We watched, uttering low-voiced and obscene conjectures,
as the strangely assorted pair reached one of the fishing
shacks on the breakwater from which a small, winch-operated
seine extended. When they stumbled inside the shanty and
closed the door behind them we whooped and jeered, but
not too loudly.

Oh, we knew what was going on inside that shack, all
right; but we did not dare, as we urgently wished, to try and
peek between its rough boards actually to witness it, for we
were afraid. The big guy was dangerous. We had not only
seen him wham grown men so hard they fell down uncon-
scious, but some of us had felt his bare, hard toe in our be-
hinds when we had failed to keep our distance, or got fresh
in some other way.

But I cannot remember that the girl's blackness had particular significance. She was just another of the women
Whitey was always bringing out to his shack and what had
interested us most was that the lake wind kept blowing her
thin red cotton dress so that we glimpsed most of her lower
body, and she had what the bigger boys called "a swell

shape," and they spoke knowingly of what they would do
with her if they were in Whitey's place.

The only thing I can recall which might have given me
a clue to the shape of things to come was one winter afternoon when I was eight or nine, and Uncle Albert had taken
me to a performance of light opera full of wonderful music
and exciting duels, with swords that clanged and shone like
polished silver. Nor was the opera spoiled for me when the
antagonists kept right on singing while they fought, or,
mortally wounded, lay dying on the stage.

Afterward we stopped in a nearby *rathskeller*, which is
what Uncle Albert called it, but it was really only a basement saloon with lots of bright lights and paintings of almost
naked women on the walls.

The paintings didn't shock me, for I had seen real, live
naked women at the Art Institute. But I must have looked at
those saloon paintings pretty hard, because only when I heard
the crash of glass did I notice what Uncle Albert was doing at
the bar. When I saw the broken glass in front of him, I
thought he had dropped it or knocked it over, and I couldn't
understand why he was just standing there, exchanging cold,
angry looks with the bartender.

Then Uncle Albert said in a queer, tight voice, "I'd like
another drink, *if* you please."

The bartender poured it and left the glass at the back of
the bar. Uncle Albert slowly reached across and picked it up
and slowly drank and stood there for a few seconds just turning the glass in his hand, staring at the bartender.

I noticed it had gotten suddenly quiet and that the other
men had stopped drinking to watch Uncle Albert and the
bartender.

A sigh went up when Uncle Albert finally set down the
glass atop the bar. The bartender, his eyes pinned on Uncle
Albert's, picked up the glass, held it for a second, then
smashed it on the bar rail.

Uncle Albert put a bill on the bar and started to leave, but the bartender hissed, "I don't want your goddam money, coon," and Uncle Albert stopped, turned and said the only dirty word I'd ever heard him use. Then he went out, stiff-legged, his shoulders back, forgetting me so completely I had to dodge through a sea of adult legs to catch up with him; and although he took my hand, he didn't say anything and his face had a terrible frozen look.

Outside he flagged a Yellow Cab. It was the first time I'd ever been in a taxi; I felt proud and rich and the incident in the saloon was completely forgotten until decades later when, to explain and justify the present, I dredged deep into the past.

I do not know when, perhaps lulled by this second recollection of a not unhappy youth, I finally slept. My awakening was sudden. I was supposed to be in New York by morning to meet my wife and children. I feared I'd overslept, but a glance at my watch reassured me, for it was only eight-thirty. I'd make it down to the big city in plenty of time.

CHAPTER *five*

I T WAS CLEAR AND COLD, A GOOD NIGHT FOR driving. I thought how wonderful it was going to be to see Helen and the children again. They were always a part of my thoughts, my plans, for the freedom I wanted for myself, I wanted more for them.

It had been like that with my mother too. After my father's death she had moved to Chicago mainly to give me a chance to grow up in a less prejudiced atmosphere than existed in Kansas City.

But *my* plan had been to take our children to Haiti, a country where there would be no anti-Negro prejudice at all, since it belonged to colored people. Yet, I hadn't done it.

My mother had not completely carried out her plan for me, either. For when I was twelve we moved back to Kansas City, not because she wanted to, but because my Uncle Bill, himself a physician, kept urging my stepfather to come there and set up practice in his office, and that is what my stepfather did.

I, of course, knowing nothing yet of such things as prejudice and segregation, was enchanted with the city of my birth. We lived in a nice house all our own. Best of all, it was right across from Spring Valley Park, a lovely four-block expanse of greenery bisected by a valley in whose center was a little lake.

34

During my first week, while playing in the park with Jake, a new acquaintance, he called me a bad name and I hit him. We were the same age, but Jake was taller, heavier; and I was surprised and relieved when he backed away and began crying.

"What'd you hit me for?" he whimpered. "I didn't do you nothing."

"You did so," I charged vehemently. "You called me a dirty name."

"Why, I did not, neither," he yelped indignantly. "I never even *said* no dirty word."

"Oh yes you did," I insisted, advancing warily. "Just say it again, I dare you!"

"Did you two li'l boys have any words before you fell out?" That amused drawl came from my rear. I whirled and there was Mike, a grin on his heavy-featured brown face, his muscular arms akimbo.

Apparently encouraged by Mike's presence, Jake suddenly ran at me, but when I pivoted to face him, he stopped abruptly, his mouth working as he wailed, "I didn't do nothin' to him and he hit me when I wasn't even lookin'!"

Mike laughed. "Well, Jakie, you're lookin' now, ain'tcha? What's a matter, you chicken?"

I glared at Mike, wishing urgently that he wouldn't egg us on, for despite my show of belligerence I quaked inwardly. I did not really like to fight.

But I had been conditioned to it in Chicago. In those first years of my life the choice was of fighting almost daily, or of becoming one of those boys whom we scornfully called "yellow" and tormented unceasingly. Worse, cowardice brought exclusion from one's gang. In preference, one fought.

Members of different gangs challenged in various ways, but the favorite and the surest way of starting hostilities was name-calling. I cannot remember that we exercised much selectivity in the choice of epithets, especially we younger kids. All were merely fighting words to which we reacted indiscriminately. A Pastelino would bristle and start swinging if taunted as a "kike," as would a Findlebaum if called a "dago" and a Donegan if jeered at as a "nigger." I would fight at any name including wop, christ-killer, catlicker, harp, shine, or son-of-a-bitch.

Later, without doubt, all of us learned that those curses had personal application to various of us, but at the ages of seven to twelve we automatically struck out when *any* of those epithets were hurled at us.

And I had automatically struck tar-skinned Jake because he had called me one of those dirty names and his barefaced denial of it made his offense seem doubly heinous.

"Aw you're talkin' crazy, li'l ole nigger," he had jeered in response to some probably fabulous brag I'd made about my former home.

And so I had hit him instantly.

And now here was Mike, who was fifteen, with the shoulders of a young bull, who wanted us to continue the fight.

"Jake called me a nigger," I explained, "so I hit him."

Jake's blubbering clipped off, his mouth dropped open, his eyes bucked. Mike was staring too, his face tightening into a ferocious scowl.

My eyes darted back and forth between the two and panic gripped me, for obviously I had in some way committed a most serious breach, but I hadn't the faintest idea of what it was.

"Well," I mumbled defensively, "he *did* call me a nigger."

"Oh he did, did he?" Mike growled, advancing slowly.

I began backing away, bewildered, scared enough to wet my pants, because Mike was a "big boy," out of my class.

We were in a grassy tree-studded glade above the pretty little lake and home was a block and a half away. The ground rose sharply to our rear and so hid us from the adjacent street, making our seclusion complete, and terribly unnerving.

Mike began a bitter monologue as he followed me with short, stiff steps, his huge fists balled.

"So you think you ain't no nigger just 'cause you're lighter than somebody," he rasped. "Li'l yella nigger, you think you're cute just 'cause your father is a doctor. Just 'cause you come from Shee-caw-go. An' I'm 'ona beat th' livin'. . . ."

Jake catapulted into me then, arms flailing, and I went down, not from his wild blows, but because my feet had tangled as I tried to leap backward and sideways simultaneously.

Frantically I scrambled up only to see Mike rushing at me, right arm drawn back. My left hand shot out automatically. The impact of Mike's face against my fist jarred me to the elbow; and Mike, with a bellow, stopped for an instant and grabbed his face then hurtled at me again. I dodged and ran like a rabbit fleeing for its life.

I scurried up the hill, crashed through the hedge which bordered the park and dashed toward home; but didn't gain its sanctuary, for Mike pounded so close behind I dared not try to veer in my headlong flight when I zipped past my house.

At the far end of our block I had gained a little. I took the corner fast and gained a little more when I swerved into the alley in mid-block of that cross street. Our back gate resisted my frenzied efforts. I yanked at it, shook it, and a sore big toe later indicated I must have also kicked it. But it would not budge and the now winded Mike, jogging grimly toward me at a slow dog-trot, saw my difficulty and increased his pace alarmingly.

I abandoned the gate and leaped at the high wooden fence it conjoined. Mike thudded into it an instant later, grabbing for my feet. My frenzied lunge, when I jerked them up beyond his reach, toppled me off the fence, but happily into my own back yard. I was up and into my house via the back porch in nothing flat.

Mother, not I, discovered that in scrambling over the fence

I'd ripped not only my khaki shorts but also my hide. She was alarmed and angry. How had I damaged both clothing and skin? And why was I sobbing for breath? Had I been fighting again? She had thought it would be different in Kansas City, that I wouldn't eternally be coming home with my clothes and person shredded, scaring her half to death. *Had* I been fighting?

Well, not exactly, I told her. Just sort of playing rough, maybe, with some fellows. Gazing into her pale, troubled face I saw it was sick with concern. The impulse rose in my throat to tell her how it was—how it *really* was: how a fellow *had* to fight when called a dirty name like "nigger" or "son-of-a-bitch." And I wanted to ask her what *nigger* really meant —if it meant any different in Kansas City than it did in Chicago. Apparently it did. Maybe it meant something worse than it did in Chicago.

But I knew I mustn't, for then I would have to admit that I had been fighting, that *I* had started it; and my mother would not understand—would believe I was the real troublemaker.

Then her arms were around me, her face warm and wet against mine. Her voice broke a little when she told me that she knew I wasn't really a bad boy and she didn't mean to fuss; but that she loved me and didn't want me hurt, that she wanted me to grow up and be like my father and perhaps even follow his profession.

I hadn't thought about that for a long while, not since my year at the Art Institute when I was a little kid. My father was often in my thoughts, but remembrance of his profession had dimmed.

My father had been an artist—an oil painter, my mother reminded me. I had his name, "Will Madison Thomas," and was much like him in certain ways, only his conduct had always been gentlemanly, whereas mine—well, in that respect,

I was not like my father. He was not only a very talented
man, but had been fine and sweet and gentle.

I did not often see my mother in tears, nor had I ever
before felt the shudder of her sobs. Usually, it was the other
way around. It was desolating. It tore me to pieces inside,
and I began to cry too.

That night I did not as usual fall asleep the instant I got
into bed, but lay awake for quite a while, ten minutes perhaps. I vowed to be a better boy, to behave myself, to make
my mother proud by some day becoming a great painter. I
would paint pictures of the lake front in Chicago, and as
though it were before me, I saw the wet, rotting piles of the
breakwater, its great, rusted chains; and the dank, somehow
exciting smell of the backwaters was strong and real in my
nostrils and the lake beyond was blue and sparkling, tossed
with frothy whitecaps, and I clearly heard the thunder of the
surf and how it crashed against the pilings.

Yes, from now on I *would* be a better boy. I would not
worry my dear, my darling mother any more. She was a peach
and I—I was just an old rotten apple core, or something worth-
less like that. It would not be hard to start a new leaf by
sticking closer around home for a while.

Besides, Mike, or Jake, or others of that Michigan Hill
gang, surely would be after me. And I knew about gangs.
Maybe I'd have to duck Mike a long time, all summer perhaps. Because whether I had meant to or not I *had* hit him
a good one, right in the eye.

Of course, if I happened to encounter Jake again, well, he
was an ole 'fraidy cat anyway.

But Mike—

Well, I *was* going to be a better boy from now on.

CHAPTER *Six*

INSOFAR AS KEEPING CLOSE TO THE HOUSE was a part of the vow I'd made, I kept it. I still did not know what the neighborhood gang had against me, but evidently it was something pretty bad, for almost every time I ventured into the street boys would dart at me from behind trees or rise up from the weeds of a vacant lot and chase me home.

Often, as I lolled in the safety of our front porch, Mike, one eye blackened, would slow-drag by and silently shake his fist at me and make horrible faces.

Yes, I stayed quietly home in the interests of being a better boy—and perhaps a whole boy—dispiritedly re-reading *The Swiss Family Robinson*, or some old favorites from my tattered set of Alger. But mainly I passed the time dreaming of the day when older and bigger, I would beat up Mike and chase him a thousand miles.

I really didn't want to stay around the house though, for on those warm days of early summer the cool, green park, so temptingly near, called to me constantly.

I don't think either my stepfather or my mother noted anything amiss. He was busy most of the time setting up his office with Uncle Bill and she was busy, too, unpacking barrels of paper-wrapped dishes, trunks, crates, buying new furniture, getting our house in order.

Most evenings she and my stepfather went out, for there were many parties, dinners and dances in their honor, since Mother was a popular hometown girl returned and her new husband, a handsome "professional" man from the elite East.

I did not much mind being alone nights, for I'd grown used to it in Chicago, nor was I afraid, or lonely to the point where it hurt inside, as so often I had been in Chicago when I was a little boy.

There were things to do; I could plunk on the piano, or fry bacon and eggs for sandwiches and go unreproved if I filled the house with smoke and smell, for I usually managed to burn everything I tried to cook. There was also a new phonograph, and I could play beloved familiars like "The Glow Worm," "Humoresque," or "Poor Butterfly" if my mood was nostalgic. There were records by a gravel-throated man named Bert Williams which were very funny. And then there were books, lots of them, neatly arranged on shelves along one living-room wall; and among these I discovered many I'd never seen which had been my father's for they contained his signature. I checked every one until I had found all with his autograph and I arranged them together on the bottom shelf.

Somehow it seemed necessary to do that when I was alone, but I did not know exactly why. I still resented my stepfather, but to please my mother I hid that feeling as best I could; and perhaps I felt that any display of interest in my real father might in some way reveal what seemed best to conceal.

Often I tried to read some of my father's books. Ruskin, Thackeray, Shakespeare, Thoreau and such authors were beyond my comprehension. But Tennyson I read avidly, especially his *Idylls*, and was entranced by the sweetly flowing lines, even when their meanings were unclear, for to that music one could always provide meanings of his own. And I read my father's worn *Rubaiyat*, and felt blasé, believing I truly understood such lines as "The Moving Finger writes; and having writ, moves on . . ." for I *saw* that gigantic finger stirring letters into Time's sand.

But understood by me or not, I cherished those books, including the ones in German and French that had belonged to the father I never knew.

Such were some of the possibilities for filling those evenings when I was alone, although I cannot say I found them really satisfying, for often, beneath the corner street light, the neighborhood boys would gather and no matter how much I longed to, I dared not join them.

When my exile dragged into a second week I wished very much for it to end. Every day boys would straggle past our house en route to the park and threaten me in elaborate pantomime. I began to have hope, however, when they carried it to such lengths that I had to laugh, and so did they; and I thought maybe they did not hate me so much any more.

But Mike! His unforgiving glare made me squirm inside with fear; and the way he wiggled his big fists at me didn't make me feel good either.

At such times I'd stare back at him expressionlessly, but one day I snickered, because Mike had *another* black eye, a real beaut.

My amusement died when Mike, infuriated, recklessly charged across our lawn toward our porch. I had to move briskly indeed to get inside the house before he reached me.

After that I dared only a sly grin when he passed and Mike's piggy eyes, once again red and swollen, would flame and make me quake. I thought sadly I'd probably never be a member of the gang, and wished we'd move from the neighborhood. Or, better still, that Mike would.

However, the matter was nearer resolution than I knew, for one afternoon shortly afterward a tall, slender brown boy stopped in front of our house and called, "Hiya, Willie."

I knew him. He was Jess, leader of the gang; and I suspected his friendliness was a ruse, so contented myself with
a cautious, "Hi, Jess."

"Hey, how about coming on up to the park?" he invited
casually.

Silently I shook my head.

"Aw, heck," Jess laughed, "nobody's gonna bother you.
Come on, kid." He paused, adding in a lowered voice, "We're
gonna have a rock fight with the Pecks. They're tryna run us
outa the park. You game?"

Again I shook my head.

Jess climbed the terrace steps slowly, hands in hip pockets,
ragged cap back on his narrow head. I hopped up from the
porch swing and stood by the front door, my hand on it.

"Aw, I'm not tryna trick you, Willie," he assured me in his
soft, lazy voice while his greenish-brown eyes twinkled at
me. "I guess you don't trust me, hunh?"

He was right, but I dared not say so. I didn't need to, for
Jess laughed and said, "Never trust nobody, kid."

He had gotten to the porch steps and to my relief he
stopped there. "Hey, you like to play in the park, don'tcha?"
he asked.

"Sure."

"Well, them Pecks don't want us to, see? They think the
park belongs to them. So we're gonna show 'em it don't." He
paused, then chuckled. "Hey, Willie, you sure gave Mike a
shiner that time. What you hit him with?"

"Why—with my fist."

"I mean," Jess said patiently, "how?" His long left arm
flashed out and I jumped. He laughed and said, "Like that,
maybe?"

"Why, why, yes," I admitted, wondering how he had
known.

"A straight left will do it every time," he nodded approv-
ingly. "If you was only a little heavier and your arms was

a little longer, you could have cut that hunk of blubber to pieces with it."

Encouraged by his words I asked, "Who blacked his other eye?"

"Me," Jess grinned, holding up his left fist. "With this."

"Gosh," I said, awed. "Mike's a lot bigger than you."

"Ah, he ain't no trouble," Jess said negligently. He tapped his forehead with one long forefinger. "When you got it up here, Willie, you don't need so much of it here," he explained, touching his lean bicep. "So if *I* tell Mike to leave you alone, he'll do it, see? Because he knows I can knock him on his ass. So come on up to the park, Willie. We need *good* fighters today."

I hesitated, torn between the flattery and my fears.

Jess shrugged. "Willie, you're chicken," he said, starting away.

Had his tone been jeering I might have yielded to the suspicion which warned I must not go with him; but his words had been a sigh of disappointment with an overtone of surprise that I had not proved up. I ran after him.

"Hey, Jess, wait a sec. I'm—I'm coming!"

Jess paused and, turning, smiled and said quietly, "I knowed you was, Willie, because I can tell when a guy is chicken, and I didn't think you was."

He dropped an arm around my shoulder and we started up the street. As I matched steps with his I felt a fierce determination to prove to Jess—and to myself—that his confidence was not misplaced.

"I just didn't want Mike beating up on me," I said breathlessly, adding, "He's a lot bigger than me."

"Ah, forget him," Jess ordered. "He ain't gonna bother you, not when I tell him not to."

And my fear of Mike died.

We walked rapidly toward the park, and when we reached the corner Jess stopped and started hurriedly loading his pockets with chunks of rock from around the base of a newly installed light pole.

We were diagonally across from the entrance to the park and I gazed in that direction warily, thinking maybe I'd see one of the Pecks peeping from behind a bush and Jess said, "Hey, Willie!" He needed to say no more, for the sharpness of his tone set me to filling my own pockets with rocks.

Jess did not enter the park at its nearest point just across the street, but strode swiftly uphill on Woodland Avenue, which flanked it. In midblock he suddenly cut over to the other side and crawled beneath a mass of heavy shrubbery, with me so close behind I could see his dusty pink soles through the holes in his shoes.

We emerged just above the glade where I'd had the trouble with Jake and Mike. When we appeared, Jess was quickly surrounded by boys who popped out of the bushes, from behind trees, and dropped down from the lushly foliaged trees themselves.

One of them breathlessly pointed downhill toward the little lake. "There's some of them Pecks, Jess. An' more sneakin' in from over by the tennis courts."

"Well, don't wet your britches," Jess said. "Them Pecks ain't no trouble."

But they were! They were big trouble. There were a lot more of them than of us; and quite a few were big guys, fifteen or sixteen years old, and they had plenty of rocks; and, worse, some had air rifles.

It was my first glimpse of the Pecks and it stirred within me the same dread thrill soldiers must experience when first the enemy is sighted.

I remember wondering why the gang below was known as "The Pecks," but that trifling matter swept from my mind when Jess eased up from behind the bush where he had been studying the foe, grimly hefting a rock, shaking it around in his hand getting the feel of it.

There were perhaps eighteen of us, mostly shabbily dressed boys in our early teens. Our eyes were pinned on Jess; we imitated his venomous snarl and took courage from him because he was our leader, Chief of the Michigan Hill Gang.

I didn't know I'd been holding my breath until Jess seemed to coil and uncoil in one fluid motion before the rock whizzed from his hand. My heart leaped when in the center of the rival gang a husky blond youth reeled back, clutching his head. Jess's long throw had scored.

The members of the other gang froze, stared numbly at the boy who had been hit or fearfully gaped up to where we still remained hidden.

Then Jess threw again, scored another hit, and yelled, "Lettum have it, men!"

We did, furiously, wildly, whizzing a hail of stones down on the foe who broke and ran. Jess plunged downhill with a harsh, jubilant cry, and we poured after him, screaming, charging in for the kill.

The big blond boy, victim of Jess's unerring aim, blood trickling from a cut cheek, ran toward us rather than away. A few of his followers hesitated, then edged after him, and began returning our fire with stones of their own.

Jess raced straight toward the blond boy. Unable to check his speed on the slippery grass, he ran right into the boy's powerful swing and went down.

Even as he hit the ground and began rolling away from the blond boy's vicious kicks, Mike smashed into the enemy leader at knee level and flattened him.

Meanwhile, encouraged by their leader's prowess in felling ours, some of the Pecks swarmed back.

Despite my size and age, I was no amateur at this type of combat and I moved about cagily, circling to protect my rear, fending a wild thrust here, ducking a ferocious swing there, getting in a lick of my own when I could.

It became quickly evident that we had made a tactical error in attacking so impulsively, for we found ourselves almost surrounded as more and more Pecks joined the fray with wild whoops.

Jess, again on his feet, realized the situation, and even as a foe tumbled down from his blow, he yelled for a retreat— an order that some of our boys had not awaited. The rest of us rallied behind Jess, backing up the hill from which we had attacked. We would have been overwhelmed except for the restraining effect of Jess's deadly fire upon our pursuers.

But the blond boy wasn't deterred by it. He burst ahead and swung at Jess. This time, Jess had firm footing and he leaned away from the blow and I heard the *splat* his fist made against the blond boy's face. The boy staggered back, pawing wildly, trying to keep from going down. But he did go down and when he tried to get up he couldn't and we took advantage of the ensuing brief, shocked lull to further retreat.

We ran uphill, across our glade, through the thick, bushy hedge which marked the park boundary, and when we hit the street we were fairly flying. Most of our gang slashed through the tall weeds of the big vacant lot on the corner and kept going despite Jess's yells for them to stop.

I was right beside Jess and although I also wanted to keep going I stopped when he did and dropped down beside him in the weeds.

Mike, his thick chest heaving, dirty, sweaty face fiercely contorted, was the only other who stuck with Jess and we three lay flat on our bellies, peeking toward the park, waiting to see if the Pecks would follow us.

When they appeared, a shrieking pack of triumphant young savages with shirt-tails flying wildly, they jumped and danced and jeered, screaming invitations for us to return and fight again.

It was then I began to distinguish words, phrases, in the jumbled din the enemy was making, such as "goddam black

sonsabitches," "scary-cat nigger bastards," but above all else
a shrilling chorus of "nigger-nigger-nigger-nigger."

Someone must have summoned the police, for a patrol car
came clanging up the street. Jess said softly, "Uh-uh!" The
Pecks broke and ran and we lay as still as death among the
weeds.

The police lumbered into the park after the Pecks, but soon
returned, red and sweating, and after looking up and down
the street, climbed back into their car and departed.

Jess released a whistling breath, stood up and said, "Come
on, men, let's get out of here."

We went, a disheveled trio, defeated but not downcast,
our faces cut and lumpy, Jess in the middle, Mike and I flanking him. There was a swagger in our unhurried pace, a de-
fiant set to our shoulders.

"Next time," Jess said, thinking aloud, "we gotta have more
men. I didn't think them Pecks would have so many." He
chuckled and gave Mike a hard shove. "Man, you sure
knocked the taste outa that big yella-haired Peck."

Mike clumsily caught his balance and his wide grin showed
how pleased he was by Jess's praise. "Well, you touched him
up lightly and po-litely yourself," he replied, "an'," he added,
patting my shoulder, "this here li'l ole yella nigger didn't do
so bad, neither."

A flush of pleasure warmed me and I knew I should let well
enough alone and I meant to, but the words came out any-
how and they were, "Don't go calling me any dirty names,
Mike."

Mike stopped, hands on hips, his grin fading into an angry
glower. "Who called you a dirty name?" he demanded. "Are
you crazy? Here I try to say something good about you and
you-you. . . ." He took a step toward me, fists balled, and I
backed away. Jess stepped between us and shoved Mike back.

"What dirty name you talkin' about, Willie?" Jess asked,
regarding me curiously.

"Well, he called me a *nigger*," I said, trying for truculence and managing only a low mumble.

"Well, if you ain't a nigger, what are you?" Jess didn't sound angry at all, just puzzled.

Mike tried to edge around Jess to get at me, but Jess said casually, "Let him alone, Mike," and Mike stopped, but he was almost doing a jig of rage, and tears started at the corner of his eyes. His mouth shot out and he looked like a balloon on the verge of bursting.

"Looka here, Willie," Jess said quietly, "how come you don't like to be called 'nigger'? You don't think you are a Peck, do you?"

"Yah, he thinks he's a Peck," Mike yelped, half crying. "Thinks because he's light he's better'n us. I—"

"Shut up, Mike," Jess ordered gruffly. "Well, what about it, Willie?"

"Well," I said, fumbling to explain what I did not understand, "it is a bad word. You fight a guy that calls it to you."

"You fight a *white* guy that calls you that," Jess corrected. "You fight a Peck when he calls you that or 'darky' or 'coon' or 'Sambo' or 'snowball.'"

A dim light was dawning, a foggy understanding. I said, "Those guys we were fighting—they were all white? Is that why you call 'em 'Pecks'?"

"Well, gah-ah-ah-dam!" Mike exclaimed unbelievingly. "You tryna say you don't know what a Peck is—a Peckerwood? Where you been all your life, man?"

"Why—why, in Chicago," I said bewilderedly.

Jess laughed. "Hey, Willie, didn't you sure 'nough know what a Peck was?"

"I thought it was the name of a gang," I confessed, ashamed of what now seemed colossal ignorance, "like in Chicago. We called our gang the 'Dearborn Street Sluggers,' because we lived on Dearborn Street. But mostly we just called

ourselves 'The Dearborns.' So when you said we were going
to fight the Pecks, I just thought—"

Jess laughed. Mike whistled as though amazed. Jess
dropped an arm around my shoulders and said, "Willie, you
got a lot to learn." I tried to hold back the tears, but they came
and I began to blubber and Mike gave me a punch in the
back, not hard, and said, "Well, it ain't nothing to cry about,
Willie."

It was a good moment, but also one of confusion about
many matters still unclear. I gulped and scrubbed away my
tears and Jess and Mike sat down on the curbing, with me between them, and Jess put his arm around me again and gave
me a squeeze and said gruffly, "Everything's all right, Willie,"
and Mike said wonderingly, "So *that's* how come you popped
Jake that day in the park! I'll be doggoned. You *sure* got a lot
to learn, boy."

I began learning right then, and when my instructors had
finished that day's lesson, I knew that I should not hit a
member of "our race," or even resent his calling me "nigger"
or the like, for it was just a kidding way we had of using a
hated word.

But it still was not at all clear.

I learned many new, complex, and perplexing rules that
morning, among which were: that because my skin was fair
I must not refer to darker boys by *their* color, must not give
reason to make them think I thought myself better because
of my lightness. And that just because my stepfather was a
doctor, I'd better not act like that made me any better than
the other boys. Because packing-house laborers, Pullman
porters, cooks and maids and porters were just as good as anybody, including doctors.

Mike thawed completely during that strange session when
I was initiated into the society to which I had not known I
belonged, for I had not known it even existed: The Dark
Brotherhood.

When that day began, I was but a boy. At its end I had become a *Negro* boy, and as such, for the first time, troubledly glimpsed walls which, like morning mists, arose between people different in something called race.

In the end I still could not grasp all that, and all I *knew* was that I really hadn't thought myself better because my stepfather was a doctor, and certainly not because my skin was fairer than that of most of my new playmates; for I had not given a thought to my looks until then, except back in those tormented days when my mother had made me wear my hair in curls.

I also knew that the word *nigger* was not, as I had always thought, just one of the bad words which could be used indiscriminately. Even so I was still confused about it because it was all right for colored people to use it in reference to one another, yet it was wrong when white people used it in speaking to, or about us. But we did not use that word in reference to them, or to them even when we cursed them to their faces.

CHAPTER *seven*

SUCH WERE MY RECOLLECTIONS DURING
most of the time I was driving down to New York from
that Vermont village where I'd bought a house and so had
ended my home-hunting trip to New England. It was but
the second time I'd been away from my wife and children
even overnight, and as I paced impatiently amid the throng
in the vast Grand Central Station's waiting room the next
morning, I resolved that never again would we be separated.

I had arrived in New York sooner than I'd planned, creating a two-hour wait before the arrival of my family at eight
o'clock. I bought newspapers, but found no interest in them.
I tried playing an old game: observing the scene, speculat-
ing about those who caught my attention, trying to guess
what was beneath their public masks, and whether life for
them was tasteless, or tolerable, or possibly quite fine.

I soon ceased that. At that moment the only thing in the
world I was interested in was my family, and for some reason, possibly because I had long since fallen out of love with
Manhattan Isle, I was thankful we neither had to nor
wanted to live on it. And I thought how strange that this
great city, which for me, a writer, ought to have been Mecca,
was instead the Valley Hinnom.

By contrast, even the little Vermont village where we

would try to live seemed preferable. Possibly I'd peopled it with devils of my own making. But—had I? And bleakly I thought were I free to choose within my native land the section in which I'd really prefer to live, certainly it wouldn't be in austere New England, but rather somewhere in our warm Southland.

My imagination flitted over that sweet, drowsy land down there behind the sun. Again I beheld scenes of dreaming loveliness, moss-draped trees, dark bayous, sun-sheened lakes, rivers great and small twisting and singing toward the tropic Gulf.

It was another world, where time ran slow, giving the best to its own sad, grieving song, a harmony of mourning dove and nighttime weeping and high noon laughter, and of a wailing fiddle in a cabin doorway at dusk, and of a murmurous lament for a love and a life that never really was and could never be. It was like a hand at my throat.

But, alas, the South had a different, uglier side and it was not for me; nor, reminded a postcript thought, was the North, not really, nor anywhere in my native land.

To think that, to believe it, was saddening. I sighed and looked at the big station clock: half past seven. The thought that in only thirty minutes I'd see my dear ones again banished all disturbing thoughts.

And when at last they came I ran to them, heedless of the crowd, and swept my wife and my children into one vast embrace amid a joyous babble from us all, and when I kissed my wife both our faces were tear-wetted. Then I lofted and kissed each of our children, and when I put down the last one, Anne, she asked what I was crying about and I said I was not crying, my face was just raining a little because I was so very glad to see them all again.

We breakfasted in the station where, as usual, our fair-skinned youngsters, two with taffy manes, attracted some little attention from the other diners, but it was not of an unfriendly kind and for once we did not mind it at all.

Then we went to Brooklyn for an overnight visit with one of Helen's sisters, and when at last Helen and I were able to be alone, her first question was, "Well, Daddy, how is it up there in Vermont?"

I wished she had not put her question just then, but knowing the anxiety which was back of it, I said offhandedly, "Oh, I think maybe it is going to be all right," and I added, "Gosh, honey, you sure look fine."

Helen smiled. "Uh-huh," she drawled, "but right now I'm more interested in how *Vermont* looks."

"Wonderful," I said briskly. "Just now the trees—"

"Oh, hush," my wife bade. "You know quite well I wasn't asking about anything like that."

"Well, truthfully," I replied, "I'm not really sure yet. These things take a little time."

"Have you had any—trouble?" she asked quickly.

"No. Of course not. It's just—well, you know. Things not seen nor heard, but sensed. Maybe it's just that I was a stranger. I mean—"

"Uh-huh," my wife sighed. Then, brightening, she asked, "How about the house? Is it nice?"

"I guess it could be called that," I replied. "I don't mean it isn't essentially okay. It's quite modern: furnace, city plumbing, electricity—"

"Brick or frame?"

"Uh—frame."

"How many rooms?"

"Well—five. But the bath is quite nice and—"

"Has it a fireplace?"

"No fireplace, honey. Sorry."

Helen murmured sadly, "No fireplace. Not even that."

"Heck, I'll build one," I rashly promised. "Really, honey, the house isn't all *that* bad."

"I'm sure it isn't," she laughed. "Have you missed me—much?"

To my relief, there, at last, was a question which I could answer without the least equivocation.

I had not expected that Helen would like the Vermont scenery, but during the drive up from New York she found much to admire. The children were also much impressed, especially with their first close-up of real cows. They got a good one when, just beyond Bennington, we poked along interminably behind a large, unhurried herd being driven up the highway.

"Maybe we'll have one or two like those," I remarked.

"Oh yeah?" my wife drawled.

"Can you milk a cow, Daddy?" Anne asked eagerly from the rear seat.

"How do you milk a cow?" young Will demanded. "How many are we going to have? As many as all those ole cows in front of us?"

"Heaven forbid!" his mother exclaimed.

"Hey," I demanded, "what've you got against cows, anyway?"

"Well, one kicked me when I was a little girl."

"Did it hurt, Mother?" Anne inquired anxiously. "Where did it kick you at?"

"No, it really didn't hurt," Helen laughed, "and never mind whereat it kicked me. Anyway, it scared me half to death. So tell your daddy I'll have nothing to do with cows."

"Ah, you're just prejudiced," I charged. "Cows are gentle things."

"And how would you know?"

"Well, I've read a lot about them and—"

"And I've been kicked by one. If we do have any you'll take care of them."

"I'll milk 'em," little Will offered eagerly.

"So will I, Daddy," his sister seconded.

"Me too," Bradley, our youngest, chortled.

Helen said dryly, "Now that problem is solved; how about solving this one?" She nodded ahead, but even as she spoke the herd which blocked us was shunted off into a pasture by the herdsman.

As we drove along Helen began to ask about Vermont and why I hadn't looked at possible homes in other states.

"Truthfully," I confessed, "I didn't stop to look until I was in Vermont."

"Why not?"

"Oh, I guess I got to thinking about things. Like the way that cop in New York State shot and killed two of those three brothers, those young colored sailors last year."

"And for that you passed up the whole state?"

"Of course not. But after all—"

"What did you have against Connecticut?"

"Ah, prices and taxes are too high there."

"And Massachusetts?"

I shrugged, intent on negotiating another of the unending curves of the Vermont highway. "Oh, I really don't know, Helen. I mean, like New York and Connecticut; they had slavery there. And Sam got a pretty rugged deal."

"But didn't you once tell me Massachusetts had a Negro Governor?"

"Yes, and it's true even though our histories for the most part fail to mention it. But that was in Colonial times, under the British, and there were reasons for it strong enough to override the color bar. The guy was very rich."

" 'Fess up, now," Helen laughed. "You were decided upon Vermont right from the start, weren't you?"

I laughed too. "Maybe so. I hope I didn't back the wrong state."

"Well anyway," Helen observed, gazing out at the countryside, "I must admit Vermont certainly is a beautiful state. And just how far are we from home?"

"Less than a hundred miles now."

"Then we'll live at the northern end of the state?"

"Yes. Actually, we'll be very close to the Canadian border."

"Will, was proximity to Canada a factor in your choosing that location?"

"Could be."

"Still looking for big racial trouble, eh?"

"Not looking for it, no. But still not ruling it out, either. In times like these anything is possible. For instance, my impression is that the example of Hitler in the murder of six million Jews may not have equally horrified all Americans. A lot probably figure Hitler had the right idea. I've heard that feeling expressed more than once."

"So have I, Will, but goodness—"

"Look at it like this, Helen: over here, Jews are no serious problem, especially numerically. But *we* are. And in the kind of jungle the so-called civilized world is becoming, would you say it can't happen to *us* right here?"

"No, but—"

"I'm just adding it up. How many times in recent months have we read daily newspaper prognostications of possible widespread racial violence? If that sort of stuff is a reflection of how the white folks feel, who am I to say they are wrong?"

"I hope they are. God knows I do!"

"I hope so, too. But since we did elect to stick around in the U.S.A. I don't see the point in disregarding a single possibility which may affect us—not our race, but you and me and our children. *Us!*"

"An avenue of escape? A back door to Canada? Should we need it? Is that it?" she asked quietly.

"Yes."

"It does seem that with Hitler's example, so fresh, our

white folks would learn at least a little from it," my wife sighed.

"Maybe they did," I told her, "only not in the way we would like. Because at this very moment anti-Semitism in America is supposed to be at an all-time high. And that doesn't figure, except as an indicator, that a helluva lot of Peckerwoods think Hitler was on the beam, like I said before. Is it such a long jump to application of that idea to the dark brother? Is it?"

"I don't know, Will. I just don't know."

"Nor do I. But I do know the white folks probably don't like the idea of the gains *we've* made during the war years, and maybe they suspect we're not going to give up those gains as we did during the period after the First World War. Hence those predictions of trouble between the races. All that crap about 'Eleanor Clubs.' The way they malign Mrs. Roosevelt, simply because she's a grade A human being. The stories the dailies print about caches of arms we are supposed to have. It makes me sick."

"Oh dear!" Helen exclaimed. "Let's talk about something else." She glanced over her shoulder. "The kids are all asleep." Tenderly she added, "I wish you could see them. The boys have their heads pillowed on Anne's little lap and they're all snuggled up together, bless their hearts."

"It's been a long day for them."

Helen shifted to a more comfortable position. "I'm going to nap a little, if I can."

Except for the throb of the motor we sped in silence between pine-clad hills, nearer with each turn of the wheels to the real start of our adventure.

The day had been crisp, sunny. Now great splotches of late afternoon shadow lay athwart the twisting highway, and the soft blue haze on the hills was rapidly deepening to purple. Soon we'd be—home. *Home?*

I wondered if it would ever be home to us. And I thought

sadly that we would be approaching it with pleasurable anticipation instead of apprehension, if things were—different; if I
did not have substantial reasons for my feeling of invading
an alien and unfriendly land.

As twilight sifted down, lights glimmered in the infrequent
houses, and I thought about the people who lived in those
houses, their settled lives, secure status, their freedom from
the special fears and restraints and insecurities to which,
purely because of our race, we were inevitably subject.

Did they, I wondered, understand and appreciate what a
precious thing they had, even the poorest, the most lowly of
them? Probably they did not. Broodingly I thought that they
never would until they lost it. Then it would be too late. And
I thought, perhaps vengefully, the unique kind and degree
of personal freedom enjoyed by most white Americans was
taken as much for granted as the water they drank—and would
not be missed until the well ran dry.

Helen awakened just as we entered Vermont's "Queen
City," Burlington. The kids awoke too and for a short time
the car was filled with excited chatter.

They gradually quieted when, having passed through Burlington, we again were on the dark highway. And when, a
half hour later, we topped the rise which brought the few dim
lights of our village into view, they were asleep again.

"Well," I announced with false heartiness, "there it is,
honey. Our town, our journey's end."

"*Ah, wilderness,*" she sighed.

"Oh, come now," I chided. But I was thinking she was
right. It *was* a wilderness, only not in the way I thought she
had meant.

But I had misjudged her, for she replied, "I wasn't speaking of the woods and things like that, Will."

I wanted to make some light reply, but hadn't the heart.
Neither of us said anything during the few minutes before

we reached the house. After I'd stopped the car in the drive-way we got out and stood silently looking at the boxy little structure. I sensed something of my wife's feeling and took her in my arms and gently kissed her.

"Don't feel too badly, sweetheart," I begged. "We'll get a better house."

Helen said a little forlornly, "It isn't just the house, dear. It's—it's being away up here, away from everybody—everything . . . "

And then she wept. I held her close, knowing what she meant. "Maybe it won't be so bad," I said. "Anyway, we don't *have* to stay here, you know. We still can sell this place and get clear out of the U.S.A."

Helen pulled away and I gave her my handkerchief and she wiped her face. "I'd settle for Los Angeles right now," she sighed. "Why in the world did we ever leave there, anyway?"

"Because," I said gruffly, "your darn fool husband had a brainstorm, that's why. He——"

Helen put her hand against my lips and said, "*We*, not he, dear. Anyway, we're here. Let's get the children to bed in our—our house and—and stop worrying. Everything probably will be all right."

We got the children into the house and to bed, but I couldn't stop worrying; and I knew I wouldn't stop until I got the right answer: whether we *could* live with the dignity of full-fledged human beings in our own country; or whether we *could not*.

CHAPTER *eight*

Helen slept almost immediately we retired that first night in our Vermont house, but despite my own weariness, I never felt more awake. Thoughts of all kinds racketed through my mind, but the most clamorous were those which concerned the resurgence of doubt which had tormented me the day before my trip to New York to bring back my family.

I'd been so sure, when we were in California, that things were going to work out well for us in Vermont. Now I felt just the opposite. Why? From where had come the seeds of which my fear and suspicion were the bitter fruit?

I had at least determined that those seeds had not yet sprouted during those first years of my life in Chicago. Had the fertile soil of my young mind received them that memorable day in Kansas City when Jess and Mike had initiated me into the ranks of Negrohood?

Possibly, but not certainly. For while that experience had enlightened me in some ways, it had confused me worse in others. Then where *was* the point at which it all began, this bitter realization that the accident of birth had cast me in the role which for so long I had to play before I rebelled?

Possibly it had begun the year after we came to Kansas City, when, in the eighth grade, our class was required to learn by heart the *Declaration Of Independence*. Its grand phrases struck sparks of pride in my breast because I was an American and they made me sense some great, vague glory. We had no tyrant kings in *our* country. *We* held it as self-evident that *all* men were created equal and were endowed with certain *inalienable rights* by our Creator, among which were *life, liberty and the pursuit of happiness*.

That is what I was taught, and what I believed, then.

When, the next fall, I entered high school, it was a new world both educationally and socially. Soon I became really aware of the racial segregation which existed in Kansas City. I had known that white and Negro children attended different schools, but that previously had no special significance except perhaps as a local custom.

It was not only my youth which had until then prevented me from knowing segregation, it was also the isolation of living in a solidly Negro community beyond whose borders I had seldom found the need to venture. When I went to the movies, it was within those borders. If I wanted a soda, I got it from one of *our* stores.

But in high school my social horizon widened. High school boys sometimes squired their girls downtown to the Orpheum Theatre, where there was vaudeville. I did that too and at first took for granted the fact that we could sit only in one special section of the balcony.

Then one day I accompanied a schoolmate to a downtown store to buy a tennis racket, and while there I had to use a rest room. When I asked my friend if there was one in the store he said yes, but *we* were not allowed to use it.

"Why not?" I asked.

"Boy!" he exclaimed. "You know they don't let us use their toilets."

I hadn't known, but it didn't take me long to learn "they" didn't let "us" do a lot of things. I soon stopped expressing surprise, or resentment when I made such discoveries, for my

companions did not understand why I did so because that is
how it had always been for them.

That is why, I suppose, that when we studied how our
country came into being, and as a part of that learned about
the United States Constitution and its Amendments, I knew
something was very wrong somewhere. But our history teacher
never discussed the difference between what we were being
taught and the way things really were for *us*.

One day the subject came up between myself and a classmate who had recently come from Alabama, and he shocked
me by scoffing at the Constitution.

"Willy," he jeered, "Don't you *know* that thing ain't nothing but a lot of white folks' words they don't even believe
themselves?"

I asked, "How come, Peewee?"

Peewee laughed. "If you'd 'a come from where I come from
you wouldn't ask no fool question like that. Boy, down yonder
the white folks really got things fixed. Us colored can't vote
and better not even act like we want to. The white folks feel
like putting you in the jail house, they just up and do it
whether you done anything bad or not, it don't make *them*
no difference. An' the ole white judge feel like giving you four
hunnert years in the pen, he does it. And if you just even ac-
cidently bump into somebody, some *white* somebody, they beat
your head. And if them white folks think you done something against one of them, don't care if you didn't, boy! they
don't fool around with no court trial: they just hangs you up
to a tree and sets a bonfire under your behint—and sometimes
they cuts your privates out too."

Peewee had said all that in a laughing, bragging kind of
way, but I knew he wasn't kidding, and I guess the way I
felt showed because he laughed again and said, "Shucks, that
happens all the time down where I come from."

"Did you ever see them do that to anybody?" I demanded.

My classmate's face lost its laughing lines and the twinkle

natural to his dark eyes died, and he said, "Sure. I seen 'em. Leastways I did oncet. From away back amongst some trees and bresh I seen that big gang of white men whoopin' and hollerin' round a big old tree where they'd hung 'em a man."

He paused, remembering, then added in a subdued tone, "That's how come we moved up here, Willy. Because the man they lynched was my uncle. They done it because he went after some ole white man that had knocked up my cousin, Rowena, when she was oney thirteen."

That conversation was of an October afternoon in the carpentry shop, after class. Peewee and I stood by a work bench, ankle deep in wood shavings. As he talked I saw the black figure writhing in the noose, flames roaring up from beneath him and I shivered and grew sick as though an icy hand had touched my heart.

Was it from this the seeds dropped which in time germinated, cast out tiny root fibres? Or was another happening of that period responsible? I didn't know. Perhaps both had contributed.

I was christened in St. Augustine's, the Episcopal Church for Negroes in Kansas City, just before my mother took me to Chicago, when I was six months old.

When we returned to Kansas after my mother had married again, I served that church as altar boy until I was sixteen, then I was confirmed. What I remember most vividly of that ceremony is that at its most solemn moment, when the bishop sprinkled my brow with holy water, I was more conscious of his race than anything else and I wondered why a white man was administering this sacred rite.

Later I asked our rector about it. He was a tall, dark man, grave but kindly and I liked him very much, but of all he said in explanation as we sat in the cool quiet of the church sacristy that summer morning, the only thing which really registered was that a white bishop had conducted the rite because there were no Negro bishops of our faith.

Certainly he did not intend that to be the answer to what troubled me, but it was.

Possibly the effect of that incident might have worn off except that soon after, while poking through an old history book of my mother's, I read that the Episcopal Church had flourished in the South because it had condoned slavery.

And I thought, "No wonder there are no Negro Episcopal bishops."

From that day until many years later—until I went to Vermont, in fact—I did not again enter an Episcopal Church, or few of any other denomination, and then not to worship.

I made no issue of it. There was no one with whom I felt free to discuss it; and even though I knew I was shoving something very important out of my life, I could not bring myself to alter the course I had chosen.

It was but a step then to rejection of the whole idea of God, for having already had my attention focused on the segregation by races on a temporal level, I could not escape noting the same thing on a spiritual level.

Perhaps even then I might have escaped the morass of contradictions in which I was floundering had not my vague but growing resentment been fanned into a blaze by something I read in our local weekly newspaper.

As I brought the paper in with the rest of the mail one day during this disturbed period, my attention was caught by the head over a front page story:

NEGRO LYNCHED BY GEORGIA MOB

Perhaps I might have paid no attention to it had I not become so sensitive to things like that since Peewee had told me of his uncle's lynching. Doubtless similar stories had appeared regularly in the publication, but I had not previously noticed them.

I shrank from reading this lynching story, but I had to. A Negro sharecropper and his landlord had fought over shares of what had been raised and the Negro had fled. A possé with bloodhounds soon captured him, hanged him, riddled him with bullets, castrated him and set him afire.

They had also done all that to me. At least that is how I felt. And later I wrote:

They hanged John Brown to a sour-apple tree.
But did they castrate him, burn him?
And Patrick Henry cried, "Liberty or death!"
So that is what they gave him down there in Georgia,
That black man swinging from a fire-blackened tree:
Death?
They, with liberty, lynched him.
Is that what liberty means?

I thought maybe it did.

After graduating from high school, my folks planned for me to attend Lincoln University in Pennsylvania, and then study medicine at the University of Pennsylvania as had my stepfather.

I wanted to go to college, but not to a Negro institution, such as Lincoln; nor did I wish to become a physician.

But by then I had become very fond of my stepfather and did not want to offend him by objecting to the schools he attended or by revealing that I did not want to follow his profession. I was almost eighteen and felt strongly about racial inequities, which is why I shied from attending Lincoln University, for I saw it as self-chosen segregation. But for a year I did attend there, and it was a fine experience, except that I could not forget my original objection to it.

The following summer I got a job as a dining car waiter when I learned crews were being recruited in Kansas City for work on the West Coast. After making several trips out there, I quit. I didn't like the work and my fellow waiters thought

I was crazy because I didn't like being tipped by our white patrons and objected to being called "boy" by them and having them snap their fingers to get my attention.

Portland, Oregon, was the base for the runs for which I and others from Kansas City had been hired. At the hotel where the dining car waiters and Pullman porters were quartered during their layovers, I became acquainted with several professional boxers who also lived there.

My trailing around after them and watching them train at the gymnasium drew me to their attention. After I revealed that I had boxed a lot as an amateur back home and wanted to learn more about the game, four of them more or less adopted me, even to paying my hotel bills. They said they'd make a "pro" of me if I had what it took.

I did not tell these new friends I'd already made my debut as a professional. At least, without my parent's knowledge I had appeared in a bout at a fight club in Kansas City. I was doing all right too, in my match, when my stepfather invaded the ring during the first round and led me out by my ear.

But in Portland I could do as I chose, and I chose to try the prize ring. Why, I am not sure, except that I thought it important to be able to defend myself well, especially if attacked by whites.

So my pugilist friends started teaching me; in the process they batted me around pretty roughly to see if I could and would take it, and somehow I did, although many times I felt more like crying than fighting.

A few months later I made my start by scoring a first round knockout of a more experienced opponent. But I wasn't congratulated by my sponsors when I returned triumphantly to our dressing room, for I'd been instructed to box, as they had taught me, but after the first exchange of leather with my foe I'd stood and traded punches with him until he fell. My mentors said that I had just been lucky, and that rightfully I ought to have had my brains splattered over the ring.

I boxed for a year with some success, then had to give up the ring because of a split brow which threatened the sight of an eye. Ironically, the injury came not from a blow in the ring, but from having crashed into a metal stanchion while playing basketball with some school kids half my age.

CHAPTER *nine*

A FEW WEEKS AFTER I LOST THE DECISION
to the iron post, I left Portland and headed for Mexico. En
route I stopped briefly in Los Angeles. I don't remember being much impressed by that city, but I must have been, for
over the years it drew me back a number of times.

I'd been away from home a year and a half, and while I'd
written regularly to my mother, I knew she worried about
me. But stronger than my concern about that was the urge to
continue living on my own. I wanted very much to go to sea,
perhaps because of the books I'd read by Joseph Conrad and
others. But since Mexico was so near, I meant to visit it first.

To husband my funds I'd "beaten" my way on freight
trains to Los Angeles, and I continued to San Diego the same
way. By simply walking across the border into Tijuana I entered Mexico. Just to be on foreign soil was a thrill. And to
see so many faces ranging from dark brown to faintly tinted
bronze was an even greater one; and even though we were of
different countries and spoke a different language, I felt a
kinship with them, felt at ease, knowing the color of my skin
no longer mattered.

I'd had two years of Spanish in high school and another in
college, but at first there seemed no similarity between it and
the Mexican version. There was, I discovered, once my ears

became better attuned and I began to grasp the idiom. Almost at once I began to get a lot of help with the latter, and of a most delightful kind from the dark-eyed senoritas whom I met as I traveled at a leisurely pace toward Mexico City by truck, bus, wagon and ofttimes by foot.

When I reached that wonderful metropolis a couple of months later, I fancied myself a real *Mejicano*. By then my Spanish was much improved and I could express myself with some degree of fluency, although I still made mistakes.

I learned later that prowling about in a foreign land as I did, without papers could have caused me trouble with the authorities, but happily no situation ever developed requiring me to show a passport or any other identification; and when I re-entered the United States, I merely walked across the border, this time from Juarez into El Paso, Texas, without being questioned by either Mexican or American immigration officials.

In Mexico City I'd developed a friendship with a Mexican youth named Pato and we were going to San Francisco together where he said we could sign on for a season's work in a North Alaskan salmon cannery. He had done it before and I was all for it, not only because Alaska sounded interesting, but because the trip would be made in a sailing vessel.

Aside from being cast away in the middle of the New Mexican desert one broiling noon by a heartless brakeman from the fast freight we were riding, Pato and I reached 'Frisco without incident and signed up for the Alaska work.

The cannery to which we sailed on the *Admiral Flint*, a 750-ton three-master, was located at Ekuk on the coast of the Bering Sea. We were thirty-one days reaching it. Much of the time, especially as we neared the Aleutian Islands, the weather was tempestuous, but I enjoyed every minute of it, even when, having squeezed through the Unimak Pass, we were blown so close to the Siberian coast that its dark, rocky shores were quite visible.

I was never afraid, regardless of the storms we encountered. Indeed, I was always a little sorry when they ceased. I spent every possible minute on deck and never got enough of the smash and roar of the angry seas, even when we careened along at such an angle that had I lost my grip on whatever I was clinging to I'd have slid right into the sea. Nor was I ever seasick.

Our crew, mostly Mexicans or other Latin Americans, was quartered in the forecastle, or "glory hole." We would do the work of canning the salmon, which would be caught by the sailors who manned the ship, mostly Swedes and Norwegians. There was little fraternization between us. I don't know how the white crew felt about us, but we had no use for them, or any other whites. *Bolil-yos* we called them. I never did know exactly what that meant, but it was the harshest epithet possible to apply to another human being, much worse than *hijo de la perra:* son of a she-dog.

That dislike, even hatred, for whites, by these pigmented sons of our sister republics, as expressed so freely among themselves, was to become familiar to me as the feeling of other non-whites everywhere I went. And after this first taste of roaming, I worked on steamships which took me to many distant lands, mostly Asiatic, where I heard the same kind of bitterness many, many times.

I remember that in Burma I struck up an acquaintance with some young English-speaking Burmese recently graduated from the university at Rangoon, and was shocked to hear their opinion of not only Europeans, but Americans. They also spoke with contempt of the upstart religion, Christianity, which, they said, was merely a hodge-podge of the various Eastern and Near-East religions, many of which existed thousands of years before our Christian era began. And when I made an attempt to defend Christianity, I was silenced when asked how we in America would receive Oriental missionaries in our land who sought to convert us to their religions. They

pointed out that the white Christians came to *their* countries
to convert *them* to Christianity just as though their ancient
religious beliefs were as nothing. That, they said, was arro-
gance of the worst kind. And I thought that perhaps it was.

After a three-year absence I returned to Kansas City. It
was good to be home, so good that I agreed to go back to college. So for two years I attended the University of Kansas, at
Lawrence, but could not stick a third year in order to receive
a degree.

The trouble was again racial. The University practiced
segregation on all levels except that of the classroom. Negroes
could not even try out for the athletic squads, nor participate
in any other extracurricular activity. They were required to
eat in one section of the school cafeteria, and while colored
men could use the swimming pool, colored coeds could not.

The town of Lawrence also barred Negroes from its public
places except for the few which admitted them on a segregated
basis. This did not seem oppressive to most Negro students
because they were used to it as the way of life normal to their
own communities. But I had not been able to accept it. I had
learned how it felt to be free. So, instead of returning for my
final year at the University, I took a job on the Kansas City
Call, a rapidly growing weekly newspaper.

That was the start of a newspaper experience which over
the next dozen years was to take me to Chicago, New York,
Atlanta, Memphis, Houston and other cities.

If I desired to learn in detail the scope and the infinite
manifestations of racial prejudice in my country, I certainly
chose well.

But if I had wanted to avoid that subject, then I could not
have made a worse choice, for it was the very blood of most
Negro newspapers. Indeed, it seemed to me to be the chief
reason for their existence.

I do not think it was an inner need to find expression for

my wish to protest the inequities from which my race suffered
that drew me into newspaper work, although it may have
been. I believe it was more likely that the somewhat romantic
flavor with which my reading had endowed newspaper work
was responsible, even though at first I did not differentiate
between such reading, which of course was of the white
world, and the fact, which was of the Negro world.

Too, newspaper work was supposed to be good training for
one with ambitions as a writer of fiction; and regardless of
what else I did, to be a writer, a novelist, was my real ambition. I considered that everything which happened to me was
grist for that mill.

In Chicago, in the early thirties when I was employed by
the Chicago *Defender,* then the largest of the nationally circulated Negro weeklies, I began selling serials with a racial
background to the Illustrated Feature Service, a newsprint
magazine insert which appeared in sixty or more of our weeklies.

My serials usually had twelve two-thousand word chap-
ters for which I received seventy-five dollars a chapter. That
was very good pay for those days, a fact I did not fully appreciate until I tried my luck in the general market where my
initial sales to the love and adventure type pulp magazines
brought only a half-cent a word.

However, to sell in that market, regardless of how little the
pay, was most heartening, for then I was in competition mostly
with experienced writers, whereas in the extremely narrow
market where I'd sold the serials, the competition was not so
severe.

But what I wanted most to do was to write a novel which
would depict Negro characters struggling against adversities
arising out of their position as a depressed minority. I had
not read any books by Negro authors with that theme, except
some by Charles W. Chestnut, who had published *The
House Behind the Cedars,* and a few other such books with a

racial theme written before I was born. It was high time somebody did the job and I felt qualified.

I suppose I was seeking a larger forum for the release of my
strong feeling of racial injustice, by then considerably en-
larged because of the daily handling of news which dealt
with it. But our papers were addressed to Negroes, and I believed that not only did few white people read them, but in
the main they were not even aware that many Negroes could
even read or write, much less publish newspapers.

The roots, the dark, poisonous filaments, were creeping
down, slowly, imperceptibly. But I didn't know it. I was not
even aware they existed.

I thought of all that, of all those years since boyhood, as I
lay sleepless that first night my wife and children spent in
the house I'd bought in Vermont. I was comforted that we
were together again, but it was that fact which disturbed me,
for it meant we were actually embarked upon an experiment
which now I feared was only going to prove what I had
already believed: that *nowhere* in our country would we be
able to live as first-class citizens, not even in Vermont.

I wondered tiredly if I really were justified in believing
that. Yet what else could I believe? Certainly that is how it
seemed if I judged by the facts.

I lay still lest I disturb Helen. I was bone-weary. My head
ached. Why could I not forget all this stuff and sleep? I tried
to, closed my eyes, but I continued to remember other years.

In California I'd thought I surely had the answer. If I
hadn't thought so, we would not now be in Vermont, or anywhere in my native land, but in Haiti. But now I was terribly
unsure.

Where was the key which would unlock the truth for me?
Had I neared it when I made that return to Los Angeles in
the mid-thirties?

I didn't know, but possibly I *was* near to it, for at that time I was smarting from the experience of having been almost literally chased out of Memphis, Tennessee, because my editorials in the semi-weekly newspaper I headed angered the Mr. Big of local politics. Race again. And again, protest. Protest of the system by which so-called justices of the peace, politically appointed without regard to fitness or training, preyed upon the poorest, least informed class of Negroes who were arrested not because of crimes they had committed, but because they could be hired by labor contractors to work out their "fines."

And so I had departed Memphis abruptly, glad of a whole skin, but angered and shamed by the ignominious nature of my rout. All Mr. Big had needed to do was to summon three large minions and tell them he wanted that nigger editor of that nigger newspaper down on Hernando Street to get out of town or else.

I got out of town. I could have stayed, but it would have been permanent, beneath six feet of earth.

I didn't want to go home, for at that moment, Kansas City had too strong a Southern flavor. So I went to Los Angeles, hoping its languorous charm would wash away the bitter residue of my newspaper years to which I had decided the Memphis incident had written an emphatic *finis*.

Making that decision wasn't easy. I'd loved newspaper work, but aside from one brief stint on a New York daily and a space rates deal with another in Chicago, my experience was with Negro weeklies; and to work on them had been to crusade for racial justice, often at pay barely enough for existence.

I hadn't minded that. I'd thrilled to the challenge, the odds, knowing that most often hammering at the "enemy" was productive only of battered fists. Yet I'd done it for quite a while and I thought I'd quit now, and at last devote my efforts to writing.

But I was depressed, not alone because of the nature of my farewell to the Fourth Estate, but because just before it, my literary agent in New York had finally given up on a novel I'd written. It had been refused by enough publishers to convince us both it hadn't a chance. Most hurting was that the main objection appeared to be its racial theme.

This race business! Why could I not forget it? In every direction I turned, there it was. My agent had suggested that my book might be accepted if I would change the complexion of my characters, let its protest theme be simply of beset people. Why could I not do that? I did not know. I just couldn't.

My agent had sold quite a few of my magazine stories. No race there. Nor anything else, for that matter. So I thought I'd write pulp material again. Not the kind of writing I wanted to do, but better than not writing at all. Nor need I be ashamed of it, for had not many successful authors risen from the pulp mines? Sinclair Lewis, Rudyard Kipling, Agatha Christie, P. G. Wodehouse and others?

Besides, not everyone who tried could produce salable pulp. Or anything else for which editors would pay money.

Probably I was a bit smug when I got to thinking like that. I'd sold quite a few short stories during the past two years. Had I known the probable reason I would not have been able to use *that* salve.

Those were tough times for all publishers, especially on the popular magazine level, many of whom depended upon their distributors for pre-publication advances to keep in business.

But the distributors were also hard-hit, could no longer continue that arrangement. That killed many titles. The editors of those surviving had to pare expenses drastically. One way was to stockpile stories by new writers, who were happy to accept the very lowest rates, willing to wait for their pay until publication of their pieces, rather than upon acceptance.

My idea was to get a small apartment in Los Angeles and

turn out the stuff at a great rate. So I got a small apartment, but I did not turn out the stuff at a great rate.

At first I attributed the trouble to the lazy, romantic flavor of Los Angeles, its semi-tropic clime. But soon I decided my inability to produce had a different cause: a subterranean conflict between what I was trying to do and what I wanted to do. And there came a day when I could not even approach my typewriter because in it was the last page of a probably salable story which needed only the usual happy ending.

That half-written page stayed there for a week. I was about broke but my subconscious revolt was not. A few days thereafter, down to cigarette money, I attacked my typewriter suddenly, viciously, and so finished my first fling as a "manufacturer."

Then I wrote what I wanted to write, stubbornly using the racial theme again and approached each writing session with eagerness, sometimes even arising in the night to set down a paragraph, a page, or several which could not wait for morning.

That was fine. But having deserted magazine fiction as a means of livelihood, I had to find something else which at that period inevitably had to be one or another of the various government projects. Mine was for newspaper writers.

For reasons which I could only surmise, I was given few assignments and was not required, as were others, to report daily at the project office. I didn't care so long as my monthly ninety-five dollar check kept coming, for at that time such an amount went far, and by it I was enabled to write when and about what I pleased.

Life wasn't too bad, was often a lot of fun. It cost little to squire a pretty girl around and there were plenty of them, especially in Hollywood. Too, there generally was a choice of parties in that section and others, where each guest brought food or drink, mostly the latter, in collective entertainments which sometimes turned out spectacularly.

It seems to me there was a great deal of that sort of thing going on, as though in hectic, almost desperate gaiety, we sought to escape the insecurity, uncertainty and fear which so many felt in those dark days. Too, the depression had a leveling effect, for practically everyone was in the same fix.

Many months later there came an offer of a trouble-shooting job for a faltering chain of Texas weeklies, and despite my vow never to do newspaper work again, I was off like a shot.

CHAPTER *ten*

IT WAS GOOD BEING IN HARNESS AGAIN, DO-
ing a job I knew, particularly since the owners of the Texas
string gave me complete freedom to revamp their publications.
In that involved process I was so busy the first few months
that the kind of news most characteristic of "our press," which
I handled despite my vow never to again, was simply news.

But gradually, like a surgeon's probe in flesh from which
the anesthetic is fading, it began to get to me again as the
familiar panorama of lynchings, fantastic punishments for
trivial offenses and the like, unrolled once more. And this time
racial news horizons extended beyond our shores, for Italy
was invading Ethiopia, while England, by treaty its protector,
remained silent.

I wasn't alone in viewing the Italian action as an unpro-
voked act of aggression which would not have gone unchal-
lenged in Europe or America had its victim been a white
nation, a conclusion of disturbing significance.

Even more disturbing was the *League of Nation's* rejection
of Haile Selassie's plea that the Italians be stopped, as well as
the Ethiopian Emperor's grim prophecy that were it not, world
peace would soon shatter.

At home, another disquieting development was the Hitler-
inspired anti-Semitic campaign to set Gentiles against Jews.

For Negro consumption the chief accusation was that while themselves a persecuted minority, the Jews were just as prejudiced against Negroes as white Gentiles.

This charge was not new, for it had long been held by many Negroes. What was new was its active propagation and probable wide acceptance among the uniformed of our race.

The Negro press and our racial organizations might be ineffective in the matter of Italy and Ethiopia, but at home, among our own people we could be effective in counteracting the vicious anti-Semitic propaganda, and we were. Spearheading the counterattack was our most powerful organization, the *National Association for the Advancement of Colored People* —the *NAACP*. Other organized groups such as the *Urban League*, and our press in general, also swung into the fray.

Our reasoning was that while some Jews practiced and supported prejudice against Negroes, the majority did not; and in any event, especially in proportion to their numbers, infinitely more help and friendship had been extended us by Jews than by white Christians; and finally, that it seemed folly to allow ourselves to be turned against another minority which shared in some degree the kinds of intolerance which we suffered.

There were a few bright spots. One was the knockout of the German, Schmeling, by Joe Louis, in their second fight. Another was our victory at the 1936 Olympic games in Germany, in which Jesse Owens and other Negro athletes had a large share.

But mostly, the prospect was bleak. It seemed that Negroes need not expect their lot to improve, for in this year of 1937 an anti-lynching bill which had passed in the House of Congress, was killed in the Senate despite the record of almost one hundred lynchings during the previous seven years alone, and a total of 3,394 lynchings in the fifty-five years since 1882 when accurate records began being kept.

I cannot know to what extent my acute, personal awareness of this, and infinitely more like it, contributed to the serious illness which struck me several months later, but I believe it was considerable. Of course, I had worked hard and for long hours, but that was nothing new; and besides, I loved what I was doing, for it challenged in many directions. At least, I loved all but the upsetting news which I could not escape processing, for after all, it was the lifeblood of our product.

In any event, I awakened one morning in agony, stricken with ulcers and I almost died. Probably I would have, had not my mother hurried to my side to draw me back to life after the doctors had given me up. I'd suffered a series of hemorrhages which left me almost without pulse and my mother disregarded medical advice and took me home to Kansas City.

There, my stepfather, Dr. Howard M. Smith, then superintendent of General Hospital No. 2—the city hospital for Negroes—went to work to bring me through, and although several times it was touch and go, he did it. I spent four months in bed and two more in ambulant convalescence and then I was ready for work again.

I returned to Texas in an old roadster bought for the purpose, because I had never and meant never to ride a Jim Crow train. But returning was a mistake. My work there was done, had become mere routine, and my interest swung in other directions and I involved myself in a romance which ended unhappily. Then I went back to Kansas City.

Shortly afterward, my stepfather contracted pneumonia and died within a week. Until then I had not realized the depth of my affection for him. His death was a surprisingly heavy blow.

It was a time when my mother and I needed one another and I stayed with her that winter and spring. Then I bought a new car and headed for California, hoping a change of scene would lift a continuing depression, only a part of which was due to recent events and sorrows.

What was bothering me, deep down, was a weary conviction of the futility of fighting a white Goliath immune to my puny sling. The better way was to forget the whole bitter business. Many seemed able to do that, to concentrate upon the pursuit of life and happiness, if not liberty. But could I?

Somewhere in New Mexico I spent a night in a tourist camp. When I departed at dawn, I left beneath a pillow in the cabin I'd occupied practically all my money, about five hundred dollars. I didn't discover my loss until hours later and by then had no idea how far I'd come. Worse, since I'd arrived at the motel after dark, I hadn't noticed its name or even what it looked like.

So it seemed hopeless to go back and hunt for it, yet not to do so seemed foolish. The few bills and coins in my pocket came to seven dollars and I was tempted to use them to reach Los Angeles. But I backtracked, spent most of the day doing it, the only result being a serious depletion of what money I had.

I doubted I'd make it to Los Angeles, but I did. I got as far as Fifth Street and Broadway before the fuel, bought with the last of my money, ran out. I found one nickel in my pocket and used it to telephone the one friend whose welcome I was certain wouldn't be affected by a three A.M. distress call. Nor was it, for within twenty minutes Nate whizzed up in a new convertible bringing gasoline and overflowing with wisecracks about my contretemps.

Refueled, and heartened to find my friend the same old zany, I trailed him to his apartment in North Hollywood where his wife, Belle, was not only up but had coffee, eggs and toast ready. We had not seen one another since my departure for Texas two years before, and we chattered at a great rate bringing each other up-to-date.

Nate produced brandy. We laced the coffee, ate, and I forgot my weariness, and was quickly kidded out of the disgust

I felt at the witless loss of my money. Somehow my two friends managed to make my mishap seem amusing, what with Nate's absurd badinage and Belle's dry recital of his even worse lapse when he had blithely driven away from a filling station in Acapulco, leaving her stranded in its rest room, on their honeymoon trip.

"I guess we all do dopey things sometimes," Nate grinned unabashed. "Even old experienced billiard-ball drinkers like us, Willie."

"Well," I grumped, "I haven't doped off like that since I was a young, inexperienced billiard-ball guzzler. That time I hid two months' ship pay under a carpet with red and purple roses and never did find it again."

"Purple roses!" Belle exclaimed. "Ugh!"

"Purple roses, purple clotheses," Nate said. "How come you didn't find your dough, Willy-Bill?"

"That," I sighed, "I'll never know on account of I never located the house that went with that particular carpet."

"*Purple* roses, yet," Belle murmured.

"You never found the house," Nate prodded, "so what kind of house?"

"Well—uh—" I flubbed, conscious of Belle's faint grin, "a half dozen of us were celebrating our first night back in Seattle, our home port, and well, you can imagine the kinds of places guys rod around at a time like that."

"I don't have to imagine," Nate leered, "Because I *know*: cat houses, hey, William?"

"So you know, huh?" Belle said severely. "How?"

"Oh," her husband said airily, "a guy once told me. But I still want to know why our prodigal stashed his wad under that beflowered carpet in the first place."

"Go on," Belle ordered, "tell all or Nathan will never get his mind out of the gutter."

"Hah!" Nate snorted. "Which gutter?"

"It was this way," I said. "For some reason I felt a bit dizzy, and—"

"You felt drunk," Nate charged.

"Dizzy," I said. "I felt dizzy and stuck my money under the carpet as a precaution in case my—illness—increased."

"Illness, indeed," Belle sniffed.

"So who was going to rob you when you passed out?" Nate wanted to know. "Your shipmates? Or one of them kitties in that cat house?"

"Enough," Belle said decisively, "of that low talk, you low characters. It is six o'clock. To bed with you both."

"What for?" Nate demanded. "I—"

"I-I-*I*," his wife mocked. "In case you've forgotten, you've got to be at the studio this morning by nine and you need a few hours more sleep or they'll be dragging you off Marie's bed again."

"Marie's bed!" It was my turn to leer at Nate, but he leered back and said triumphantly, "Yanh-yanh-yanh and go wash your evil mind, Willy the weaser. It's not what you think."

"He took a nap on the set where they were making the Marie Antoinette picture," Belle explained. "It was empty at the time—I hope."

"When I dozed off on that big dais-type bed, it was," Nate said. He shuddered, rolled his eyes and added, "But when I woke up! Yeeow! I'm surrounded. The producer, director, star—everybody is standing around the bed discussing if I am or am not dead, and if not, why I ought to be made so."

"You could have lost your job," Belle warned. "So—" She made a shooing motion, "to bed, Genius. And you too, Will. I guess you need the rest more than any of us."

"Well," Nate muttered, backing toward their bedroom, "you will maybe be sorry for your snide remark, woman. Because maybe I *am* a genius. I—"

Belle shut the door on him and took me to their guest room and after seeing me installed, went to bed herself.

I awakened around noon and Belle fed me and we talked
of the change in their circumstances while I'd been away,
which was due to the miracle of the job Nate had gotten as
an assistant musical director at one of the motion picture
studios; and we spoke nostalgically of the good old days in
Chicago when we had almost starved, and where, among
other memorable events, Nate and I had once been arrested as
suspicious characters when police found us wandering about
in a dark alley while trying to find the Dill Pickle Club, a
writers' rendezvous which really was located in an alley somewhere in the neighborhood.

A silence fell between us then, as our thoughts drifted back
over that period. After a while Belle asked quietly, "What
is it, Will? What is wrong?"

"Something is wrong?" I asked. "I'm losing my hair,
maybe?"

"This is not a stranger who asks," she chided gently. "Is it
perhaps the same old trouble, Will?"

"Perhaps," I muttered, avoiding her level blue gaze.

"Let it go, Will," she said earnestly, "or it will destroy you."

"I know," I said heavily. "How's it with Nate by now?"

Belle said softly, thankfully, "Not as it used to be, Will.
It will not destroy *him*."

"He has you to thank, Belle. He's lucky."

"*We* are lucky. We have each other. Together we are
strong. Certain things no longer have the power to hurt you.
At least not so much, like dying. Now we make stepping-
stones of them. For instance, we are buying a home out in the
Valley."

"And the stepping-stone?"

"This building changed hands recently, and the new owner
—perhaps because we're Jews—has asked us to move." She
jerked her thumb shoulderward in a baseball umpire's signal
for "You're out!"

"A goy, of course."

"Who else? But now I feel like thanking him. Now we'll have our own home and *nobody* can do that to us again."

"Better you should feel like breaking his neck, not thanking him."

"Let it go, Will. Remember!"

"Okay," I growled. *"Okay.* Only—"

Belle raised a silencing hand. "Only I shouldn't have even mentioned it. Would you like to hear some of Nate's new records?"

"You're not so smooth these days," I jeered.

"Let it go," Belle said again. "You feed on it and yet you must know by now it's poison. You do know that, don't you?"

"You talk like my old man," I told her. "And yes, I know it's poison. What I don't know is how to get it out of me."

"There is One bigger who could help you."

"Ah, Belle. That old stuff? I've evolved beyond superstition."

"Evolved, Will? *Evolved?"* She clucked sadly and shook her head. "I think you've got the wrong word."

"Perhaps," I agreed.

I stayed the weekend. Nate wanted to lend me money, but I begged off. Instead, en route to the Central Avenue hotel where I meant to live for a while, I stopped at a finance company and borrowed a hundred dollars on my car. That would hold me until I made more. Being broke and jobless wasn't alarming. It had happened before, sometimes in strange cities, alien lands. I'd manage.

It had been good, seeing my old friends again, but it had also been a strain, trying to match their gaiety, when all the time, down deep, there stirred that harsh old ache that no laughter could erase. So I was relieved to get back to my world, to lose myself in the dark ghetto which was both of the flesh and the spirit, even though the perplexing fact was it held none with whom I could claim a friendship as true and warm as that of Nate and Belle.

CHAPTER eleven

I WAS STILL ABED LATE THE SECOND MORN-
ing after I'd checked in the hotel when my phone rang. The
desk clerk informed me a reporter from the California *Eagle*,
a Miss Helen Chappel, wished to speak with me. I groaned
and said please tell the lady I haven't gotten up yet, then I
hung up.

I wondered why the editor of the *Eagle* suddenly considered me worth interviewing. Something fishy there. I rated
no interview, had done nothing good or bad enough for that.
So what and so why? I hadn't an idea. Besides, there were a
couple of girls in town I'd just as soon not know I was back
and therefore I certainly wanted no mention of my return in
the weekly news columns.

When I came downstairs that afternoon, all I had on my
mind was a small brandy from the bar, a copy of the New
York *Times* from the hotel newsstand, and a table in the
hotel café where I could read it during a belated breakfast.

At some point midway the latter, I glanced up and saw a
slim, attractive girl enter the café. Our eyes met and held as
she approached my table and I thought, "Uhuh! That's
her!"

It was. She strode directly to me, a trim, tweed-suited figure, tawny brown of skin and hair, and brown of eye, too.

She was blazing slightly around the edges, but her manner and voice were quite impersonal.

"I'm Helen Chappel, of the *Eagle*. You're Will Thomas?"

I arose, admitted my identity, lied a trifle as to my pleasure at meeting her, and unenthusiastically invited her to sit.

"Thank you," she said primly, seating herself across from me on the very edge of her chair.

"Drink?"

"Thank you, *no!*"

"Cigarette?"

She shook her head and I noted how close-cropped was her hair, almost like a boy's, and that plus her severely-tailored suit typed her in my mind as a career girl.

"All I want," she stated, "is a few minutes of your valuable time."

I didn't like the way her tone underlined "valuable" and I said more brusquely than I intended, "My time isn't valuable, Miss Chappel, and I fail to see why I rate an interview, anyway. I didn't when I left here a couple of years ago and since then I've done no great works, committed no great crimes. So what's the score?"

"I really don't know," she replied coldly. "I was told by my employer to interview you, and if you would be so kind—"

"Okay," I said almost curtly. "Fire away."

"I understand you've been working for a Texas newspaper. Do you plan to return to it?"

"No."

"Then what are your plans?"

"To rest."

"Is that why you've returned to Los Angeles?"

"Among other reasons, yes."

"And the other reasons?"

"My toast has gotten cold. I'm going to send your boss the bill."

Miss Chappel's lips tightened and she shoved up from her

chair. "You are," she announced, "the most insufferable man I've ever met."

I didn't get up that time. "I'm sure I am," I said, repropping my newspaper in front of me, and fixing my eyes upon it. "It was nice meeting you, Miss-uh-uh—"

There was a small feminine snort and Miss Chappel sailed away, shoulders stiff, heels clicking angrily. I could not remember when a good-looking girl had so grated on me. I thought defensively, that had not her manner been antagonistic right from the start, I would not have been so ungracious. Besides she needed to learn a better approach if she ever expected to get anywhere as a reporter. Also—

Then I thought, to heck with it, and almost forgot the whole episode by burying my nose in the book review section of the *Times* again. But it continued to gnaw at me and I vaguely resolved to make amends at the first chance.

That Friday I bought a copy of the *Eagle*. After scanning it swiftly I was relieved that Miss Chappel had not made the *Eagle* peck me. But, as I discovered later, *she* had ripped me in her column, "Chatter and Some News," only what she had to say of me was hardly chatter, nor was it really news.

But I wasn't sore at her, and was even able to chuckle at her deft thrusts for I deserved them. Had I tried, I might have brought her around, might have accomplished what I wanted, which was to know the real reason shrewd Charlotta Bass, the editor-publisher of the *Eagle*, had sent a reporter to interview *me*. For I was certain Mrs. Bass did not waste her shots—or her news columns; and what she was sniffing around for had nothing to do with my newsworthiness.

The one bright spot of that first week back in Los Angeles came the next morning when my mail caught up with me, and in it was a check from my agent for a pulp novelette written so long ago I'd forgotten it. It enabled me to take up residence at an address unpublicized by Miss Chappel's acid pen. I checked out of the hotel that afternoon and before

night had found and moved into a tiny two-room cottage in
the rear of the owner's house on a quiet street.

I might have saved myself the effort for I soon learned
the two young ladies from whom I considered myself to be
fleeing, lest either or both seek me out, were probably not
giving me a thought. One had married and the other had
gone East to try show business.

I had occupied my little retreat no more than a week before I discovered something else: Miss Helen Chappel resided
less than a block away. For that and other reasons, our paths
crossed frequently. And so, at first, did our swords. After I
had apologized for my rudeness when we first met, our ex-
changes softened to friendly, if wary, raillery.

Our encounters, at first by chance, often took place in a
Father Divine café in our neighborhood where, for fifteen
cents, substantial tasty meals, including Sunday chicken dinners, were served.

That low price was a favorite topic when we met: how was
that feat managed? We speculated, often fancifully, on the
economics involved, agreed that while Father Divine might
not be God, as his followers devoutly believed, he certainly
fed his flock and anyone else who was hungry whether or
not he had the fifteen cents required. And we learned to respect the stock greeting of his followers which was: "Peace,
it's wonderful!" for obviously it was to them something more
than words. It seemed to reflect a way of life. Secretly I
wished I might find that kind of faith, that kind of peace.

One mutual interest was, of course, newspaper work. We
often discussed it, agreeing that only true love or a sense of
duty made most Negro journalists stick to it, since neither its
financial rewards nor its opportunities for advancement were
alluring. And I finally learned that Mrs. Bass had wanted me
interviewed because she had suspected my return to Los Angeles meant that I was going to start a California edition for
the Texas publisher for whom I had worked.

Miss Chappel confessed her own newspaper experience was limited, since she had but recently been graduated from Wilberforce University in Ohio. She told me that while she liked newspaper work best—except her chores as social editor with the *Eagle*—she was leaving it to handle publicity and advertising for the Golden State Mutual Life Insurance Company.

I twitted her about that, but she held that she had plenty of use for the better pay her new job would yield. Besides, she said, she would gain valuable new experience.

From this I gathered that all she had in mind was a career. When I told her that was how I had catalogued her at our first meeting she replied that she had worked hard for her education, that her parents had sacrificed for it and she meant to use it to get somewhere.

Where?

Well, the sky was the limit, wasn't it?

Oh sure—for the white folks.

Agreed. But even so, one had better sense than to aim for its apex. Even to brush its lower edges would be near enough to glory.

Although I personally did not admit to such limitations, I agreed with her, admired her clear-eyed ambition, her will to achieve it; and perhaps I envied it, too.

But what really fascinated me was the picture she gradually filled in about her family, her musician-turned-preacher father, her resourceful mother who always managed to make a home wherever her husband was assigned by his church—the African Methodist Episcopalian—and of her brothers, sisters and other relatives, including her white-looking Virginia grandfather who once had bitten off the ear of a white customer of his grist mill who had insisted that *his* corn be ground ahead of that already brought in by Negro patrons.

Pressed for the sequel, she told me that the sheriff had jailed her grandfather and that not only was there some hot lynching talk among local whites, but a number of them gathered near the jail, bent on carrying it out. But numerous stalwart sons and other male clansmen of her grandfather's also gathered at the jail, and like the whites they had weapons and everyone knew that they would use them.

And what then?

Why, the sheriff released her grandfather and told him to go on home and behave himself and take all those mean-looking, gun-toting "nigras" of his along with him before somebody got hurt.

—And take those "nigras" of his. Of *his?* Wasn't her grandfather a Negro?

Helen didn't seem to know. Nor, apparently, did anyone else. He was married to a handsome, dark woman, and lived with her and their large brood. Helen had known him only after his hair and magnificent beard, both worn long, had become snowy. Then in his eighties, he was still a broad, powerful man who worked every day in his grist mill just below a dam on the Bannister River, in Halifax County.

I asked if there was any connection between the respect her grandfather apparently enjoyed among whites and their possible suspicion that he might actually be one of them, even though a "renegade."

She said she didn't really know, but that it was more likely due to her grandfather's county-wide reputation for living up to his avowed intention "not to take any stuff off nobody, be he who he might, short of Gawd-A-Mighty Hisself." He died, she told me, at the age of ninety-seven, two years after his children finally persuaded him to stop working in his mill.

What, I asked, was the color range of his children, offspring of a near-black mother and a blue-eyed, white-skinned father?

Her own father was the darkest of them, Helen believed,

his color deep brown. An aunt was the fairest, could "pass" as white. The others were "in between."

That was a familiar pattern among our people and we speculated on the number of fair-skinned Negroes who each year passed over into that mass of Americans who are "legally" white. We spoke of those we had known who had or had not crossed the color line, and why.

In time our meetings were not always by chance. Gradually we discovered other mutual interests: plays, literature, music, although often our views were dissimilar. Hers generally conformed to her academic background, that of an English "major" and a one-time music student. Mine were considerably less orthodox, and usually reflected my thought and feeling as a member of a depressed race.

In consequence, I often revealed a cynicism which seemed sheer heresy to Helen, especially when I charged that the subject peoples of the world, all non-whites—the yellow Mongols, brown Indians, black Africans—were held in thrall by white Christian nations. Was that, I asked, conduct befitting those who claimed to be children of God?

Helen, the minister's daughter, was shocked by the irreligious implications of these remarks and stoutly insisted the trouble was human, not divine.

Since I had begun to suspect that my interest in her might be more than casual, I took care lest she should suspect that I was an "unbeliever." When I began accompanying her to the AME Church she took it as proof that at worst I was only a backslider. Apparently it did not occur to her that I might have attended church merely to be with her.

But a few of Helen's friends saw something sinister in my sudden church attendance and warned her of my dubious reputation "with the ladies," and of my general "instability." Following that, she started to work on me. I wore my hair too long, she said, and I countered by suggesting that she

wore hers too short. And while she didn't accept my suggestion, I did hers and submitted to a closer shearing.

She regarded my usual jacket-slacks attire as not appropriate for the slightly starchy social affairs we were beginning
to attend and dutifully I wore more appropriate clothes.

Yet she seemed to enjoy rodding around with me, although
certain of my favorite haunts aroused her apprehension, and
the kinds of people I knew, her open dismay.

I liked to hang around the shop of a friend, a commercial
engraver, on North Broadway. In that neighborhood, an old
Mexican section, were cafés and clubs and stores and perhaps
less respectable enterprises, operated by Mexicans, Japanese,
Filipinos and other pigmented folk, many of whom I knew.
But Helen saw it as a dangerous section, peopled by vil-
lainous-looking characters; and she always expected something terrible to happen when she accompanied me to it. The
worst thing that ever did happen was when, one noon, as she
waited for me in my car outside the engraving shop, a near-
naked woman ran screaming out of a dingy rooming house
across the street, a pint-sized, half-clad man stumbling in pursuit. Nor would she believe *that* was *most* unusual. She
never went to that section with me again.

Then there was the time we had stopped on Central Avenue for barbecue and as I returned with it, an acquaintance,
a hustler, fell in step with me, grinning and shaking his head.
We were within a couple of feet of my car where Helen
waited when he went into a routine by then grown familiar.

"Man," he said, "that little brownskin from the Insurance
Company has got you wearing a four-cornered hat. Oncet a
knocked-out little chick from Boston had me squaring up like
that. Man, you better slow down."

"Man," I laughed, knowing Helen could not help hearing
our badinage, "man, sometimes being a square is fine, like
wine."

"Man, git," my acquaintance jeered, "because you're *hit!* When a cat gets to talking out of his head, Man, he's *dead!*"

Then with a sly grin in Helen's direction, he strolled off.

"Another of your pals, eh?" she asked as I got into the car. "What's his racket? Stickups? Or burglary?"

"What's the diff?" I laughed.

But I knew Helen thought it made a lot of difference; if you were respectable you knew and spoke only with those like yourself.

I took a lot of kidding from acquaintances both respectable, according to Helen's code, and otherwise, for most of them knew how freely I circulated between the various levels of our society. I knew all kinds frowned upon by the more fortunate. Some I liked. Some I respected and some I loathed, but I could not escape feeling that they were all shaped by unfavorable circumstances in a world of shadow and poverty, in so many ways a facsimile of the larger half-world in which all Negro Americans were constrained.

Frequently these shady characters were interesting, often capable, and I thought of what many might have become if they'd had even the opportunities possible to many of our race, let alone those which white Americans take for granted.

This viewpoint didn't quite click with Helen. To her a gambler was a gambler, a prostitute just that, and forever beyond the pale. She was shocked to learn a young college graduate whom we knew made his money as a partner in a numbers racket which provided his extensive wardrobe and expensive automobile. He held a degree in Business Administration and came of a good family. When he failed to find a job which could utilize and pay for his training, he drifted into this illegal work which paid highly for his specialized abilities. Having tasted its fat rewards, he soon forgot his ambition to become a certified public accountant.

I knew him well and had often heard his cynical philosophy, which was to get the do-re-me, the gold, the money, which was all that counted regardless of your race. Because wasn't that what everybody was after?

The law, he argued, said gambling was wrong, but what was the stock market but high-class gambling for big stakes? And look what a hell of a shape the whole country was in because those big-shot gamblers messed up in 1929. Craps and cards and the numbers game never did that much damage, did they?

Helen couldn't see it that way. Her ideas were as strait-laced as my mother's. Nevertheless, despite our differences in outlook and personal philosophy, something was growing between us. She learned that I was not quite the dissolute character of whom she'd been warned and perhaps discovered that buried not too deeply beneath my cynical shell were beliefs and ambitions of which she could approve. And after a while, to the dismay of some of her friends, we became engaged and in due time, we married.

CHAPTER *twelve*

For THREE MONTHS AFTER OUR MARRIAGE, Helen and I lived in an apartment with maid service, and ate in restaurants, which was not my idea of married life. This situation, which Helen rather liked, was then remedied, because I bought a house. It cost only one thousand dollars and it was a mere shell.

Helen's friends obviously felt sorry for her when they saw it. Small, in complete disrepair, its floors gaped with missing boards, its unplastered walls were so warped that in some places we could see through them as freely as through the unpaned windows. And all the plumbing fixtures were missing.

Of a type known as "California" the house had no foundation and at one corner the mudsills had rotted, allowing that section to sag alarmingly. It was set on the rear of a deep, narrow, weedy lot and it was a forlorn little house and I didn't blame my wife's friends for thinking it was hardly the place to delight a bride.

But Helen bravely agreed with me that however humble, there was no place like home, if you owned it.

Besides it fulfilled the last of the three conditions to which she claimed I agreed before she would marry me.

These conditions were enunciated by Bishop R. R. Wright, president of Wilberforce University in Ohio, when my wife was a student there. She related how he advised of three things a prospective husband ought to have before being seriously considered: a health certificate, life insurance and a title to a home.

I qualified on the first two items before we were married.

We were not perturbed by what anyone thought when I bought that wreck of a house, for I'd assured my wife that we could make it comfortable and presentable.

However, we hadn't much free time to work at it. Helen handled publicity and advertising for the Golden State Mutual Life Insurance Company, and was also working on her Master's degree at the University of Southern California and was active in her sorority. So she had little time for her new home, nor for that matter, for her husband, either.

I was operating a small advertising agency which kept me busy, also. Still, within a few weeks we fixed up our house enough to occupy it.

Money was scarce, but we secured needed materials such as bathroom fixtures from wrecking yards. Evenings I repaired floors and painted woodwork while Helen measured for curtains, window shades and floor coverings. We secured plasterboard for the walls, electrical fixtures and other items "on time." And with a couple of automobile jacks I raised the sagging corner of the house so that the roof line was level, almost.

Despite its low price, our property was really a bargain because of its Westside location. Unlike the Eastside where the bulk of the Negro population was concentrated, the Westside had no slums, no ghettos. A few Negro families had lived in our section for years, usually in homes they owned. The drift of other Negro families to this area had been slow but steady. When we joined it, the tempo was quickening.

Westside neighborhoods were often quite mixed. Some whites moved out immediately a Negro family moved in. Some did not. Many of these neighborhoods were protected by restrictive covenants regarding the race, and often the religion of those who might occupy them. Ours was unrestricted.

On our street lived the Suzukis. The father and mother were Japanese nationals. Their daughter Tokikio and their son Johnny were American-born. Mr. Suzuki, who operated the vegetable concession in a supermarket was very religious, a deacon in a Japanese Baptist church. His wife, frail, tuberculous, managed the household with the help of "Toke," her daughter, who was sixteen. Johnny, seventeen, a husky high school senior, helped his father after school and on Saturdays.

On our right in a neat white cottage lived the Walkers, an elderly Maine couple. They had remained even after their neighborhood became more colored than white and were well liked because of their unpatronizing friendliness.

Both they and the Suzukis were most helpful as Helen and I strove to transform our ugly duckling of a house into the modest swan we envisioned. Mr. Walker taught me how to shingle our roof; and the know-how which eventually converted our weedy front yard into a smooth lawn bordered with bright flowers, came from the Suzukis. I managed to paint the exterior of the house on my own.

After a while our little place looked quite nice. There were two palm trees in the parking strip and midway the lawn there was a scrubby orange tree which never rewarded our attentions with any oranges. But except for the pleasure of having oranges from our own tree, that wasn't important, for that fruit cost little, six dozen for a quarter. Big cantaloupes were a nickel each, and fat avocados were three for a dime.

Those were good days. We often ate by candlelight in our tiny dining room, an enjoyable custom discovered one evening when our lights wouldn't come on.

The next day we made another discovery: we hadn't paid our light bill.

We were married in June. The summer months went

quickly. Our first Christmas was memorable because we were in our own home and had our own little Christmas tree, and turkey, plus trimmings.

Just before Christmas I'd sold a story and with the proceeds, we'd bought a Monterey living-room suite. The store owner made us a present of a colorful Indian rug which nicely complemented it. Helen was delighted by the gift, but puzzled.

"I wonder why that man gave us that expensive rug," she mused. "I never heard of a Jew giving away anything unless there was a catch to it."

"Why, you're prejudiced," I charged.

"Sure I am," she admitted. "But not just against Jews. I don't like the white race in general."

"Well, honey," I said, "that man in the store knew we were newlyweds and that's why he gave us the rug. Besides, I've found Jews as generous as any people, maybe more so. And what's your beef against the white race?"

"It is exactly the same as yours," she said.

Not wanting to discuss that subject, I said lightly, "Well, to heck with 'em. We've troubles enough without dragging them in."

Brave words, but foolish. Because we didn't have to drag them into our lives. In one way or another they barged into them, shaped them, and there were no barriers which could keep them out, especially those dead ones who, in the invisible ink of custom, had rewritten the Constitution in a way their forefathers certainly had not intended.

The rains came late that year. Days, Helen and I worked at our usual tasks. Evenings, to the accompaniment of drumming downpours, we often played favorite records. Once in a while we drove down to the ocean, parked on some dark rise and watched its mighty stirring and listened to its deep-throated roar, which to Helen was a symphony in monotone, and to me, a stormy-weather blues, a cappella.

It was as though the constant rains enclosed us, helped to make a world all our own. Our concern was for ourselves, especially when our doctor confirmed Helen's belief that she was going to have a baby. To us both that was wonderful news.

Sometimes while Helen studied or worked on her thesis, I wrote, determinedly concentrating on commercial fiction. That was difficult, an old struggle. As I had so many times before, I assured myself that some day I would write only what I wished. But the need for money dictated a different course. I didn't mind too much. There were compensations.

So passed that spring: gently, happily.

In mid-summer, yielding finally to our doctor's advice and to my worried urging, Helen took leave of her job. She thought both her doctor and her husband were old fuddy-duddies because of our concern over her "delicate condition."

However, when her "time" came in November, some of my fears were justified, for hers was an ordeal of thirty hours, during which her life hung in balance. I spent every one of those awful hours in the hospital where she was, fearing the worst. And when Dr. Wakataki, the Japanese head of the maternity ward, approached me at the end of that period, my last glimmer of hope waned, so certain was I he bore ill tidings.

But he said, "Your wife is going to be all right."

I could only gaze at him in speechless, unsayable relief and he grinned tiredly and said, "Tough going, eh?," adding drily, "especially for her."

Finally I mumbled, "She's really okay? I mean, *really?*"

Dr. Wakataki replied sharply, "Yes, really. And you've a fine little girl. They are both all right. But it was a near thing for the mother."

"Never again," I vowed.

"That's what I said with my first," the doctor laughed. "But you get used to it. And your wife will probably have no trouble next time."

I nodded, but I didn't intend that there would be a next time. I grasped the doctor's hand, unable to find words which would express all I felt, but he seemed to understand, for as he turned to go he squeezed my arm and smiled. "Get some sleep," he advised.

I nodded again, and stood watching his slender figure retreating, knowing he needed sleep more than I, for during all those hours I'd spent in the hospital waiting room, calls for him sounded unendingly over the loudspeaker.

I knew of his excellent reputation as an obstetrician but had not until now quite believed it, for he looked so very young and boyish. But now I was positive he was the most skilled of his profession. And I was proud that he, like myself, was a man of color.

I was also grateful to the hospital, the White Memorial, operated by the Seventh Day Adventists, for it made no racial distinctions in staff or patients. In that moment I was glad and grateful for many things, but above all that although Helen had walked through the Valley of the Shadow, Evil had not overtaken her.

Our babe was a lovely little thing. At birth and for several years her skin was as unpigmented as that miscalled "white;" and her features were well defined, her hair bright blonde, and her eyes, sky blue. We named her Anne, after my mother.

It didn't seem strange to us that our child was so fair, for in both our families fair-skinned members were not uncommon. Too, we knew that it was the norm in our racial patterns for there to be sometimes marked divergencies of this kind among children of the same parents. We also knew the genetic law that while a child cannot be darker than its darkest parent, it can be fairer than either.

But the nurses who attended my wife apparently knew none of this, for they seemed unable to comprehend how a brown girl could bear a baby indistinguishable from a Caucasian infant. And my wife is definitely and beautifully brown.

She is also normally perceptive and did not fail to sense the undercurrent of curiosity and speculation which swirled among those nurses, but managed to restrain her reactions to wry amusement at their open staring and whispering as she suckled her white babe at her brown breasts.

But despite their wonderment, the nurses were mostly kind and attentive. Yet sometimes Helen found it difficult not to flare up when one of them, as she put it, "talked all around it," used oblique remarks like hooks to try and draw forth details which would satisfactorily explain her blonde, blue-eyed child.

Helen thought that when I was allowed to visit her, the matter might become clearer. But it didn't, for while I am fairer than she, I was apparently not sufficiently so to explain our white-skinned baby.

During my first visit to Helen's room, a rather brisk traffic developed. One nurse entered, fussed briefly with a medicine tray, and departed with wide-eyed, over-the-shoulder peeks. Then came a pair to merely say "hello" to Helen, the while allowing their eyes to flick over me. Others wandered in and out, clean young kids no doubt dedicated to their profession but patently puzzled by this particular by-product of it.

"They can't understand it," Helen sighed. "They just *can't.*"

"Well," I said helpfully, "don't let it get you, honey."

"Don't worry," my wife replied drily, "it's got them, not me."

It got others, too. After Helen was strong enough to resume normal activities, she would frequently return from marketing in an angry simmer. If I saw her approaching at such times I'd know the state of her feelings long before she reached me, for she would come sailing along, pushing Anne's pram rapidly, and when she neared, I'd see how her usually gentle brown eyes were snapping.

"Again?" I'd inquire sympathetically.

"Darn it, yes!"

"Where this time?"

"Ralph's Market. Some long-nosed old white woman eased up to me and said, 'What a *pretty* baby!' Then she gave me that bright, nasty-nice smile and asked, 'Is it—yours? You know: *Yo*-urrs?' "

The very air seemed to tingle at such times, so alive did my wife make those encounters with her angry, exasperated mimicry.

"And did the white lady believe you?" I'd ask.

"Do they ever?" my wife would explode. "Because how could a brownskin like me have a white baby? Or were that possible, then the father just had to be some lowdown white man. But just wait! The next one who asks me about Anne— Well, I'll fix her!"

"Bop her with a bunch of carrots, maybe?"

"Of course not. I'm just going to return an overdone version of that phony smile they all seem to use and explain sweetly that yes, the baby is mine and that my husband is white. By golly, that'll shock 'em!"

"Undoubtedly," I'd agree. "But why libel *me?* Anyway, why let that kind of thing upset you so?"

"For the same reason you let it upset you," my wife would counter.

So I did the marketing thereafter, for Helen wouldn't leave her precious babe with me while she did it, nor even with Toke, the young Japanese girl next door who not only adored Anne, but had professional baby-sitting experience.

And when Helen took our daughter for her daily airings, she
kept within our block where she was not apt to be asked any
damn-fool questions.

And I agreed when she remarked that it seemed as if we
couldn't even have children without the white folks sticking
their long noses into our business.

Helen's frightening brush with death jarred my life into
focus, gave it meaning and purpose; and it certainly settled
me down with a solid thump.

I knew I was regarded as somewhat unstable, and I suppose I was, although not in the way many who knew me
believed. As a newspaperman I had seldom stuck to any one
job very long; and in the way such things get around, it was
known that in my younger years I'd done a lot of "crazy"
things, like prize fighting, wandering in all sorts of strange
lands, and getting into one scrape after another.

Much of that was true, but I'd never tried to explain or
justify any of it, for I knew what drove me, what I had been
seeking.

In any event, marriage and fatherhood changed all that. I
knew it if nobody else did, and I thought of it as I drove
home with my wife and child the day they were released from
the hospital.

It was one of those bright gilt mornings Los Angeles often
enjoys in November. Helen and I spoke little. There was no
need, for we were joined in a new and wonderful link which
was our daughter, and only that mattered.

I drove slowly, carefully, thinking of the future and
how to make it secure for us, and especially for our child,
our lovely little Anne. She must have many things, but above
all else, the freedom of which I'd dreamed since I first realized I did not have it. She must never go through that, must
never know the shame of being considered inferior simply
because she had been born a Negro; and she must not ex-

perience the hurt of exclusion and rejection for that reason alone. Somehow I must protect her from all that and from all the other warping racial patterns of our native land.

First, I planned, intent upon my driving, to quit piddling with my picayune advertising agency. That I did fairly well with it was only because I frequently undertook commissions for downtown agencies, such as certain types of market research. Handouts from friendly white agencies. But handouts.

Admitting that, even to myself, wasn't pleasant, but I knew it was true, just as I knew there really wasn't enough business in my own section to make my agency really profitable, and that only in my own section could I operate at all.

I thought resentfully what a hell of a thing it was not to be able to work in a field for which I was reasonably well prepared; and what a hell of a thing to see the feast and not be permitted to eat of it.

Wᴇ ᴄᴇʟᴇʙʀᴀᴛᴇᴅ Aɴɴᴇ's ᴛʜɪʀᴅ ʙɪʀᴛʜ-week with a little party and Helen baked a small cake for it, her first. But when she removed it from the oven she wailed, "It's burned!"

"It sure is," I laughed, "but since our little darling can't eat it anyway, where's the loss? Besides, once iced—"

"Iced!" Helen exclaimed.

"Cakes generally have it," I said. "Can't you make the stuff?"

"Well," my wife said doubtfully, "I can make fudge."

So we observed the twenty-first day of our daughter's birth with that little burned cake covered with chocolate fudge, and topped by three wee candles, and we sang "Happy Birth-day To You" to her, but our babe was so bored she fell asleep in her mother's arms.

"There's gratitude," I chuckled.

"Bless her little heart," Helen cooed. "I'll put her in her bassinet."

When Helen returned, we sat down to dinner, exchanging smiling glances because of our child, of the goodness of being in our own shabby little home and because of the fine, strong bond which drew us ever closer.

It was a warm December afternoon. We ate leisurely,

talked much about nothing in particular and found it enough
to stir us to frequent laughter. Afterward we looked in on our
daughter, and finding her soundly sleeping, cleared up the
dishes and stacked them in the sink.

Then, arms linked, we strolled into our living room and
Helen said, "It looks nice now, doesn't it?" and I replied, "It
sure does," and we stood regarding it, thinking of the change
we'd wrought since first we saw it.

Now its walls were smooth, painted in pastel tones. The
floor was covered by wine-colored carpeting which complemented our Monterey furniture and set off our little arti-
ficial electric fireplace and our gift Navajo rug which was
spread before it. We thought the room quite handsome and
smiled at each other in pride and satisfaction.

"Oh, goodness," Helen exclaimed, "it's time for the symphony!" She hurried to our radio, turned it on, saying,
"They're playing Beethoven this week. Let's not miss it."

I was agreeable and while she adjusted the radio and curled
up on the divan beside it, I dropped into my big easy chair
and lit a cigarette. Comfortable, and knowing the meaning of
contentment for the first time in my life, I lay back in my
chair and lulled by Beethoven's music, I drowsed. Sometime
later, perhaps only a few minutes, Helen's sharp call jerked
me to wakefulness.

"Will," she cried, "listen to this!"

I sat up, startled. The music had stopped. A charged voice
was saying,"—first reports from Pearl Harbor state that this
sudden, sneak attack by Japanese war planes has seriously
damaged the American fleet based there and—"

I listened, shocked, incredulous. But as further tense reports poured forth that Sunday afternoon, it was impossible
to doubt there really had been a smashing attack upon our
fleet in Honolulu and that many Americans had been killed.

Our Japanese neighbors seemed as shocked as we. Elder

Suzuki hurried off to his Baptist church to pray. Periodically that afternoon his wife's wailing sobs drifted from their house.

Within minutes the street was dotted with agitated knots of people excitedly discussing what had happened. That tiny Japan had dared to jump us was absolutely fantastic! Why, we'd smash those crazy Nips before you could count to ten!

Our Maine neighbors were terribly alarmed. While we discussed the news with them, over the fence between our houses, both old people kept glancing fearfully toward the Suzuki cottage. Clearly they were no longer friends of those Japanese traitors. And as to my suggestion that the Suzukis had had nothing to do with the Pearl Harbor disaster, why they were Japs, weren't they, just as were those slit-eyed devils who had blown up our ships and murdered our poor boys over there? Probably they were spies. They ought to be locked up before they cut everybody's throats!

Their fear, their instant suspicion of the Suzukis, despite years of friendly association with them, was shocking. But it seemed the general attitude even though many West Coast Japanese were native-born, were Americans.

However, at least among many of my race, there quickly crystallized a different feeling, especially as the Japanese successes mounted in the Pacific. We'd take care of those Japs in the end, but it was not really unpleasing that the little yellow nation had reared up and knocked the mighty white man flat. It was what the palefaces needed. It proved they were really not so tough as they made out to be. Maybe between Hitler and Tojo, the white folks might straighten up and fly right.

To "fly right" in our vernacular meant that the white brothers ought to get over believing they were so superior to us that they had to prove it by treating us like dirt. And some said darkly that they had better not take forever to change their ways, either, because even we could see that all over the world the colored races were stirring, straining to break free.

Two days after Pearl Harbor, Johnny Suzuki and several friends, all Japanese Americans, tried to enlist in the United States Army. Johnny returned in tears. He and his pals had been cursed and chased out of the recruiting post.

Johnny and his Nisei friends had believed they were Americans, for so said the United States Constitution. They spoke better English than Japanese and had little interest in Japan except as the land of their ancestors. Like most Nisei, they were probably more outraged by the Pearl Harbor attack than many Americans because their ancestry identified them with an action in which they had no part, but for which they shared the blame.

I knew that feeling well, for many times I'd been shamed by some ugly or uncouth action of a member of my race who was an utter stranger to me, as though I were in some way responsible because we both were Negroes. For when Negroes do certain things, steal, commit assaults, get drunk or behave badly in whatever way, it is apparently what most white people seem to expect, and regard as confirmation of inherent Negro inferiority. Nor does it seem to matter that such offenses are common to all mankind.

So when I saw Johnny slumped beneath a pepper tree in his back yard, shaken with sobs, I went and sat beside him, understanding something of what he must be feeling. His noiseless, violent weeping was shocking.

After a while he told me in detail what had happened. Then he demanded, "What's the matter with those guys at the recruiting station? How can we prove where we stand if they won't even give us a chance? America is my country, not Japan. But those white guys ran us off like we were dirty dogs."

I tried to soothe the boy, to explain, but my heart wasn't in it and I guess he knew it. Yet I'm sure he didn't understand the irony of my even trying to do so, for probably he did not realize that although browner by far than I, and of alien ancestry, he enjoyed greater general acceptance in my native land than I. There was prejudice against the Japanese, sure. But at the same time, in most sections of our land, including the South, Japanese did not encounter it in the same degree as Negroes. Often they attended schools and used public accommodations from which we were barred.

Johnny's sister, Toke, came out with a pot of ginger tea and some almond cookies still warm from the oven. She and I ate some cookies and sipped the spicy tea, but Johnny would touch neither. After a while he got up and wandered off, a lost soul.

"I never saw him like this," his sister said worriedly. "He acts like somebody is dead."

"Something, not somebody," I said absently.

"Pardon?" Toke said, brows lifted.

"Skip it," I sighed.

"Pa feels pretty bad about all this," Toke said. "Ma, too."

"You mean, about Johnny?"

"No. Pearl Harbor. They don't know about Johnny yet. Boy! Will Pa ever be sore when he hears about Johnny!"

"Who could blame him?" I asked. "He once told me the only reason he and your mother came to this country was because they wanted their children born in America—wanted them to be Americans. But even so, it looks like there is some question about that now."

"Heck," Toke said stoutly," Johnny and I *are* Americans. But that isn't what I meant. Pa will be plenty sore when he finds out Johnny tried to join the army. Pa doesn't believe in wars and killing." She shook her head sadly. "Poor Pa."

Lines from some forgotten source formed in my mind and I uttered them: " . . . *and you have seduced me with your Christian dream.*"

Toke said blankly, "Pardon?"

"Nothing," I told her. "Just nothing at all."

*   *   *   *   *

For a year and a half I'd known an increasing happiness and inner peace of which I'd scarcely permitted myself to think lest I break the spell. Then suddenly I could no longer ignore, as I had been doing, the crash of world events, for the day after Pearl Harbor, our country declared war on both Japan and Germany, and that as well as other kinds of disturbing news slammed at us from every source of human communication.

Soon afterward came the decision to remove all persons of Japanese ancestry, citizens and aliens alike, from the coastal area. They were gathered up and herded into "assembly centers," then were transported to and confined in "relocation camps" deep in the hot desert and ringed by barbed wire and armed soldiers, like the concentration camps in Europe.

This seemed keenly felt by many of the Negro communities, for we resented the manner in which the native-born Japanese were being treated, seeing in it a raw deal with which we, as Negroes, were all too familiar. What made it almost impossible for us to see that as anything but race prejudice was because white enemy aliens—Germans and Italians—were not interned, but were only required to register, even though in their countries Americans were being sent to concentration camps. Yet alien Germans and Italians, being indistinguishable from white Americans, could move about freely without exciting attention, whereas the easily identifiable Japanese could not have, even had they not been interned.

If I had wished to escape all this it would have been impossible for in homes, shops, stores, pool halls, bars——everywhere in *our* communities——all this was a main topic. But I had ceased trying to shut such things out of mind and gradually I had resumed my old habit of roaming and listening and talking with all kinds of people.

I did not realize at first why I did this, why I *had* to do it.

But gradually I understood that I sought confirmation of the magnitude of the flaws in our democracy which to me had now become so starkly visible because of the loudness, bordering on stridency, with which my country was avowing the purity of its democracy. And I took comfort in finding that I was far from alone in recognizing those flaws.

One morning an Army truck removed the Suzukis to the Santa Anita race track whose horse stalls had been converted overnight into quarters for the interned Japanese. It was called "an assembly center."

Mr. and Mrs. Suzuki, Toke, and Johnny awaited the truck on their front porch, the few possessions they would be allowed to take piled at their feet.

Mrs. Suzuki, eyes reddened with weeping, sat on a bedroll, her face in her hands. Elder Suzuki, stony-faced, gripped a paper sack of food in one hand, a worn Bible in the other. Johnny, slumped on the steps, was grimly silent, but the spasmodic bunching of his jaw muscles told something of what he was feeling. In the doorway of the only home she'd ever known, Toke wept, clinging to the door frame as though she meant never to let go.

When the truck roared up, Mr. Suzuki said in an odd, stifled voice, "If we never come back, you keep everything, Mist' Thomas. And thank you very much." Only he said "sank you."

"You'll be back," I assured him, "and your things will be right here, waiting." Our garage and attic were crammed with Suzuki possessions.

The elderly Japanese bowed ceremoniously. His wife raised her head and tried to smile. I said quickly, "Be seeing you, Toke. Take it easy, Johnny."

Toke began to cry loudly and Johnny, without even looking up, muttered, "Oh, sure. Oh, *sure.*"

I left hurriedly, not wanting to witness them being herded

into the big olive-drab truck by the gruff, hard-faced young soldiers who accompanied it. But for days I kept seeing the Suzukis during those last frozen few minutes of waiting, crushed, accepting with a resignation I hoped I would never know, the ruin of a golden dream of a sweet land of liberty, where freedom rang.

Only, not for them.

Nor, alas, for me.

CHAPTER *fourteen*

Aꜰᴛᴇʀ Aɴɴᴇ ᴄᴀᴍᴇ, Hᴇʟᴇɴ ʀᴇʟᴜᴄ-
tantly resigned her position with the insurance company from
which until then she had been on leave. I was asked to take
over her work, but as an agency account.

It happened that just then the company reached its goal
of becoming an "old line" legal reserve organization. Being
on the inside during this transition allowed me a close-up of
uncommon business acumen, integrity, courage and vision.

The vision was Texas-born in the mind and heart of the
late William Nickerson, Jr., a slender, coppery man who
came to California in the early twenties and with a few hundred dollars and a prayer, started the Golden State Mutual
Life Insurance Company.

In Texas, Nickerson first taught school, then for twenty
years engaged in insurance work.

In Los Angeles his big problem at the outset of his venture was to raise $15,000 for the guarantee fund required by
the state under an old insurance law, in order to qualify as a
Chapter Nine assessment company.

Aided by two hard-driving young men, Norman O. Houston and George A. Beavers, Nickerson was able to persuade
seven local citizens to chip in from five hundred to one thousand dollars each. And by intensive effort, these three vision-

aries and the field force they fired with their own enthusiasm, induced more than the required five hundred charter members to put up advance premiums and to apply to the proposed company for insurance.

So in January, 1925, the company began business in small, shabby quarters with an actual working capital of only $28,000.

I once asked Mr. Nickerson why he had chosen California to start such a difficult undertaking, particularly when at the time there were only about 30,000 Negroes in the entire state.

"I wanted to live and work where there wasn't so much race prejudice and economic restriction as there was in the South," he told me. "I knew California was a comer, young, bound to grow, for it was growing fast even then. I figured that the Negro population would increase proportionately with the white. And I meant to grow with the state."

Thus, sixteen and one-half years later, when I served my brief stint with his company, I was at hand to observe the realization of his dream. That was in 1942 when the company did become a full-fledged mutual legal reserve insurer, with a $250,000 capital structure.

By then there were more than 100,000 Negroes in the state. In the ensuing war years, the figure skyrocketed to probably more than the official estimate of 500,000. Thus was Nickerson's prophetic vision also fulfilled.

What I thought most amazing, as I familiarized myself with its history, was that during the difficult depression years, the tiny company had not only kept afloat, but en route, had accomplished a feat I understand was unprecedented in California insurance annals: to climb from the lowly Chapter Nine status to that of the old-line insurers, its original assets increased from $28,000 to more than $1,000,000.

The story which unfolded was not only one of dogged courage, but of determination and resourcefulness which tri-

umphed over difficulties which at that period so many business firms found insuperable all over the country. It was a
story of solid achievement, of creating jobs, of helping Negroes
buy homes and income properties when most white loan
agencies refused to consider anything in a Negro neighborhood. The company was truly a beacon of hope to the hard-
pressed people of color when, next to food, hope was what
they most needed.

Knowing that man and his associates and what they had
accomplished was a heartening experience, and a reminder
of the many Negro men and women who had successfully
created similar businesses against equally great odds in other
parts of the country.

On the other hand, those very accomplishments pointed up
the reverse side of the coin, for responding to America's urgent
need for war materials, defense plants were blossoming everywhere, but they were not hiring Negroes except in token
numbers and then for only the most menial work.

This wasn't a local or state situation, but extended all over
our nation, creating among us a widespread bitterness. It was
bad enough that we were not acceptable to industry in peace-
time, but it was worse when our country was locked in a
death struggle with Germany and Japan.

In our view, Negro soldiers were working, fighting and
getting killed in the war and were being drafted for more of
the same in increasing numbers. If we were good enough for
that, why were we not good enough to help produce the
desperately needed material for which our nation's leaders
pleaded?

That could hardly fail to be embittering, especially since
we heard constantly over the radio and read daily in the newspapers how acute was the manpower shortage, and how every
American must help. Yet, such pleas were not meant for us.
Among ourselves we spoke of that, and of the weird feeling
we had of being non-existent.

What finally altered this situation was the threat of a "March on Washington" by fifty thousand Negroes in protest of discrimination in the armed forces, another sore spot, and in the war industry. The leader of this movement was A. Philip Randolph, organizer and president of the Pullman Porters Union, who had the powerful backing of the NAACP, the Urban League, and other groups.

This threat, which its sponsors definitely intended carrying out, created a sufficient flurry in Washington to cause a Fair Employment Practices Commission to be hastily set up on the direct order of President Roosevelt. Between it and the War Manpower Commission, factory doors slowly opened to Negro labor, a process accelerated during the next two years when the vast pool of Negro labor was the only one remaining untapped.

California factories yielded quickly and almost overnight there was an astonishing increase in the number of Negro war workers, including quite a few women.

Too, especially on Central Avenue, my ears caught more "downhome brogue" than usual. The war boom had arrived, a fact made personal when we were able to sell our thousand-dollar house for $2,700 two years after we'd bought it.

I'd been casting about for a way to increase my earnings and I found it when I was offered a spot as a route manager for the home circulation department of the Los Angeles *Examiner*. My territory was large, covering most of the East-side; and while handling thirty-five or more carriers between the ages of eleven and fifteen was one continuous headache, the profits were excellent indeed.

I kept the job a year. During that time I learned much, not only about daily paper circulation methods, but what many of my people were thinking, for I had to visit hundreds of their homes. In that way I had a chance to talk with many of my racial kin, mostly newly-come warworkers. I also chatted constantly with soldiers and sailors of my race.

Out of it all there emerged a pattern of opinion which was disquieting, even to me. There seemed general agreement that: this was a white man's war and ought to be fought exclusively by them until they exterminated each other. And thank God for Hitler on account of he started all this mess and maybe he and the rest of the Peckerwoods would keep fighting until they learned some sense. But wasn't it a crying shame they made *our* boys help fight their white war? Because everybody knew the whites didn't mean them any good, no matter how fine the colored boys worked and fought. It was going to be the same old soup warmed over, like after World War I, when as fast as our soldiers came back from France, the white folks snatched their guns and put shovels and mops into their hands and made it clear nothing had changed—for them.

"But just one thing, cousin: they ain't foolin' nobody with that democracy jive. Not no more and not nowheres. Because they treats the colored soldiers so bad even in them foreign countries that them foreigners can't help seein' it and even foreigners ain't simple enough to believe Americans sure 'nough mean that stuff about democracy they yellin' all around the world, not when they treat they own soldiers, they *black* soldiers, like they was scum."

"Democracy? man, you got it wrong. Its de-mockery."

"Aw naw, man, it's de-pocrisy."

"All y'awl's wrong. It's de-pox. And, man, de-pox is a bitch on wheels. I mean, it's *bad!*"

So went the talk, constant, with laughter, but bitter underneath.

With our soldiers and sailors there was little laughter, only hard, cold resentment.

You ask: "Well, soldier, how's it going? How do you like the Man's Army?"

And he: "What you mean *like* it? How the hell I'm going

to like what they put on us? Nobody but a damn fool would. Or some brown-nosing clown, which is the same thing."

And another: "They don't treat us like men, but they expect us to act like men. And die like men, too. Mister, you can have it."

But I didn't want it. I was beginning to wonder if I wanted any part of my native land.

Soon after we bought our second home, I completed the first draft of a novel upon which I'd been working when I first met Helen. During the year I handled the newspaper route, it had gathered dust.

I read it again; and decided against going on with it because more clearly than ever it seemed evident that my theme would not be welcome, however well it might depict certain aspects of our national life, for that theme concerned miscegenation.

For a year I'd concentrated on making money. I was resolved to continue that course; and the way to do so certainly was not by wasting time writing what was unwanted.

Helen saw it differently. "You never know until you try," she insisted.

I reminded her I had tried with that other book I'd written in the mid-thirties, and that it hadn't found a publisher, apparently because its theme was similar to my present one.

"That was then," my wife pointed out. "You yourself have remarked that certain publishing taboos, particularly racial ones, have been fading since Richard Wright's *Native Son* made such a big success."

"I know all that," I countered, "but I also know my book is no *Native Son*. It hasn't a chance."

Since Helen said no more I thought the subject was dead. But it wasn't, for my wife prodded me until I reworked the script.

While doing so, I mentioned the project in replying to a

letter from a friend, a successful white writer, and he asked that when it was finished I send it to him before I tried to place it with a publisher, and I did.

My writer friend kept the script quite a while and when he returned it, his comment on my theme confirmed my own opinion as to its unacceptability.

Despite my wife's insistence that regardless of how famous, the opinion of my critic was but one, and besides, that he was a writer, not a publisher, I put the work aside. I wished never to see it again and I resolved that I was finished with writing. One morning I even started to burn the script, but couldn't quite do it. I compromised by burying it in an old box of books and papers in a dark corner of our garage. I was determined to forget it.

But every once in a while I thought of it, and every time I did I felt a deep-down ache.

A year passed. I thought Helen had forgotten that abandoned novel, but she had not. She told me one day that she'd met a girl named Jean Himes, the wife of Chester Himes whose *Esquire* stories I'd so much admired. And she jockeyed me into suggesting that we have them to dinner. Later I learned the invitation had already been extended—by her.

So I met Chester and Jean and learned of his long, dogged struggle to become a novelist, and that he now stood on the threshold of that ambition for he was completing a book titled *If He Hollers Let Him Go* under contract to a major publisher.

His book was what is called a "protest novel" although stories with the same general theme concerning whites or even other non-Negro groups are not so tagged, a matter we discussed at once, agreeing it was unfair, seeing in it the identical pattern of setting Negroes apart from their fellow Americans and their culture as was the norm on supposedly less enlightened levels.

There was red meat, for I rarely encountered anyone who

also had faced problems of this kind and who recognized in
them a cultural segregation which seemed as definite and
rigid as the Jim Crow laws of the South.

But unlike myself, Himes had simply refused to be stopped
by that, even though he, as I, found it insupportable that the
product of Negro writers, when its theme was racial, should
be classed as "Negro literature" by those who dictated the
norms of aesthetic appreciation and controlled the channels
of public recognition.

Whereas for years I had pulled back, Himes had stubbornly shoved ahead, using the theme of his choice, and
finally he had won through. I realized that was how it probably had to be done, regardless of race.

All the while I was hoping Helen wouldn't mention the
novel I'd "buried," which, of course, she did at the first
chance, taking the position that I'd not given it or myself a
fair chance.

Himes agreed, saying you had to slug until something gave
and I countered by stating my unwillingness for that something to be me; and that besides, I couldn't chance it because
of my wife and child.

One argument Himes did not voice: the acceptance of his
own fiery novel.

The result of this discussion was that he asked to read my
script and Helen at once scurried to the garage to get it and
Himes asked with a grin, "What's the matter, Will? Scared?"
and I answered, "Perhaps," and Mrs. Himes said, "Hey, would
somebody please tell me what you two geniuses are talking
about?"

Chester laughed and said, "Thunder, honey," and I nodded
and said, "That's it," and his wife shook her head and said,
"I don't get it," but could pursue the subject no more because
just then Helen returned with my dusty manuscript.

Chester read the novel, said he liked it and wanted to

write an editor he knew in its behalf. I thanked him and told him to go ahead.

I heard from the editor promptly and at his invitation sent him my novel. If ever an editor was on my side, that one was on mine, but months later he wrote that the decision was against my book, but that he still believed in it and wished to turn it over to one of his friends who was a literary agent.

I had tried to keep my guard up, but that was a blow which got past it. However, I sent the script to the agent and thereby let myself in for a series of similar blows over the next year.

CHAPTER *fifteen*

CALIFORNIA NEVER HAD SUCH A BOOM AS finally exploded when its new war industries got into high gear, for then it greedily sucked from other states, mostly Southern, an ever-growing horde of wage-hungry workers. They flooded in by the thousands, the white and the non-white, jamming all available housing, overflowing into motor courts, trailer camps, and even into vacant stores.

At this time we had lived in our second house about a year, but had not realized how acute the housing shortage was until we were offered $7,500 for it.

We certainly wanted to sell at that price, for it was four thousand dollars more than we had paid. Yet we hesitated lest we should not find another place within our means. But our luck was good and we were able to buy a much larger house for $9,500. It was a handsome, substantial structure of ten rooms, with a deep, wide lot. Better still, another, smaller house on an adjacent lot went with it.

The reason we got such a place at so modest a price was because its owner believed it, like the other houses in the block, was protected by covenant so that it could be purchased only by white persons of the Christian faith. Knowing that no whites were likely to invest in a neighborhood rapidly filling up with non-whites, he offered me the property at the price mentioned if I could find a way to legally make the deal.

Playing a hunch, I called a friend who was a lawyer and when we checked the records, we found that the covenant barring Negroes and non-Christians had expired a year previously. So the deal was made.

Helen was delighted with so fine and spacious a home. So was I, but I obtained even more satisfaction in having gotten it at such a bargain only because it had been barred to the non-white and the non-Christian by a legal process which to me seemed truly un-American.

In our communities the terrific influx aroused alarm as already teeming ghettos swelled, burst, and spread into other rundown areas.

What many locals feared was that the often uncouth newcomers would create an anti-Negro sentiment in a social climate heretofore not really oppressive. That would be serious, for the impact of tens of thousands of Southern whites would be sufficiently poisonous without our own emigrés adding to it.

Various of our community organizations joined to combat the bad effects we feared, hoping to lessen them by influencing and schooling our raucous country cousins to more seemly ways.

Perhaps our efforts helped, for as time passed, it did not seem that the impact of the dark influx was going to be ruinous after all. But to me it seemed that something else was really responsible which many of us did not take into account: an intense hunger for a better life, the identical hunger which had brought most of *us* to Los Angeles.

Many of the newcomers wanted, just as did we, the maximum of freedom and of all the good things possible to them in this wonderful California land. These worked hard, saved hard, kept their eyes fixed on what seemed a primary goal:

ownership of a home. And when there was enough money, they did buy homes, by the thousands.

These were the sober savers, the industrious, struggling determinedly toward a security and a status they had never known, but for which they had long yearned.

There were many, of course, of another type who joyously plunged into debt for flashy cars, raiment colorful in the California style, and spent their big wages to make the Central Avenue cafés, bars, clubs and joints jump with a frenetic beat.

But these fed a different hunger from that of the sober savers, for it was a starveling of the spirit, of the senses for the rich froth of life: the proud, sensuous feel of new fine clothes on flesh more accustomed to denim and butternut; and the heavenly joy of playing the high-life rôle and, righteously draped, to swagger into the flossy cocktail lounges and glittering bars, there to mingle with the big city guys and gals with their white folks' ways and white folks' talk.

Ah, Lawd, it sure were most bardacious fine!

But after saltback and hominy grits, patched clothes, leaky shacks and constant, inexorable pressures which mashed them down, body and soul, and the requirement that they forever bow and scrape and say *"Yassah, boss, yassah,"* and *"yasmam, Miz, yasmam,"* down in 'Bam, were these to be adjudged merely foolish, childish, frivolous, debauched, too quickly forgetful of grinding yesterdays? Too heedless of tomorrows inevitably just as bleak?

They were, by many of us. Those simple Sams from Alabam were acting exactly as the white folks said all Negroes acted—just as they expected all of us to act.

We, of course, were not like that, but what did that matter, with all those downhome bloobies acting so badly? Why hadn't they stayed back down there where they belonged?

That seemed a general feeling. I didn't share it, especially when most of it was expressed in accents still as thick as red

Georgia clay, or Louisiana blackstrap molasses, or Mississippi mud. For those themselves but recently from Dixie seemed most vociferous in expressing disdain for the gauche newcomers.

Once, with a friend, I stood watching the loud, garish scene at Forty-Third and Central Avenue. The regular Saturday night parade surged past, murmurous, raucous with laughter and vivid badinage, colorfully arrayed, proud-stepping; and obviously the littered sidewalks were really fine, warm, pink clouds. It seemed wonderful to me, but my companion, a Tennessean until six years previously, thought it was disgraceful.

"You know," he said disgustedly, "maybe the white folks *are* right about Sam. Just look at all those darkies cutting the fool! Throwing their money away like it was only trash. Guzzling booze. Hollering like everybody was stone deaf. They have got to go!"

"They'll smooth down," I predicted. "Just give them a little time."

"Some hell they will," my friend snorted. "Just look at that big spade in that crazy zoot suit. It's purple, man. Purple! And get that coat—hitting him right at the *knees!* Man, I'll bet that joker got sewed in those narrow-bottom britches and sleeps in 'em, else how could he ever get those big feet through 'em again? But does he ever think he's burning hell! Man, look at that steelhead strut!"

The tall, zoot-suited lad patently did think he was hot stuff, a splendiferously knocked-out character; and his gait *was* a swaggering slow-drag strut. For wasn't he dressed right down to the bricks in the very sharpest drapes?

Man, he *was!*

But it wasn't just his clothes which made him feel his oats so hard, because it derived from other things, like the genuine imitation leather wallet with a zipper in his hip pocket, which was a constant reminder of his new estate.

Inside it was evidence of the same: his *papers*, his cre-dentals, his Soshul Scurity card which was, he knew, very important even though he didn't know why.

There was also his membership card in the Jim Crow "affiliate" of the shipyard union to which he believed he belonged, and for which his employers kindly paid his dues out of his wages. There was also his precious identification badge with his picture sealed in its plastic cover, and too, a paycheck voucher which he was going to send down home to *prove* he sure enough had earned *seventy-eight dollars and sixteen cents in just five and one-half days*, and only eight-hour days at that!

There wasn't any money in his wallet, though. *That* was in his right-hand pants pocket, glowing against his thigh and pleasuring his hand when he caressed the magic paper wad, or even when his hand merely brushed against the bulge in his pants made by thirty one-dollar bills with a twenty on top, a five at the bottom.

Besides, a man couldn't as effectively flash his fine bankroll when it was imprisoned in a wallet.

Two final items: a pint of whiskey in his inner coat pocket; and in his watch pocket, a switch-blade knife, its pearl handle protruding just enough to be quickly grasped.

So why should he not have a big feeling and strut like a peacock bird?

I wondered if he ought not be more envied than condemned by the more enlightened, for his sensations, his joys and delights were vivid, were pristine, not jaded nor vitiated by sterile, repressive codes.

And what if his horizons were so frankly circumscribed? Had his "betters," by vastly expanding their own, made a sweeter world? If so, why was their past a blood-spattered scroll, and why their present a hellish nightmare of flaming death?

And (perhaps enviously) I thought: *Go along then, brown*

*lad, and brown lass, too, and strut and laugh and love in your
vital and uncultured way while yet you may, for soon, alas,
you will be taught how completely wrong is your crude pursuit of happiness.*

And my friend said darkly, vengefully: *"One of these days
all this war work will end and all these Sams will have to go
back to the cotton fields because most of 'em won't have a
crying dime left. They'll go back to corn pone and salt pork
and a white man's foot in their crack, and no damn better
for 'em, I say!"*

But you, dark lad. What say you? And what of tomorrow?

And he: *"What ole mammy-dodgin' termorrer you wolfin'
'bout, man? Get out'n my cool brown face with that there
termorrer jive, 'cause who give a good goddam about a day
you ain't yit even seed? It never done me nothin' good until
now, today, and I'm ona pitch me a bitch while I got th'
chancet. You know, man?"*

I reckoned I did.

Our new house had plenty of room, and a good thing, too,
Helen said, choosing that way to let me know our family
was going to increase again. The months between that announcement and its fulfillment seemed to fly. Helen hoped
for another girl, but seemed just as happy when the new
arrival was a boy. We named him Bradley, after Helen's
father. He was as sturdy and handsome as his brother, but
was as fair as his sister, which did not particularly overjoy us.
We were pleased that at least *his* hair was dark.

Nate got a writing job for me which proved unexpectedly
lucrative. It was "ghosting" an autobiography of a retired
shoe manufacturer who had come from Russia in his youth,
penniless, knowing no English, who wished now to tell of
the opportunities of America through which he had been able
to win a fortune. We agreed on a price for the work, and it

was most generous. When it was finished, several months later, the man insisted on paying me almost twice the sum we had set.

Another good break during this period was the sale of an original story to a motion picture company.

But my book still had not been placed, and while my agent continued to work at it, I hadn't much hope. One house kept it for five months. Then the bad news: no sale.

There might have been one, though, for my agent sent me a letter from the editor of the company to which my book was next sent. The letter stated that while my story had been turned down in its present state, " . . . we would be glad to consider it again if certain revisions are made." And my agent urged that I make those revisions at once.

But I didn't. I couldn't. Because, to indicate there had been interest in the book, the editor had quoted several reader reports, one of which said: *With proper revisions this would make a quite satisfactory novel. It is certainly publishable. I would not press for our doing it, however, because . . . I do not see a very promising future for a writer who would probably continue to base his writings upon Negro more than human situations and problems.*

Negro situations and problems.

Human situations and problems.

There was a difference?

Apparently in the white view, there was. I read that paragraph several times trying to discover if there was a meaning in it different from that conveyed by its wording, but I could not. Because, unless Negroes were not of the human species, how could *any* situation or problem involving them be of a nature unlike those of any humans, including whites?

I thought how deadly was the trap in which we were caught. For while we could and had altered our original African cultural traits to accord with the general mores of American society, we could not by so doing, unlike other ethnic groups, find acceptance. Physical traits such as color, hair texture, and other surface differences, purely functional in origin, are practically permanent. And yet it was these physical traits which branded us as inferior.

But to write of situations and problems arising out of those differences as a part—a valid part—of the American scene was to write of *Negro* situations, *Negro* problems; and these were somehow lacking in universality. Is that what the white brother believed?

In any event, although my agent thought me unduly sensitive, also foolish to pass up such an opportunity, I didn't revise my script then or later when, from time to time, he forwarded me letters from that editor inquiring how I was coming with the suggested revisions.

Looking back, this episode probably marked the point at which I really gave up on my native land, for it occurred to me that my every major contact with life had been in one way or another spoiled by the poison of race prejudice of a kind against which it was impossible to defend.

And I wondered sadly if *that* was a Negro situation, a purely Negro problem, completely unrelated to those who had created it, and therefore not a matter of interest to them or anyone else.

It was at about this time that the atomic bombs were dropped on Hiroshima and Nagasaki. That my country had done that to a foe which, in my opinion, was obviously beaten and aching to cry quits, saddened and shamed me; and if there persisted even the wish to believe in the innate goodness of America, it was rooted out with a pain almost physical.

For it seemed to me we had not needed so terrible a weapon under the circumstances; and I thought—could not help thinking—that perhaps it might have been done for two reasons: to test our new bomb's destructive power upon human beings—human beings who did not matter to us—and at the same time to serve notice to Asia, to all *colored* peoples specifically, of what might be expected if ever any of them dared emulate Japan by attacking white nations.

I'm sure that was not true. But at that time it was all too easy to believe that it was, because it seemed so precisely of the historical pattern established by Europeans to maintain control over its colonial possessions, which included most of the world's colored people. There was also an inescapable domestic parallel to the action: the American technique of maintaining control over its Negro citizens through lynching, and the warning implicit therein against violence to whites.

And I wondered why I remained in a country in which I had so completely lost faith. If I did not like the way things were, I was at least free to seek better conditions elsewhere. All I needed was the desire and enough money. Now I had the one; the other I could get.

CHAPTER *sixteen*

While Helen and I had often discussed emigration, she had never seemed to regard it as a serious possibility. But when I brought it up at this time, I discovered she had given the idea considerably more thought than I'd suspected.

Even more surprising was that beneath her placid exterior, Helen harbored an unexpectedly sharp bitterness of her own. I'd known that she disliked white people in general, but I'd not known exactly why.

At that time, when so many things seemed to confirm what I felt against my country, I learned why Helen found it easy to share my feelings.

She had grown up in a series of small West Virginia and Pennsylvania towns to which her father was called as a minister of the African Methodist Episcopal Church.

These were usually coal mining communities. Relations between whites, mostly first-generation Poles or other Europeans, and Negroes were generally good; and frequently they were next-door neighbors.

Helen's father insisted that his children apply themselves to their school studies and so fired them with a desire for education that all of them did well. Helen, the eldest, excelled from grammar school on.

During her first two years of high school in the Pennsylvania town where her family lived at that time, there were stories in the local daily newspaper about how the daughter of a Negro preacher (her father) was the ranking scholar of the high school.

Such excellence made her family proud and sparked Helen's brothers and sisters to emulate it.

But in Helen's junior year the grading system was suddenly changed from point to letter, making it impossible (on the record) for any student who had done well enough to be graded in the top classification, indicated by the letter S, to surpass others in that bracket.

Yet, at the end of the next year, and despite the abandonment of the point system of grading, the daughter of a school board member was adjudged to have won out over Helen as valedictorian by *three-tenths of a point*.

Then it was abruptly decided to have a pageant instead of the customary commencement exercises whose features were speeches by both valedictorian and salutatorian, the latter honor having been bestowed on Helen. No Negro had ever before won either honor at that high school.

The final blow was that Helen and the only other Negro girl in the class were assigned the only non-speaking parts in the pageant.

Helen refused to take part in the pageant and also, as one of the two top-ranking graduates, refused proffered scholarships to two Pennsylvania colleges. The very idea, she told me, of *ever* having white teachers or attending a white school again made her ill.

The incident had a marked effect on her brothers and sisters, who at once ceased being keen about making good grades, or learning. Why do that when the white folks cheated you out of what you had fairly earned?

Helen chose to attend Wilberforce University, a Negro school in Ohio, even though neither she nor her father knew how they would manage her expenses. But, as she put it, between themselves and the Lord, they would somehow make do.

They did. Through the help of her hard-pressed family and the scholarships she regularly won——and received——and later through getting her board and room as recompense for editing the college newspaper, and perhaps, as she said, through a nudge from Above, Helen finished her four years with high honors.

It had not been easy, but she had been happy, had enjoyed the social life at Wilberforce and had been inspired by her contact with its faculty. Her dearest wish was to pursue a career in a solidly Negro community, with as little contact as possible with white people.

So what did she think of the idea of leaving the U.S.A.?

Helen thought well of it——*if* we were going to a non-white country.

Well, how about Mexico?

Mexico? But wasn't that a white country? At least, Mexicans were listed as white in the U. S. Census.

Yeah, they were so listed——as of 1937, or thereabouts. "Good Neighbor" stuff. But Mexico was not white in the sense she meant. Many dark-skinned folks held high office down there. And many of Mexico's heroes had been dark. Like Villa. *Viva, Villa!* Not light of skin like Carranza. *Chinga la madre, Carranza!*

Hmmm. . . .

Well then, how about Brazil? Or if you wanted the *real* thing, how about Haiti?

Haiti? Oh yes, that was a *Negro* republic, *Yes!*

Haiti . . .

The decision made, we began at once to gather the information we would need to carry it out.

For the next few months our lives were unchanged, out-
wardly; but as our plans to emigrate extended into actual
preparation, I, at least, was conscious of deep inner shiftings.

We told no one of our plans.

One rainy spring afternoon as I sat reading in the bathroom, I was distracted by a succession of unusual sounds. On
the fringe of awareness I'd heard the door chimes. But soon
thereafter there began an excited yipping, initiated by my
wife and chorused enthusiastically by our small fry. Then
with thudding of a herd, a small one, they all galloped to
the bathroom door, the kids still yipping and Helen crying
out, "Will! Will! Good news! *Wonderful* news! Come out of
there!"

"I can't right now," I called back. "What's all the racket
about?"

"Your book," Helen screamed. "Your *book!* A telegram
from your agent about your book!"

"Well, for gosh sakes, read it," I shouted.

"You *would* be hung up in the privy at a time like this,"
my wife yelled back.

"Read that telegram," I roared.

There was a brief interval while Helen sternly shushed
the children. Then she read: "Have offer from (she named
the publisher) of a contract and thousand-dollar advance for
development of part one of your book as first novel of a
trilogy to be carved from the rest of it. Publication this fall."
There was a silence, then Helen added breathlessly, "That's
all."

"That's plenty!" I yelled, and it was my turn to yip, to
howl, and to break out of the bathroom. I grabbed the telegram from Helen, read it carefully, understood not a word,
then seized her and danced her wildly around the room, with
our youngsters careening behind us chanting, "Daddy's got
a bo—ook, Daddy's got a bo—ook."

But it was a book which had Daddy. At least he had to

write one, a new one, almost from scratch. It was a heavenly and a terrifying prospect. I was supremely confident I could do it and equally certain I could not.

But finally I'd got my chance. What I did with it from then on was strictly up to me.

"Will this change our plans?" Helen asked later.

"No," I replied. "It works in with them fine. Because for a writer, a new scene, a new land—"

Helen smiled, nodded, and said quietly, "For a *writer*, yes."

That was her way of saying many things she need not detail. For it was her faith which had revived mine, which had made me try once more after I'd sworn never to write again. Now a miracle had come to pass and I thought, it *was* a triumph of faith.

Helen's faith.

There then began a period of feverish work on my book, with time out now and then for other matters, such as deciding which of our goods we would dispose of and, of course, planning to sell our property. We knew the amount we would get for the latter would be very good, at least double what we had paid, since real estate was still rising.

Helen was busy, too. Getting the information we needed about the country to which we were going was in her department. We thus learned much of Haiti, its customs, climate and the all-important matter of living costs, which to us seemed incredibly low. If all went well, we would be able to live in good style there for eight or ten years on the amount we calculated we'd have after selling our property and certain other possessions.

The whole idea looked better all the time. We'd each had some college French, enough for a start. And I'd not have to depend upon trying to sell my writing for at least two years, since I was under contract to my publisher for two more books which were to be completed within that time.

And that seemed that. Practically *un fait accompli*, as the Haitians would phrase it.

But the book I was writing was not in like case. I knew well the story I wished to tell. It was based upon real incidents which had been something of a *cause célèbre* in Louisiana many years ago. So it had not been difficult to plan the framework, but it was something else again to construct it. Perplexing problems of a kind never before encountered seemed constantly to spring up at me right out of my typewriter. All sorts of fascinating by-paths continually opened before me which I knew I must not explore.

And then there were those dreadful days when no matter how long I sat at my work, nothing came, all was maddeningly blank.

Knowing that *this* book would be published was an inexorable prod. I grudged each day because I knew I had not done all that I might; and after a while it was a race with time in which I ran slowly, clumsily, like it is sometimes in dreams.

All the while I knew quite well I should try to sell my boat, *The Amazon*, for unlike housing and practically everything else, watercraft were not in short supply. But I was reluctant and dallied until my book was finished before I finally put her on the block. Nor was I overjoyed when, only three weeks before we planned to leave, the man who had made the one and only serious inquiry about her, bought her.

Not until our propery was sold did we tell anyone what we planned. Most of our friends seemed shocked that we were going to leave the country. Such news travels fast. Many who knew us began dropping by, and our telephone jingled with unaccustomed frequency. With few exceptions, everyone wanted to know if it was true that we were going to Haiti, and if so, why.

Such interest was not unpleasant, at first, for it seemed an indication of our friends' concern. Soon we felt differently, for many of them made it plain they thought what we were planning was foolish. Why did we want to jump up and leave our lovely home and income, property and everything, when things were breaking so fine for us? And why this and why that until we wished we had withheld our news until just a few days before we left.

Our two houses brought an even better price than we had hoped for, and we could have got more had we tried, but we had a guilty feeling that we were profiteering, as it was.

The next step was to sell the furniture and other personal things we would not want to take to Haiti. We felt no qualms about disposing of the rather costly furnishings we had bought after we had acquired our present home, but we were reluctant to be rid of certain cherished articles painfully gained during the first two years of our marriage when we'd lived in a little shack of a house and thought it a palace because it was ours.

Misgivings thus aroused were the first small, dark clouds upon our bright new horizon. What with my book done, our property sold, and other important matters fairly well settled, there was more time, more leisure than we had known for months. The ensuing calm seemed unreal.

There were still loose ends still to be gathered, but the need for hurry was ended. Yet I felt like a machine which could not slow down.

Helen and I needed rest, and while she was able to let down and take things easier, I could not. I prowled about nervously, trying to comprehend why I felt so gloomy when I ought to be rejoicing, for what I had wanted so fiercely would soon be mine.

That *was* what I had wanted, wasn't it?

Well, *wasn't* it?

Of course. What I wanted for myself, for my family, did not exist in our country, at least not for us. For had I not trav-

eled it well? Had I not looked closely and long upon the ugly
sores as well as upon the beauty of America?

No, I could not possibly be mistaken.

Why then the leaden feeling of my heart, the shadows
which so often drifted across mind and spirit? Why the vague
sadness I felt?

It could not be I feared the outcome of our venture. We
had enough money to carry it out, and in addition, had other
resources which could be turned into cash if and when the
need arose.

Then what? Surely, *surely*, I felt no regret to leave the
U.S.A.—not I! Because I had come to hate it, hadn't I? How
could I help hating it if only because I had been forced to a
choice of acceptance of an imposed inferiority I found intolerable, or the alternative of *having* to go elsewhere to escape
it?

No doubt had my native land been captive, like India,
while I would have hated its captors I would hardly have
wished to leave it, but would have stayed and fought for its
freedom, and thereby, my own.

But my land was not captive to any other, it was free, its
real masters were its people, and its like existed nowhere else,
for it was constituted a democracy, was founded upon the
principles of liberty, justice and the equality of all men.

Yet because that was so, the dose was doubly bitter, at least
it was for its children who were excluded, who were not admitted to that avowed equality, its dark offspring, and too,
its white offspring who were not of the Christian faith, even
though freedom of religion was also a basic tenet of America.

How could I be mistaken about all that?

It did not seem that I could. Yet when those bitter thoughts
slowed, I would catch myself listening, straining to tune up a
barely sensed murmur of doubt into something compre-
hensible, but it faded back into the silences only, when I was

again off guard, to whisper again, to vibrate inarticulate warning . . . admonition . . . and—promise.

At such times the razored outlines of my bitterness would blur and somewhere beyond I seemed to sense the existence of some wonderful revelation whose meaning, except for a maddening hair, I could almost grasp.

Baffled, disturbed, I'd close my consciousness to that mute, tantalizing thing, for I suspected it was but an atavistic echo of some ancient fear lost deep in time, which I must not permit to betray my quest for manhood or to impair my conviction of its validity. Anyway, it was only natural that I should feel *some* misgivings at the prospect of leaving my native land, intending never to return. If that was all that was wrong, why was I worrying?

After a while I discovered why. But even then I resisted allowing my mind to enunciate it, because I feared it.

With something like desperation I resolved that there must be no compromise in *this* matter. I would not even contemplate it, nor resignation either, for then I'd be lost. Nor could anything force me to tolerate any longer who or what assailed me and even though the odds were insuperable, I would never cease to fight, to struggle against all that.

No, others might think as they chose, adjust to the cruel mold if they so wished, rationalize the intolerable if they could, and on levels high and low, play the sycophant to gain small ends or large, but never that for me, for I had never been able to genuflect or to accept without an acid surge of protest the American way of life as I, and all other American Negroes must live it, *if* we wished to live.

I tried to keep what I was thinking and feeling to myself, but it was impossible to conceal my morose, irritable state, and often I felt my wife's troubled gaze upon me.

One day, a few weeks before our scheduled departure, I got to thinking about how one dreams of running away from the mother he believes is unloving, until the time comes to do it.

Then, perhaps, a disturbing discovery is made: one had not realized how strong is the natal bond, had not known the umbilicus is endowed with memory; and with dismay the heart unaccountably floods with nostalgic sorrow for a deed not even accomplished.

But remembrance dies hard; the flesh bleeds again beneath the mother's unjust lash; the old wounds ache anew; and the exile from the family circle feels again the raw, hot hurt, the bewildered lost sorrow engendered by his exclusion from it, knowing it is not deserved.

It was as though I stood miserable, outside the home I could not enter, gazing longingly inside it at my mother, my brothers, at my kin who had spurned me, and that was like dying. And that was how it had been for me in my country.

My country? No, not my country but only where, choiceless, I'd been born, and where in whatever direction I might gaze, were high walls towering between America's children, dividing them one from the other according to race, creed, color, class . . . and of those walls, the very highest enclosed all of pigmented skin.

Yes, that was how it truly was in my motherland and yet —and yet the incredible, the dismaying fact was that despite it . . . I loved her.

That is why we did not go to Haiti.

That is why we did go to Vermont.

And wonderingly, frightenedly, and with a kind of awe, I began dimly to realize love's terrible power, whether for man, or for one's native soil. And it came to me *that*, at least, was worth fighting for.

Part Two

CHAPTER *one*

A<small>ND THUS, OUR FIRST NIGHT IN</small> V<small>ER</small>-
mont: my wife and children soundly sleeping, and I, wakeful,
my mind captive to the surge of other years among which I
searched for what finally I concluded was not there. Then,
exhausted, I fell into a troubled slumber. When I awakened,
gray light outlined a window; and I stared at it, puzzled
because its position seemed so unfamiliar. It took a while for
me to remember why, and I felt no joy at all.

As my eyes became accustomed to the half-light of dawn,
I could discern how small was this bedchamber in this unlovely little house; and I could not help recalling how spacious
ours had been in our California home. But I halted that
thought right there and forced myself to dwell on the present
—the immediate present.

I'd lain awake half the night trying to come to some de-
cision about staying in Vermont, or more exactly, in the
United States. I thought I'd made that decision before leaving
California, but how quickly had old doubts revived!

Thinking of them, I groaned, and as if to escape, I eased
out of the warm bed, careful lest I disturb my wife. The chill
bit at my bare ankles and almost drove me back beneath the
covers. But soon my family would be awaking, so, in robe and
slippers, I crept quietly downstairs, intending to make a fire

in the furnace. But first coffee, if I could get the huge old oil stove in the kitchen to work.

For a moment I stood shivering in the kitchen doorway, peering at the formless black mass of that stove, my hand on the light switch. But I hesitated to switch on the light because it would announce we were awake and would generate anew speculations about us and—

In disgust at myself, I snapped on the light. This worrying, this forever anticipating the worst, it just had to go! I must meet situations as and when they developed, must strive for objectivity, form my judgments upon events and not probabilities.

All that was fine but it didn't help to meet the present situation: how to light that oil stove so I could make coffee. Cautiously I went to it and studied it for a while, thinking that it was the kind of thing I must be able to master from now on *if* we remained in Vermont.

If?

Well, since we were here, the sensible thing would be to at least give it a try. Maybe, just *maybe*—

The devil with that! I'd better get the stove started. I'd been looking at its two big burners and had located what appeared to be their controls. The idea probably was, I decided, to allow some oil to run into the burner wells before lighting. I turned the controls, waited a few seconds, then very cautiously I lighted one, and when it didn't explode, I lighted the other.

"Shucks," I thought, "nothing to it." But it wasn't so, for before the burners finally subsided to steady circles of blue flame they erupted tails of murky flame, then smoked sullenly until they flared alarmingly high and made ominous whooshing noises.

I finally got coffee made and then I had the impulse to thumb my nose at that stove and jeer a triumphant yanh-yanh-yanh, but that would have been childish.

I guess it was.

Helen appeared a short time later and inquired sleepily if I had made enough coffee for my poor, beat frau.

"Sure," I informed her. "Come, join me."

"Mmm, it's nice and warm down here," she said. "Upstairs it's freezing. Ugh!"

"This old monstrosity at least makes a lot of heat," I remarked, gesturing toward the stove.

"Well, that's good. And so is this coffee."

I was a trifle piqued that my wife did not seem to appreciate my feat in mastering the stove. But I was supposed to be able to cope with such things, wasn't I? Besides, the physical problems which would eventuate would hardly be as knotty as those of another kind.

As though she followed my thought, Helen asked, "How do you think things will be here? I mean, what should be expected from our townsmen?"

"I wish I knew," I sighed.

"I wonder how the weather is just now in Port au Prince?" my wife mused, elaborately casual.

"Low blow, beloved," I reproved.

"It is not. I was just thinking that in Haiti, we would not be starting our first day half frozen and worrying about how we were going to be received by the populace."

"Okay," I grumped, "rub it in, with salt, yet. Besides, you know perfectly well that had you not agreed with me on Vermont I'd have *never—*"

Helen laughed. "Got you that time, Pappy. How about some more coffee?"

I poured her coffee and said reasonably, "Well, the fact remains that you did agree on Vermont, you know. Besides, it is possible that Vermont will turn out well."

"Is it?" Helen asked quizzically.

"Not being a mind reader," I said stiffly, "I can't answer that. We'll just have to wait and see."

The waiting wasn't overlong. As we sat at breakfast an hour or so later, there was a knock at the kitchen door. Still in robe and slippers, Helen bounced up from the table with a muffled "My goodness!" and hastily departed.

Amid excited volleys of "Somebody's at the door, Daddy!" from our children, I went to see who it was. A sturdy woman in a leather jacket and faded blue jeans stood on the porch smiling from behind the thick lenses of her glasses.

"I'm Rene Callen, your next-door neighbor," she announced cheerily. "I thought you folks might be having difficulty with something or other." She nodded toward the kitchen stove. "Like that thing. New people usually have trouble with them at first. But I see you've got yours working okay."

"Yes. But it wasn't easy," I admitted. "Won't you come in, Mrs. Callen?"

"Well, just for a minute," she agreed in her breezy way. "And it's *Miss* Callen." She entered and her face lit up when she saw our youngsters and she called, "Hi, kids! How do you like Vermont?"

"Hi," little Will replied. "We like Vermont. Have you got any cows?"

Our caller blinked, grinned and said, "I'm afraid not. What's your name, sonny?"

"The same as my Daddy's," he informed her as he hopped from his chair and ran to a window. "Is that your house right next door?"

"It is," our caller admitted.

"Well, then," my son demanded, "how come you haven't got any cows in that great big ole barn back of your house?"

"Well," explained Miss Callen, "when my father was living, we used to have lots of cows. Do you like cows?"

"Sure," daughter Anne spoke up. "We just *love* cows. On account of they give you milk."

"Yeah," little Will chimed in, "and ice cream, too."

Bradley, our youngest, contented himself with peeking through his fingers and grinning at our visitor.

Eventually Miss Callen and I were able to exchange information not based on cows. I learned that she and her mother, an invalid, lived in the adjacent house and that until her father's death some years before, they had operated a dairy farm.

Then Helen appeared, now dressed in daytime clothes, and was introduced to our neighbor. But while her manner was friendly, I knew Helen was definitely on guard, whereas I was not, for Miss Callen seemed genuine, and even gave me the feeling of being a kindred spirit.

"It is very kind of you to come over," Helen told her. "And you are our very first caller, too."

"Well, I should hope so," Miss Callen chuckled. "I mean, at this hour. Well, I'd better get back home and let you folks finish your breakfast."

"Won't you join us?" my wife asked. "At least for a cup of coffee?"

"Thanks, but I breakfasted ages ago," our visitor smiled. "And I really must go now." She moved to the door, paused, and added, "Please feel free to call on me at any time. I know how it is, being in a strange place, a strange house. Okay?"

"That's a deal," I agreed. "We'll send up smoke signals, or something."

Miss Callen laughed and with a twinkling look, remarked, "That's really what brought me over."

"Huh?" I exclaimed.

"Smoke signals," she explained with a grin. "From your chimney."

"Oh—that," I said, hoping my falling feathers made no crash, for I'd thought I'd done a rather neat job of getting a fire going in our furnace. "I was—uh—burning some trash," I added, "and I guess it did make a lot of smoke."

Miss Callen nodded, but her tiny grin told me I wasn't kidding *her*. But she said, "Trash does make a lot of smoke. Well, see you later, eh?"

When she had departed Helen regarded me with a teasing smile. " 'Smatter, Pop? The furnace no good?"

"If," I replied, "your reference is to our neighbor's alarm over what seemed to her to be an excess of smoke, the fault was mine. The furnace was not properly regulated, that's all."

"Oh, sure," my wife laughed. "But that Miss Callen. She *seemed* nice. Could that be just the icing over the cake of curiosity?"

"How should I know?" I demanded. "But I don't believe it was. Yet, being female, no doubt she *was* curious."

"Females," my wife said tartly, "are no more curious than males. Where you lordly males get such ideas—"

"Mama, what does cur-i-ous mean?" daughter Anne inquired curiously.

So began the First Day, with me unable to rid myself of my wife's suspicion of Miss Callen. Was our neighbor, despite the solid-gold ring of her manner, a counterfeit, an enemy spy penetrating our fortress to make first-hand report on the dusky invaders?

Somehow, I just could not believe that.

But Helen could, and I am afraid that she did.

CHAPTER TWO

I HAD STOCKED UP WITH FOOD BEFORE I went down to New York to bring back my family, so it was not necessary for me to leave our premises that first day; and I was glad, for I did not want to face our townsmen again so soon. I spent the day helping Helen unpack.

The children, however, plagued us until, after sternly warning them not to go out of the yard, we allowed them to go outdoors to play.

Sometime later, I noticed Helen standing by a front window.

"I hope," she said sharply, "they see what they're looking for."

"What's wrong?" I asked.

"Oh, nothing important, I guess."

"Well, people are curious, you know."

"Yes, but they don't need to make it so darned obvious, do they?"

"Maybe they don't mean anything."

"When they stop out there and stare, maybe they do."

"Aw, forget 'em," I urged. "And just remember one thing: if it turns out we are really unwelcome here, we don't have to stay."

Helen turned from the window and said fervently, "Thank goodness for that!"

Our children trooped in then, their mouths and hands full of cookies.

"Where did you get those?" their mother demanded.

Anne said muffledly, "From Miss Callen." Then, after swallowing a couple of times, she added more clearly, "She sure makes good cookies, Mama."

"Yes, but didn't Mother tell you *not* to go out of our yard?"

"Yeah, but Miss Callen *called* us," little Will explained. "She's got a lot of cats, Mama."

"One of them hasn't got any tail," Bradley said, cramming his mouth with another cookie.

Helen looked at me in exasperation and I laughed. "Well, it was nice of our neighbor, wasn't it? Friendly-like?"

"Just the same," Helen said severely to our brood, "the next time Mother tells you not to do something and you disobey, you are all going to catch it, understand?"

The children nodded solemnly, still munching.

The next morning we had another caller, a ruddy, white-haired old fellow bearing a huge bunch of carrots.

Extending the carrots he said, "These are right out of my garden. Thought you might like 'em. Big 'uns, ain't they?"

I agreed they were indeed big 'uns, and I thanked him and invited him to come in. His hesitation being perfunctory, he required little urging.

"But I can't stay only a minnit," he said. "Heard there was some new folks moved in here and I had the thought I'd just drop by and say hello."

But old Roy stayed much longer than a minute. We could not help liking him and the children were fascinated by his continuous chatter, the way his blue eyes beamed, and by his manner of teasing them. They gathered around his chair and he rode Bradley on his leg.

Sometime later, when we finally had to shoo the children off the grandfatherly old man despite his protests that they

weren't bothering him, I offered him a drink and he chose gin
and water. After an hour and another small gin, old Roy departed, ruddier and certainly more spryly than when he had
arrived.

"Did you just have to offer him a drink?" Helen demanded
the minute he left. "Now he'll be telling people that we—"

"It's a crime to offer a drink to a caller?"

"No. But this isn't Los Angeles, or a city, remember. Up
here—"

"Up here, honey, we're exactly the same people we were
before we came. Right?"

"Oh—I know what you mean," Helen admitted. "But after
all—"

"After all, 'take me as I am, my love, for that is what I am,
said Sam'."

"Even so," Helen argued, "we don't want to give the
wrong impression, do we?"

" 'Take me as I am, my love,' " I began again and Helen
snapped, "Oh for heaven's sake, hush. You and Sam. You
don't have to use a hammer. I get the general idea."

"Nice going."

"But *please* put away that gin bottle, won't you?"

I laughed and obeyed and Helen said snippily, "It's not
funny, honey. Not under present circumstances."

"Okay, so it isn't," I agreed. "But if we've got to put on
an act hoping to impress these people with our great virtue,
then where's the gain?"

Despite our suspicion that old Roy might be a gossip, he
was definitely another entry on the credit side, Miss Callen
being the first, a fact Helen freely admitted as we grew to
know her better.

Almost at once a considerable traffic developed between our
houses. What won our increasing regard was not just Miss
Callen's unvarying cordiality and refreshing freedom from
the subtle (even though usually unwitting) patronage so

many of her race reveal toward colored people even when they mean to be kind, or tolerant, but a mutual interest in books, world affairs, and for a clincher, the discovery that she, too, had been in newspaper work.

Helen and I agreed it was a terrific bit of luck that our only near-neighbor should be someone like Rene.

We were delighted by her complete indifference to show, her lack of pretense, and her way of speaking with what seemed a complete disregard for conventions.

We wondered why Rene, whose talk revealed such liking for newspaper work, no longer followed it. We did not ask and Rene didn't explain. But we learned from others that she had given up her job on a Burlington daily in order to stay home and take care of her aged, ailing mother.

We each had many books the other had not read and we were soon swapping them back and forth; and soon Rene and I were often embroiled in friendly arguments about them, or anything else.

We often battled thus in her cheery, cat-inhabited kitchen, while from an adjacent room, her frail, white-haired mother would inject a quietly humorous comment when the spirit, or the subject, so moved her.

Mrs. Callen, in her mid-seventies, had for fifty years taught in local schools, and her mind was quick, perceptive, her commentary always gentle, kindly, tolerant of man's foibles.

I often visited with Mrs. Callen, too, listening with pleasure as she told me of her girlhood days, of her family that had resided in the town since 1805, and of the people and the town.

I knew, before I saw faded photographs which proved it, that Mrs. Callen had been lovely in her younger years, for she was still lovely in a way time could not erase. Her fragile, silver beauty was more than matched by the loveliness of her spirit.

Mrs. Callen was quite aware that her span was nearing its

end. In fact, during our first winter as her neighbors, she was several times so ill that everyone, including the newly-come woman physician who attended her, expected the worst at any time.

There must have been a good deal of pioneer toughness in her, for she willed to see another spring, and she saw it, and several more.

She often chuckled and said that we all worried about her more than she did herself. To her, death would come as an angel-guide to heaven and of that, and the thereafter in God's golden realm, she was serenely and completely certain. Her pure, unwavering faith, although she never knew it, I'm sure, was a continual rebuke, stirring, as nothing else ever had, an uneasy doubt of the validity of my own agnosticism.

One morning during our first week in the village, we awakened to fields glittering with the season's first frost. Our children were delighted, thinking it was snow, and wanted to dress immediately and go to play in it. They had never seen snow and had looked forward to it as a main feature of their new environment.

What I didn't know was that frost was a catalyst which almost overnight set the somber countryside ablaze, with each new day revealing progressively more vivid hues.

At first I thought it must be terrific contrast to the forever green of California, of which ofttimes I had grown so weary, that made this new scene seem touched with such sheer beauty, so rich, so immense I could not quite credit what my eyes beheld.

Yet it wasn't that, nor yet an unfamiliarity with like scenes, for practically all my years had been lived in the North where seasonal changes are always as marked. Too, I'd spent some time in Canada, whose autumnal garb I'd thought magnificent.

But my reactions to that first Vermont fall were not

thoughts, critical or otherwise. They were of feeling, of emotion.

That bothered me, made me wonder whether it all was but a subtle trick of Fate to seduce me with a painted jade who loved me not and never would. Because if I came to love her beauty, might I not, lover-like, overlook her flaws?

I sought a counter, summoned other scenes which had moved me: amethyst, tropic dawns, murmurous with gentle breezes stirring among palms . . . the diamond glint of arctic sun upon a blue-white Alaskan glacier . . . and the ineffable emerald twilight of a foliage-laced swamp at day-up, in the American South. Surely only time had dimmed those scenes so that now they seemed lusterless before this brilliant Vermont canvas.

But after a while, all I knew for sure, was that no scene, anywhere, had affected me as did the blaze of maple and sumac, thousand-fold splashes of gold and scarlet burning in sculptured flame against the dark backdrop of pine, spruce and hemlock, and the purple peaks beyond.

Too, instead of the severe cold and heavy snows I had momentarily expected during those first few weeks, the weather remained mild, frequently sunny; and the frosty nights were often lit by a clear cold moon and myriads of stars.

I wandered much along the local roads: narrow, rutted aisles twisting between multi-hued tree walls; or followed the bouldered course of the same noisy little river which curved around our land and flowed beneath the covered bridge just downhill from the village store, and surged with a crash over the dam a few hundred yards north where once, long ago, had been a grist mill, its site now a crumble of weathered stones.

Sometimes I came upon other ruins in some wild, brush-grown spot; or found on a lonely road an abandoned farmhouse with fallen roof, sagging timbers, paneless windows,

its nearby outbuildings having become anonymous piles of
rotting wood. Always I wondered about those who once had
dwelled in these places and why they had forsaken them.

Ofttimes I wondered how it was—*really* was—in the early
days and later; and in this or that desolate spot. I speculated
on what grim drama might have been played out there, between long-dead men, white or red, or perchance a vagrant
black, such as a slave skulking beneath the Northern star
toward Canada, and freedom.

Freedom! That was what all men had sought in those harsh
yesterdays: white men grimly determined to break their thrall
to king and priest, daring the vast and dangerous seas, seeking this great, rich land, and the freedom they so fiercely desired.

But was it not freedom for themselves alone they really
sought? Else why had they denied it to the red men from
whom they tore the land, and to the African blacks whom
later they had kidnapped to be their slaves?

But in Vermont, I reminded myself, men had not been
like that then.

Yes, but what of now?

I did not know, not even as weeks became months. I
wasn't sure, wasn't at all sure.

On our balance-sheet there were entries for the credit side.
After a while there was one for the debit column. I wanted
to convert the side porch to a playroom for our children and
inquired about local craftsmen who might undertake the
work.

There were several. Each listened politely to my needs and
politely evaded undertaking the work on the score of commitments already made.

I didn't know whether such pressing commitments really
existed, but I tried to accept the refusals at face value. However, in the following weeks, I noted various of those artisans

standing around in idleness and I concluded I'd gotten the old familiar brushoff.

I was tempted to gripe about it to Rene, but refrained, for there had been no mention of race between us and I wanted our relations to continue simply as between people, between . . . friends.

But the thing ate at me, seemed evidence of a kind to shadow the cautious hope I'd begun to feel. It was a small matter on its face and elsewhere it would have been the norm —the kind of thing to which, as a Negro, I was conditioned, even though that had never lessened my resentment of it.

I tried to shrug off the matter. I didn't discuss it with Helen. I didn't need to. And I knew her belief that Vermont would really not prove out for us was strengthened.

During the month before our household goods came, we visited Burlington several times to shop. We both got the impression that clerks in most of the stores were noticeably slow in serving us.

That wasn't true in all the stores, only those owned by Gentiles. When we entered one operated by Jews, we were made to feel that we and our business were welcome. The contrast was so marked that thereafter I patronized only merchants who were Jews, with whom we spent fifteen hundred dollars that month.

But when my wife and I hashed it over, I found certain of her prejudices unchanged.

"Sure, the Jews treat us well in their stores," she agreed. "They are smart. Our dollars look like any dollars to them, and so—"

"And believing that, you're still willing to give them our dollars?"

"Not give. Spend. Sure, I'm willing to spend our money with them. At least, *they* want it. Why force money upon somebody who makes it obvious he doesn't particularly want it?"

"Why, indeed," I agreed. "But I'm also against spending it with those of *any* particular race or religion. It makes me sore to *have* to do so in the interest of my own self-respect."

"Hmmm. So you're not so sold on Jews as you used to be. Don't tell me you've come to feel like I do?"

"If you mean that I believe our welcome in non-Gentile stores is solely because of the money we spend, the answer is 'no.' Because *that* I'll never believe. And to keep the record straight, I don't claim, nor have I ever, that all Jews are without prejudice against us. That would be silly. Plenty of them are just as prejudiced against us as most Gentile whites, and it would be strange if they were not."

"Hah!"

"Don't jeer, Mama. I mean, why should *all* people of whatever race or religion be unprejudiced against Negroes when we know perfectly well that even some Negroes are prejudiced against others?"

"Oh, Lord," Helen exclaimed in mock resignation, "he's off on one of *those* again."

"Well, one thing sure, we don't have to be eternally on guard around Jews."

"Maybe not," Helen laughed. "Anyway, it's nice to know our dollar has its face value in some quarters, regardless of why."

I shrugged, changed the subject. Only time and greater experience would bring my girl a better understanding of such matters.

But I was sorry Helen felt like that. And, as I so often did, I thought of Nate and Belle back in Los Angeles, for they had long since proved themselves true friends, the best I'd ever had. But Helen had not really liked them, not because they were Jews, but because they were white.

CHAPTER *three*

I UNDERTOOK THE REMODELING OF OUR porch myself and Rene often kibitzed as I worked. She claimed the job was pretty good. I knew it was not. We argued, as usual.

Rene remarked that if I was going to gripe so much about my own work next time I'd better get some of the local professionals to do it.

Sourly I replied that I had tried to but that the "professionals" had been too feverishly busy for my unimportant job.

Not so, Rene insisted, for hadn't they been standing around with their hands in their breeches for days on end that fall? And I said well perhaps those were rest periods with which my work could not be permitted to interfere and Rene exclaimed, "Oh, pish! They're always like that about new people, especially city people."

I wanted to believe her, but it didn't make sense to me and I told her so.

Rene chuckled, "Get off your horse before you fall off and break something hard, like your head, which might be a good thing, at that. And quit sneering at our local customs. Because around here, nobody thinks he is any better than anybody else, or if he does, he'd darn sight better not let anyone know it."

And I asked what that had to do with the price of eggs and Rene said, stroking at an imaginary long white beard and using a quavering voice to match, "Well, now, young man, I'll tell you: we hire out to each other when we are needed, but we don't call it working for somebody; we *help* one another."

"So you help each other," I said. "So what?"

"So," Rene said, "now that you have proved you don't think yourself too derned good to work with your own hot little hands, you won't have any trouble getting somebody to *help* you next time you want to build something."

And that *is* the way it was, as I came to know.

In January, Helen was invited to join the Ladies Aid and, after only a mild session of soul-searching, accepted the invitation, thereby suddenly expanding the circle of her acquaintances. However, when she had attended a meeting, she remarked, "Those women remind me of a bunch of jigs, fussing and arguing and carrying on. I thought *we* were the only ones who are supposed to act like that! Humph! Whoever said the white folks were so perfect, anyway?"

"They did," I replied, "and they've had us believing it. On the other hand, dames are dames, whatever their coloration."

"Now you just look here—" Helen began heatedly.

"And so," I added hastily, "are men."

In February I was asked to speak in Rutland at the winter conference of the Vermont League of Writers.

I didn't want to do it. I had done a bit of public speaking, but didn't like it. More important, I suspected the invitation had been extended me more because of my race than because I was a writer. I would be something of a novelty, I reckoned, like a talking dog or a literate donkey.

It was then Helen's turn to prod me into accepting the invitation, even as I had needled her into doing the same in our town.

"But what in the world will I say?" I demanded.

She laughed jeeringly. "Why, whatever comes into your head, darling. As usual."

"A great help you are."

"Well, after all, you have had quite a lot of experience as a writer, haven't you?"

"On the low reaches, yes. But—"

"Maybe most of your audience will not even have had that experience. It isn't a professional organization, is it?"

"No. But pulp's about my speed and I understand it is not in good odor with the non-pros."

"Even so, what's wrong with pulp? How many times have I heard you defend it?"

"Yeah, but—"

"As Rene would say, oh pish!"

By then I was banging away at another book. The little room in the barn where I wrote remained frigid, especially at floor level, despite the thick chenille rug I'd appropriated, and the rather expensive electric heater I'd bought especially for my workroom. Taking the advice of a new friend, I bought heavy woolen stockings, thick felt shoes, a pair of galoshes, and thereafter I never did quite freeze.

Out there in my cold, lonely exile, the speaking engagement would come to mind from time to time and as the weeks passed I still hadn't the least idea of the line I would take. It was a real shock when Helen warned me it was but four days away. I felt sunk.

But on the morning of the unhappy day Helen was very ill, had been so all night from ptomaine poisoning which followed after she'd eaten chicken salad the evening before at a wedding reception in a nearby town.

The affair had been at the home of the groom's mother.

Our invitation had come from his aunt. We had met the aunt the previous fall when, seeing her standing on a Winooski corner where the buses stopped, we rightly presumed she was waiting for the one which went to "The Junction," and invited her to ride there with us, since it was on our route home.

Before doing so, however, we had quite a time trying to decide if she was or was not of our race, for she was olive-skinned, thin-featured and could have as easily been white as not. In a way too subtle for detailing we decided that she *was* of our race.

Then Helen prodded me into finding out, because she had met no colored woman so far and wanted to, for one thing because she said she just *had* to find out if there was a beauty shop anywhere near which would serve *her.*

So I climbed out of the car and somewhat diffidently approached the woman and even before I spoke, she smiled and then I *knew.*

She accepted a ride and en route to "The Junction," where she told us, she and her husband, a retired soldier, were the only colored residents, she enlightened us on several other matters, one being that in so far as she knew, there was no beauty parlor in which, as she politely phrased it, "our folks are catered to."

How were they treated in "The Junction?"

Fine. They'd never had a speck of trouble. People were friendly.

Did her husband do any kind of work now?

Oh, sure. They both worked in the Winooski woolen mills from which she had just come. They'd worked at the mill for many years.

She was a pleasant, smiling, intelligent woman. We liked her, invited her to come to see us and promised that we would soon visit her. Hence, when later she invited us to her nephew's wedding reception, we said we would come.

However, when the time came, it was storming, and we decided that we must pass up the affair. But Helen changed our minds when she remembered the reception that night to be held at the Congregational Church parsonage for the new minister—"a woman"—and that we had not been invited.

Helen was piqued not only because of that snub, but because the Ladies Aid as well as the men, including me, had pitched in to redecorate the parsonage. I had painted the ceiling of the parsonage living room.

That is why, at the last minute, my wife decided, bad weather or not, we were going to the wedding reception.

So we went. The groom was handsome, pale-skinned, and so were his mother and his New Jersey bride. Most of the guests were white, friends of the groom, but even so, the eight or ten persons of color present were more than we had thought lived in the entire state.

We had a pleasant time. After a while I got off into a corner with the retired soldier, husband to our friend in "The Junction," a soft-spoken dark man, and we talked of many things: guns, hunting, automobiles, and, somewhere along the line, "lodge business."

I asked whether he belonged to a local lodge of our ancient order, and he said he did not; and when I inquired if that was because of his race, he presumed that it was; and when I told him that I had been invited to attend a forthcoming meeting of our order with some of my townsmen who were members, he could offer no explanation except that in Vermont you just could never tell about things like that.

When refreshments were served I passed up the chicken salad in favor of potato chips and beer. Helen had a plateful of salad and said it was delicious.

Shortly after we got home, pain and nausea hit her. I administered massive doses of bicarb and water and telephoned the doctor, who was abed, but who dressed and got to us quickly and did what she could, but Helen had a horrible time and so did I, because she suffered so.

That was why I did not speak at the writers' confab. In fact I forgot it entirely until noon the next day when, despite her distress, my wife reminded me of it and I hastily telephoned its president, Leon Dean, a U.V.M. professor, that I could not make it, and why.

Not until Helen recovered did I have time to think about it, and then, I'm afraid, I was relieved that circumstances had rescued me from the ordeal.

With the coming of "The Lady Preacher," church again became a part of town life, at least for the Protestants, who had been without a minister for several months. The French, of whom there were many in the township, attended the Catholic Church in an adjacent town.

By then something of Helen's background had become known to her Ladies Aid sisters, including the fact of her minister-father and her own considerable participation in the work of his church. She was asked to teach a Sunday school class, and did; first a young group, and later one of adults.

For a while thereafter, she chipped at me about my nonattendance. A part of her desire for me to go to church, I suspected, had nothing to do with the good of my soul, but rather with her wish for me to conform, to be as others, and thereby prove something.

That alone would have kept me out of church. And having already made such token appearances as I thought necessary, I went no more, for ours was the Lady Preacher's first charge, actually a trial assignment as she had not yet been ordained. Perhaps it was her lack of experience which made her sermons seem so deadly. In any event, I did not propose to endure each Sunday two hours of anything like that, regardless of what might be thought of me by the townspeople.

Finally my wife let me alone about the matter, exasperated,

no doubt, by my invariable ritualistic reply to whatever argument she made, which was: "Take me as I am, said Sam—"
That was as far as I usually got, but eventually it was enough.

Because my attitude remained inflexible in that respect,
Helen finally accepted it as genuine and not just an unneces-
sarily belligerent and unyielding reaction to my bitterness over
the whole business of race. Increasingly she was being drawn
into town life, was becoming interested in it, was cautiously
discovering that friendship might really be possible between
herself and her white sisters; and while she was still quite
aware of the gap she felt between herself and them, it was
far from the immeasurable chasm it once had been.

It had quickly become apparent that because of her abilities she need not play second fiddle among them. She had
always been a leader: in church, in school, in college, and
in community life.

When we first met in Los Angeles she was *Basileus* and
a founder of the local chapter of her sorority, the Zeta Phi
Beta; and she had just been appointed a member of the Los
Angeles Youth Commission. She was much in demand as a
speaker. Too, she had planned and managed successful affairs of various kinds and had chaired so many organizations
that to her the tempo of our local ones must have seemed a bit
slow.

Still, she could not help remaining on guard, continuing
warily to watch for telltale nuances, discordances more to be
sensed than heard.

Even so, I could see in her changes of which she seemed
unaware. In a way, she fought against what even then was
becoming apparent, her acceptance by the other women as an
individual, somebody who had something to give which they
wanted—and welcomed.

But while still not fully convinced that behind the smiling
faces, the friendly actions, there might not be something else
quite different, Helen turned the tables on me in a way I

found significant. At first it had been she who spoke most of Haiti, in case things didn't work out for us in Vermont; nor was it the other way around because of my fear of being lulled into acceptance of the half loaf, or even three quarters of it.

More than ever then, I was determined it would be everything or nothing; and while the inescapable fact was that we had substantial reasons to hope for the former, I meant to keep clear of entanglements which might make it difficult to break free in case the latter proved true.

It wasn't always easy to maintain that balance. As when some time after the parsonage reception to which we had not been invited, we learned that nobody had—that the announcement of it had been an item in "Town News" in the Burlington *Free Press* and was all that was considered necessary, according to local custom. If you wanted to, you came, and were welcome.

And as when along about that time, a young matron of whom Helen was quite fond dropped in one day, explaining that she had meant to do so sooner, but couldn't, because she had been "working like a nigger."

I could almost see Helen swelling up. I could see how her lips tightened into a straight, angry line, how fire glinted in her brown eyes.

But the young woman didn't notice, was not in the least aware that she had said anything amiss nor, indeed, anything which had personal relation to us. Then she really crossed Helen up by warmly urging us to go dancing that night with her and her husband.

By then, thank goodness, we had ourselves come a little down the road of understanding. Like Helen, I had shriveled inside to have that ugly word *nigger* spring so unexpectedly from a white person's lips. Yet I was afraid that our young friend would realize that what she had innocently said was terribly offensive to us, and that she would be helplessly embarrassed. But she did not suspect her *faux pas*. Nor did others, so far as we could tell, who made slips of the same kind when talking to us, such as when a person we regarded as more than an acquaintance described her cat as "nigger black."

Of course, while Helen knew that those who used those epithets to us or in our hearing obviously meant no offense, she could not and still does not understand why they seem so entirely unaware that such references reflect unfavorably on the race of which she feels she is so obviously a member.

To a degree I share my wife's failure to understand why most white people seem not to know that, or to know that Negroes bitterly resent having such terms as *nigger, darky* and *coon* applied to them, for it does seem to me that we have lived together in the same land long enough now for so basic a fact to have become more than slightly apparent to everyone concerned.

CHAPTER *four*

T HE NOVEMBER DAY OUR FURNITURE FI-
nally arrived, with the house, as a consequence, in utter confusion, a small, elderly lady, beautifully dressed, came to call.
Her *savoir-vivre* seemed alien to our forthright region.

But Myrtle Robb was native to it, as we learned during her
visit. She was related to our neighbors, the Callens, and had
heard much of us from them. She brushed aside Helen's em-
barrassment over the upset state of our house, sat down in
our cluttered kitchen, crossed slender, nyloned ankles and as
soon as she was settled accepted a light for the cigarette she
took from her case.

"I have been meaning to call," she informed us, "but I
thought I'd give you a chance to settle down a bit first." She
glanced at the crates and boxes by which we were almost surrounded, laughed and remarked that perhaps she had not
waited quite long enough.

"Well," Helen said speciously, "if you don't mind, we
don't."

Mrs. Robb seemed not to mind, and soon had us laughing
with her dry, gently caustic humor. It quickly became apparent that she was interested in my book and its author. I
sensed that here was not mere curiosity, polite or otherwise,
but a genuine desire to learn of us both.

Mrs. Robb didn't mean to cause me to evade some of her questions, for they were perfectly natural, as for instance, what was the title of my book? Under other circumstances I would have stated it without hesitation. But not to her, for the title was *God is for White Folks* and I found myself regretting it for the first time, but not the last. Aside from its obvious implication, that title was like a target in a shooting gallery to those who had not read it.

So to Mrs. Robb I said the book was yet untitled, which was not entirely untrue, for my publishers had not then made it the final choice. I managed to change the subject by mentioning a bit of late news: that publication of my novel had been deferred from the coming spring to the next fall.

I spoke of my disappointment about that, for I'd been secretly counting the days until I would, at long last, publish, for it would be an important milestone in the career now only just begun.

Helen, who'd kept working as Mrs. Robb and I chatted, stopped to join us. But almost as soon as she sat down, I caused her to rise in horror by my casual inquiry as to whether or not I might make our caller a drink.

My wife's eyes flashed storm warnings as well as consternation; and had her surprised look been seen by Mrs. Robb when she casually stated a preference for a martini, Mrs. Robb would likely have been a bit flabbergasted herself.

As I made the drink, I grinned smugly at Helen and, deadpanned, asked her what she'd like. Then she laughed, although not very heartily, and explained that I was just having my usual corny joke, for I knew quite well she never drank.

"That," I explained to our guest, "is not out of moral scruple, but because one little shot puts her to sleep."

Mrs. Robb chuckled understandingly, spoke of someone she knew who could not indulge for the same reason and thereby smoothed the troubled waters a little.

When Mrs. Robb departed, having made us promise to visit her soon, I departed also, my destination the workroom in the barn. It was not the disturbed atmosphere of the house which made my departure somewhat brisk. Not entirely.

We were intrigued by Mrs. Robb's sophisticated manner and wondered how she had achieved it in a town where practically all the residents were farming folk. Had we perhaps been mistaken as to the nature of our community? For as much as we had been surprised by finding Rene in it, we were literally astonished by Mrs. Robb, her aunt. How and when and where had she acquired the background, the poise, the cultivated air?

Rene solved the mystery. Her aunt, after graduation from the University of Vermont, had married and soon left her home town. She and her husband had dwelt in urban areas, for Mrs. Robb never could abide small towns. Rene also explained that her aunt and uncle had been back only a short time and would not have returned at all had not Mrs. Robb promised her husband that they would come back to the town and to Mr. Robb's family farm after their middle years.

I began to understand another matter when Rene told us that Mrs. Robb had always wanted to be a writer, had written a lot of verse about her state and its people, some of which had been published. That explained Mrs. Robb's interest in my work.

But what confused us was Rene's casual mention that the return of the Robbs, which she had previously referred to as recent, had actually taken place twelve years before! We continued to be confused for a while when we discovered that everyone spoke of the Robbs as though they had come back home but yesterday, or at least, on the day before.

We found it surprising that Rene dealt so lightly with a dozen years. But we learned that to Rene, where the people and the town were concerned, time was nothing.

We talked one day about the restlessness of returned soldiers, and Rene spoke authoritatively on the subject. Only after the conversation was well developed did it dawn on me that *her* soldiers were of Civil War vintage, and her ancestors.

Similarly, talk of the grist mill by the dam was as though it had been operative until quite recently, whereas it had crumbled to a jagged heap of debris since its wheel turned for the last time fifty years ago.

So too with the cheese factory, of which we heard frequent mention and which we thought was a going concern, only to learn eventually it had not been operated for more than thirty years.

Slowly, slowly, the town was opening up for us its history, its people, past and present, although for a long time we continued to have trouble figuring which was meant, past *or* present.

During our shopping trips to Burlington that autumn we had always taken the children with us. But when December came, shortages being what they were at that time, we thought to do our Christmas buying early and did not wish our brood along, for it would be their gifts mainly which we would purchase.

That was a major complication. It was too cold to leave the children in the car while we scouted the stores; and besides, they always clamored to accompany us and usually got their way. We thought longingly of Clemmie, our girl of all work in California, who had tended our babes so well, and wrote to her, hoping to entice her to us again, but she wasn't available.

Then we casually mentioned our trouble to Rene, and certainly with no thought that there would be a remedy for it within our bailiwick. But Rene came up, as usual, with a solution. There was, she said, a local girl, Jeanne Wherry, who did baby sitting and no doubt we could secure her services any time after school, or on Saturdays.

"Is Rene ever unhepped!" my wife exclaimed when later we discussed our neighbor's suggestion.

"The word is *unhipped*," I corrected. "An even better word is *unbooted*."

"Well anyway, Rene means well. But *I'm* certainly not going to ask any of these people to work for *us*."

I wasn't as positive as Helen that the thing was so impossible, but I agreed that whatever needed doing in this white land, we'd just have to do ourselves, as I was doing in the matter of glassing in our porch.

By then the snows had started. One day when we were all at the local store, little Will developed a chill, just as the storekeeper's wife was introducing Helen to Mrs. Wherry. I picked up my son, said I was sorry to interrupt, but that I thought we'd better get him home at once. Mrs. Wherry, a handsome, matronly woman, looked at the snow outside and offered to drive us home, and we gratefully accepted.

That afternoon we tried repeatedly to reach the newly-come physician, but could neither get her at her office nor locate her anywhere else. Our little boy now had a high fever and we were quite alarmed.

Although we didn't learn at the time just how it happened, the doctor arrived within an hour, and while we were delighted and relieved that she had come, we were mystified how she knew we wanted her, especially when she told us that she would have made it sooner except that she had been on a back road visit.

We liked the slim, attractive doctor and the children fell for her at once, even feverish Will Junior, who didn't even flinch at her deft needle jab when she administered the penicillin.

"The Lady Doctor," as the townsfolk called her, had a boyish look, wore heavy woolen ski pants, and a hooded coat. She was, she told us during a short chat after she had treated our son, a Vermonter and a graduate of the University of

Vermont's famed Medical School. This was her start as a practicing physician.

And we told her how glad we were that she had chosen to settle in our doctorless community. Knowing the heavy urban demand for physicians, I could not refrain from asking why she had chosen our town when she might have gone into lucrative practice in a city, or commanded a fancy institutional salary.

She shrugged and said offhandedly that there were too many rural areas in Vermont whose need for doctors was acute and so she just thought she'd take on country practice.

I remarked that it would probably be pretty rugged at best in this hilly section of treacherous backwoods roads, but the Lady Doctor shrugged again and dryly said she knew it. She wasn't big physically, but there was a bigness about her, inside.

We forgot to ask the doctor how she had known that we needed her. Later we learned that a "near neighbor" happened, as usual, to be listening in on the telephone line and, noting our inability to locate the doctor, had done so herself. Eventually we met her. She was the self-elected historian of the town and what she did not know about it and everyone who lived in it was very unimportant indeed. She recorded all important events, including births and deaths, and whenever there was an argument about who did what when, Lennie Willer was the one to settle it.

A couple of days later Mrs. Wherry and her daughter Jeanne stopped by to inquire how Will Junior was, and they visited a while. Jeanne, then about thirteen, a pretty, lively, dark-haired child, was as clear and forthright in her talk as her mother, and herself brought up the baby-sitting question. She and Helen talked it over, and our "sitter" problems were solved for the next couple of years, until Jeanne entered high school and no longer had much time for anything else.

We liked the Wherrys. Jeanne quickly won our affection.

She was, for her years, steady, sensible, capable of thinking for herself, of acting quickly. Our children adored her. Her parents were well-to-do and allowed their daughter to baby-sit in order that she might learn the value of money by earning some for herself.

Soon after Mrs. Wherry's visit, we had another caller, a tall, stately woman whose simple graciousness hid no guile of any kind, we were sure. She was Cora Ball, and like Mrs. Robb, was related to the Callens.

Mrs. Ball came to invite Helen to the annual dinner meeting of the Ladies Aid Society, and such was her sincerity and sweetness, that for the first time I could remember, Helen didn't try to hedge when association with "the other group" was involved. She agreed to attend and was sincerely cordial to Mrs. Ball, but when she had gone my wife exclaimed, "My goodness! What *have* I done?"

"Oh, just what comes naturally," I said airily. "Why not? Those dames won't bite you. At least not very hard. Not if they are anything like Mrs. Ball."

"Oh, no?" my wife said tartly. "Perhaps not. But will they ever give me the once-over!"

"So what? I can't see anything about you that you need be ashamed of," I said. "After all, you don't need to take low to any of them on any count."

"Just the same, I still don't relish the idea of a bunch of old white women looking me over, whispering about me, speaking to me in that patronizing way they reserve for us, as though we were a cross between some dumb animal and a child. I——"

"Has Rene acted like that? Or Mrs. Robb? Or Mrs. Wherry? Or that nice woman who just left? Or—anybody?"

"Well, no. I guess not."

"Well, give it a whirl, honey. The only way we're ever going to find out the score is to play the game. Maybe—just maybe—"

"Okay, master," Helen sighed in mock resignation, "I'll go. Don't beat me."

Flanked by mesdames Robb and Ball, Helen did go and was pleasantly and, apparently, sincerely received by the other members of the Ladies Aid, and even her delicately attuned antenna failed to pick up the least overtone of anything to the contrary.

In a tone indicating she still could not quite believe it, Helen told me afterward, "Why nobody even mentioned my race." She stared at me and added slowly, "In fact, after a while I forgot it too."

"Well," I said, "what do you know!" But if there was wonderment in my tone it was not due to my wife's experience that day, but was because of her reaction to it.

At Christmas, several people we had met casually, or not at all, telephoned to say "Merry Christmas." We had some callers, too. Most of those who dropped by were the town's well-to-do citizens, but some were not: old Roy came early, his ruddy face beaming, with presents for the kids; and another elderly man, Mr. Porter, also brought gifts for our youngsters—three neatly wrapped handkerchiefs.

We had of course expected Roy, and had his hot toddy all ready, but Mr. Porter's call was unexpected. We were touched by it, and his gifts, for he was in poor circumstances, unable to get out for even a day's work because he had to tend his bedridden wife, to whom he was devoted. We sensed that beneath his worn garments was a sincere heart; and behind his grave manner there had to be a perception of our position beyond that of mere strangers in the town.

Other friends had not forgotten us; there was a deluge of cards, letters, and holiday telegrams, mostly from Los Angeles; and on Christmas morning there came the usual telephone call from my mother in Kansas City.

Beneath the tree in our living room there were loads of

presents, mostly for the children. In the oven there was a turkey, and in the refrigerator, a big bowl of eggnog.

We were surprised that we did not really miss having old friends around, or visiting them or not making the gay parties and dances, as for so long we had been accustomed to do at this season.

When we retired Christmas night, Helen and I spoke drowsily of this, weighing it and other evidence of like kind, and deciding that it was good.

But we did not overflow with optimism, for we knew our experiment was only begun, that it had yet a long way to go, and that in view of our experience elsewhere, it would be indeed incredible if there were not deadfalls waiting somewhere farther along the way.

But so far, so good; and for that we were grateful.

CHAPTER *five*

O<small>UR FIRST</small> V<small>ERMONT</small> <small>WINTER WAS OF</small>
the "open" variety. Little snow fell, nor was it very cold.
Perversely, I was somewhat disappointed.

Our kids enjoyed it, though, and in their new snowsuits
frolicked gleefully in the snow that did fall. Anne wished to
send a big box of it to California so that our friends out there
might know how wonderful it was; and she and the boys
devoured it like candy and at first crammed it into their
pockets before they came in the house. They could not understand why it always had vanished when they sought it later.
Nor could their parents understand at first why the children's
water-repellent pants were always wet *inside*.

In one respect, however, that first Vermont winter lived
up to its reputation, for it hung on forever. Or so it seemed,
especially when long after the time we thought of as early
spring, the snow still sifted down, temperatures still hovered
low.

As those frosted months dragged on, Helen spoke nostalgically of California and wistfully of those tropic countries
we had forsworn in favor of this land of eternal winter.

But gradually the snowdrifts shrank; and often in midday
the potholes in roads thawed to a watery mush, only to freeze
again in later afternoon. And ofttimes in the fields, or in an

open spot in the forest, the ground had a sodden feel, although when I dug into it with my hunting knife, the blade met iron hardness just below the surface. Still, there was a muted pleasure in the infinity of shadings of this frost-locked land, in the white shine of the meadows and bare hills against the dark woodlands beyond, and still a quiet pleasure to walk in the cold, soundless nights.

Sometimes I'd complain to Rene about the never-ending winter and she would soberly agree that it did become a dreadful bore after a while. Then, as though she had blasphemed, she would reverse her field and brag about the very thing she had deplored, and to it ascribe the willful stubbornness she claimed for Vermont people, ending on the note that the weather would not break until it got good and ready, so one and all might as well make the best of it, for that's how it was, and please God, how it would forever be, for like it or not, such was Vermont.

Then I'd jeer, and we'd argue, and once in a while, from the adjoining room, her mother's quiet, enjoying laughter would counterpoint our extravagantly acrimonious duet and we would laugh, too, at ourselves, but more because our crazy talk had amused that lovely frail woman in the other room.

So far as I was concerned, spring never came at all, for it arrived in stages so imperceptible I never did know when winter yielded to spring.

After the new minister came, we joined a club of young married couples; it was a social club, connected with the church.

I went to meetings once in a while, but Helen was faithful in her attendance, due, I claimed, to my self-sacrificing nature, which made me elect to stay home with the children while she went abroad on pleasure bent. Helen said I could lay off that line, because I was just too lazy to dress and go with her.

Then, one day it was June; there was genuine warmth in
the air, an earthly fragrance in the greening fields, and they
were touched with dabs of color: the sullen red of "devil's
paint brush," the hard, green heads of adder's tongue, later
to blossom into big fluffs of white and orange; and the pale
pansy-purple of tiny "spring beauties."

And in the woods, beneath spruce, pine and hemlock,
from beds of fine rock moss, glowed tiny, exquisite blue vio-
lets, miniatures of the flower my mother loved best.

Just as there was no definite boundary between winter and
spring, neither could I discover one which marked when summer came. Seasons merged so unobtrusively, so gradually,
that even in July I had not yet lost the feel of winter.

By then, though, the land was mossy green; there were
flowers everywhere, some unexpectedly brilliant in color, surprisingly varied in type, and they flourished in sun and
shadow, in field and meadow, and gleamed along every road-
side. I hadn't known Vermont was capable of such lush color-
ations.

It was during that month that I made my debut as a
speaker, for another invitation had come from the Vermont
League of Writers, this time to address its summer conference
at the University of Vermont. Since the University was in
nearby Burlington, I had no excuse, nor was one provided by
any such emergency as Helen's illness which had saved me
in the winter.

However, this time I did not fret about what I would say;
my speech would be impromptu. It certainly was. Helen loy-
ally said I did all right, and the newspapers were kind enough
to mention my talk and publish my picture. But my main
reaction was relief that the ordeal was over. Had I an inkling
of things to come, my relief would have been much qualified.

As it was, I hadn't the least idea that other groups would
think me fitting as a speaker; but some did, and however
much I shrank from it, there was no escape, for having ac-

cepted the first few such invitations, I was afraid to refuse others lest I seem ungracious.

Sometimes the group to which I spoke was comparatively small; sometimes it was frighteningly large, but always when the moment came for me to rise and shine, I wished I were elsewhere, preferably Haiti.

In the following months I spoke to various groups: church organizations, Rotary Clubs, and a teachers' gathering. On one memorable occasion at their request, I spoke before a gathering of gentlemen on the legal status of American Negroes.

Fortunately I was familiar with that subject, for after having expounded my views of it, pausing here and there to carefully define some legal phrase, I discovered that my listeners were all lawyers.

Some fun, for *them!*

I soon gathered that audiences were usually interested most in our experience in Vermont. I was glad I could honestly tell of the warmth with which we had been received, could in truth say that we had no regrets that we had come to Vermont.

Such reservations as I had, I kept to myself.

In time I found myself dealing more and more with matters of American racial and religious prejudice, in all of America except, of course, Vermont, and the relationship of prejudice not only to democracy as an American ideal, but its immediate and increasingly important bearing upon our relations with the rest of the world.

Perhaps that choice of subject stemmed from my own preoccupation with it, for it seemed to me that in that year of 1947, changes of great significance were in the making, particularly in the non-white lands.

I saw the global picture thus: the Second World War, like the First, had been fought in freedom's name, but unlike the First it *was* accomplishing its avowed objective, although *not* as envisaged by the major powers. For freedom was a magic word that this time echoed around the world, awakening three-quarters of the world's people who were of colored skin to their opportunity to break their chains and win it for themselves. To me it seemed inevitable that they would burst those chains, for I had more than an academic idea of how fierce the thirst for freedom could be.

It seemed obvious that leadership of the non-communist world was up to us—the United States—and since our avowals of democracy had been so loud, that leadership could not bring peace to the world unless we practiced at home what we had preached abroad.

Thus, in my view, it was up to American citizens to tackle at once the problem upon whose solution might well depend not only our opportunity to restore peace in a troubled world, but in the end quite possibly our own existence. The battle would not be won by guns and money, in which we were so rich, but rather by our position toward the issue paramount in the world—human freedom. For clearly this was a battle for men's minds, and we were opposed by a great foe who already recognized it as such; and that foe had a great advantage over us because we were allied with the Christian nations which had for so long held captive the dark, non-Christian peoples.

In my view, while we had not been guilty of the imperialism which had generated the deep, dangerous hate its victims felt for the Christian nations, our denial, by a rigid pattern of racial segregation at home, of the democracy we preached made us doubly suspect in the eyes of the dark world, and provided our powerful enemy with a weapon which in the end could very well defeat us.

Karl Marx long ago had enunciated ideas of such vitality that they had spread throughout the world and, indeed, had already effected great and visible changes not only in men's thinking, but in men themselves, in their lands and systems of government. Even in our own land we were beset by it.

It was these ideas which we must overcome. Neither gold nor atomic weapons could destroy them. Only a better idea could win. It seemed tragic to me that we already possessed that idea; indeed, it was the very heart of our American Constitution; and that because we had not proved for ourselves our own belief in it, we could not prove it to others.

So it was along these lines that I most often spoke, but when I did it often seemed to me as though my words, my thoughts, rebounded like pebbles tossed against a wall. This sometimes made me wonder whether the facts were really as I saw them, the danger of which I warned was more imagined than real; and if perhaps I was not building a straw man to belabor more in my own interests than in those of my country.

But I knew that was not true, even though the world situation was shaping so that it did in a way make a whipping boy for my own desire for equality in my own land. The truth was, I was compelled to speak as I did through an unsuspectedly strong concern for it, for all its people, even those whose deeds against my race—against *me*, therefore—I hated.

Now there was a strange development. Sometimes I was angered by it, and baffled. For ever higher was the sun of hope rising for *all* dark peoples and I had only to wait, and perhaps even in my time, noontime would blaze and . . . my eyes behold the execution of a vengeance well earned, well deserved, long due.

Vengeance is mine, saith the Lord.

Yet, according to my opportunity, I continued to plead for an understanding of our peril, our nation's peril, as I saw it.

B<small>Y</small> <small>MIDSUMMER</small> I <small>HAD RECEIVED GALLEY</small> proofs of my book for correction. That was a thrill. Too, it was evidence that come October I'd really be published.

It wasn't that I doubted it, but rather that I had really not accepted its actuality until those galleys were in my hands. However, when I read them, I was dismayed. My editor had taken liberties with my copy of which I violently disapproved. My reaction, justified or not, wasn't merely that of an outraged author, but of a Negro author angered when his delineations of members of his own race are in any way altered by a white editor. Because, what did he know about Negroes?

Actually that editor had, with some exceptions, done an expert job for which I ought to have been grateful, but then it seemed another gratuitous slap which I was receiving simply because of my race. And I wanted to return the advance I'd received and withdraw the book from publication.

The famous Vermont author to whom I appealed for advice soothingly agreed with my objections to certain aspects of my book's editing, but saw as unwise my hot desire to interfere with its publication. Getting published was the important thing, she said. It was the start. Besides, what had happened to me had happened also to writers she knew, many of them famous.

Her words were wise and I believed them, for I believed in her. I'd read many of her books and in all of them she had enunciated convictions based upon understanding and compassion for those segments of humanity disadvantaged by impersonal circumstance.

It was not easy, but I took her advice.

I was very grateful to that famed woman, Dorothy Canfield Fisher, for her generous help, and even more so when later I realized it was given at no small cost, for the demands upon her were dreadfully heavy. Yet she had read my script and had given me valuable advice.

Because of her continuing and friendly interest in me and my family, we cherished her long before we actually met her.

Perhaps in my letters to her I revealed a continuing bitterness and resentment because of the inequities of race; and in the following months and years Mrs. Fisher not only continued to correspond with us and to send us quantities of books and magazines, but often forwarded clippings or articles relating incidents or developments reflective of improving race relations in our country.

I am afraid that, at first anyway, my reaction to those clippings and articles was tinged with smug tolerance. The lady meant well. But didn't she know that such happenings thus called to my attention were but drops in a sea of exactly opposite composition? Sometimes I was sorely tempted to counter by sending *her* clippings which would prove that. Such as:

HOODED ORDER RIDES AGAIN

ATLANTA—The Klan is riding again in Georgia. "We are four or five times stronger than last year" boasts Grand Dragon Dr. Samuel Greene . . .

Despite revocation of its state charter June 13, the Klan has stepped up its membership drives and Columnist Drew Pearson reported that several Atlanta policemen who belong to the order were given prizes last week for recruiting new members.

and:

S. C. Slayer Acquitted

Barnwell, S. C.—William Craig, local white farmer, who confessed slaying a Negro, James Walker, last Aug. 12, was acquitted of murder charges in general sessions court here this week.

Craig had already been freed by a coroner's jury ruling that although he had followed Walker home and shot him in the back, he had acted in "self defense."

and, on less violent levels:

Mixed Group Discussion At Tenn. U. Barred

Knoxville, Tenn.—University of Tennessee students known as the World Affairs Discussion Group, were yesterday denied the right to hold a discussion of the President's Civil Liberties program in Ayres Hall on the university campus because a Negro, Dr. J. Herman Daves, TVA director of colored personnel, was scheduled as a speaker.

Clippings of that kind might be garnered day by day from both white and Negro press. They did not, in my view, attest to improving race relationships.

Thank goodness, I did not argue that point in my letters to Mrs. Fisher, and in her letters to me she never discussed the subject, but in her friendly, cheerful way, spoke of pleasanter things, of her family, of people she had known, of her beloved Vermont and its curious ways.

Nevertheless, through all her correspondence there was woven a gentle philosophy which held that in order to see clearly, one must look beyond horizons which possibly had been circumscribed by one's own self.

I understood her point but didn't accept it, believing that because she was of the white world she could not really know how it was in mine.

Still, I was pleased I could write to her that we continued

to like Vermont, and could relate happenings, great or small, concerning the progress of our acceptance in our community.

During the summer Helen and I lost much of the feeling of newness as residents of our town, a process considerably aided by the friendliness of its people and the consequent enlargement of our circle of acquaintances.

Too, there had not been one real incident having to do with race, a circumstance I found so singular I began to develop a feeling of marking time, of waiting for an unpleasantness which I was entirely certain had to occur, eventually.

But the only incidents we did experience were more annoying than hurting, and were based we were sure more upon ignorance than animus.

The new minister was responsible for the first.

The club to which Helen and I belonged decided to give a play. The minister had ideas about it, assumed the function of choosing it, and giving out the parts.

The play she chose had as a minor character a Negro maid, and our lady preacher thought Helen and that part were made for one another.

Helen didn't. It wasn't that she objected to being cast as a member of the race to which she belonged, but rather to being singled out because of it; for aside from other considerations, it called attention to differences which she felt needed no added emphasis.

The minister's choice of play and her casting were received without enthusiasm by the club members, and even she apparently perceived this. When none found the words which would make the group feeling explicit, Helen, burning inside, quietly pointed out that there were actually more parts in the play than members in our club; and that was that.

I don't know if the minister ever realized how revealing her attitude was to us, and perhaps to others of whom we were beginning to think of as our friends; but I do know that Helen and I agreed that the lady just didn't know any better.

Another play was chosen, this time by the club members, and soon thereafter when it developed that Helen had a considerable experience in such things, much of the responsibility for its production settled upon her shoulders.

The play was staged late in the spring in the town hall before a packed, highly appreciative audience. After the curtain, Helen was surrounded by the cast, and in the general jubilation was hugged by several of the girls.

It made a curious warmness flood over me to see my wife the center of such spontaneous affection. I marveled that she returned it freely, as though she were among girls of her own race. It seemed to me that in that moment when they were all so happy, so elated over their success, Helen completely forgot that her friends were white and she was not. I resolved not to mention that to her, for there was growth, delicate, but definite, which would not be encouraged by critical examination, for that was my way: to examine, weigh, assay, and I knew I'd be much happier were it not.

The other "incident" wasn't much.

It resulted from an article in one of the Burlington newspapers wherein the Reverend Richie Low, originator of the famed Vermont Plan, told of visiting us, of how much we liked Vermont and its people.

We had liked Reverend Low very much, were much more interested in listening to his experiences than in telling of ours; and as I remember it, we kept him relating them most of the time during that first visit. Our paths were to cross many times thereafter, but then, although I had been taken with the man and his intriguing Welsh accent, and with his great good works which bespoke courage as well as Godliness, I regarded him much as I did Mrs. Fisher.

That was because even though Reverend Low had traveled both North and South, had mingled freely with members of my race in both sections, he seemed not to know the score any better than she. For it was the good man's belief that if one did not anticipate rebuffs, one did not receive them, in evidence of which he cited several experiences of his own.

It seemed to me he did not realize his experiences could not be applied to us, to our experiences. Because the way he figured, if we went, for instance, into a public place, say a restaurant, North *or* South, with the expectation of being well received, we would be.

But, he thought, if our attitude were hesitant, or in any way reflective of fear or expectancy of being refused, then that is what might happen.

The catch was, we *knew* that almost anywhere in the North we would probably be refused, and in the South for a Negro to even *act* like he wanted to be served in a white restaurant would result unpleasantly, to say the least, for the Negro. The customs of Dixieland, of which the complete social separation of the races was Article One, were also the written law, specific and detailed.

In any event, another minister, of a neighboring town, a more recent newcomer than we, having read Reverend Low's article about us, came to meet us, to welcome us to Vermont, and to let us know that we, also, were welcome at his church.

We appreciated his good intent, but we did not appreciate his constant harping on our race, upon which practically every one of his remarks was predicated.

"You colored people . . .

"I used to know a colored man very well, a fine fellow, named Sam Watkins, in Newark, New Jersey. If you've ever been in Newark, maybe you know him. He was the janitor of the building where I had my first charge. Sam Watkins. You never happened to meet him, did you? . . .

"Now you take your Marian Anderson, a fine Negro singer, a credit to your race. I guess you people are pretty proud of her, aren't you? . . .

"What I was wondering, aren't you awfully lonely up here? I mean, there not being any other colored people, and all?"

There was no offense intended in anything he said. The man was trying his best to show how he felt about us, that he was for us.

Knowing that made me, at least, exert myself to prevent our real feelings from showing. I suppose I succeeded, although there were times, when the going got a bit too thick, that Helen rolled her eyes so eloquently I feared our visitor surely must catch on.

Our relief was immense to have him finally depart. That may sound unkind, and perhaps it is; but to us even frank hostility is preferable to the smug patronage of those well-meaning white people whose every word makes explicit what they really think and believe of us, which usually seems to be a cross between a child, an animal, and a fool.

Those two incidents were the only ones which had happened in our town to remind us that, as my wife acidly put it, we were the only flies in the buttermilk.

Neither of us could remember a single instance where one of our townsmen had brought up the matter of race. Nor had any of them deemed it necessary to drag in Marian Anderson, the great contralto, because she happened to be a member of our race, or the boxer Joe Louis for the same reason. And we wondered: "What kind of people are these?"

What kind? A good kind.

Yes, a good kind, no question about it.

But it just didn't make sense. Not in the U.S.A.

Yet my own attitude didn't make sense either, maybe. Why did I still resist the feeling that we were being accepted and in a way with which we could find no fault at all? And in a manner which ought to have engendered increasing feeling of belonging?

And sometimes I wondered what it was I really wanted.

CHAPTER *seven*

I WAS BECOMING DISGUSTED WITH MYSELF because I could not get rid of my distrust of our acceptance. Constant distrust certainly wasn't pleasant, nor was it sensible, for by then I knew I did not need always to be on guard. But after all, the total of my pre-Vermont experience outweighed by far the favorable things experienced in the short time since we had settled in the state.

What I must do, I told myself, was to stop digging into the unhappy past; now only the future really mattered.

It was at a time when I was riding out another recurrence of doubt and depression that Chester Himes came up for a visit; he hoped to rent a place where he might spend the rest of the summer working on another novel.

The pleasure of seeing him again drove away the mental conflict which had been troubling me.

A few days after his arrival, Chester and I set out to find a place for him. We left after breakfast, expecting to be gone only a few hours. Somehow we ended up in Montreal, which made our return very late.

Helen took a rather dim view of our trip despite our explanation that our search had led us so near the Canadian border that we decided to continue to Montreal so Chester might check on how his last book was being handled in that city.

Chester and I made a few more house-hunting forays, all dutifully short, but without result. Then someone told me of a local possibility, a big brick house whose owner might be willing to rent it.

From my informant's casual mention of it, I didn't recognize the house as one with which I was already familiar. Located three miles from the village, on a high rise, it commanded a sweeping view eastward over a wide valley to the mountains.

Helen, the children and I had driven by the house several times and approaching it from far below had gazed admiringly up at its mellow red mass outlined against the summer skies; and we had followed the road as it curved up a long hill between flanking rows of giant maples to the very top to admire the view, and seen the stately old house at close range. It was the kind of house we had always wanted.

So it was there that Chester and I went. The owner didn't wish to rent the house, but he told us he might sell it. He showed us through the place and I liked it. The house was well-built; its ten rooms were spacious; the floors wide-boarded, the windows multi-paned; and some of the hardware was hand-wrought.

Before leaving, we discussed price and I said that we would buy his house if we could sell ours.

Helen liked the idea, too, but we doubted that we could find a buyer for our house before somebody else snapped up the other.

I fretted, wished for a small miracle, for in addition to the big brick house, there were one hundred and fifty acres of land and the price wasn't too much more than I'd paid for our village home.

We got the miracle. At least that is how it seemed. The town clerk and his wife had sold their farm, planned to build a house in the village but could not before winter because of unexpected material shortages. Everyone but us knew about that. And since I had spoken of our wish to sell our place and buy the other, the solution of the town clerk's problem and mine was obvious to our townsmen: he'd buy my house, then I could buy the other. It was all planned before I heard a word of it.

Both transactions were closed in late July. Everyone seemed pleased, although a number of our friends couldn't understand why we wanted to move 'way out in "the sticks." Then Helen had some belated thoughts of the same kind.

However, her objections to what she called our isolated location were not serious. We agreed that we had gotten a much better property, and we were pleased that now our daughter would go to the little one-room school near our new home instead of to the village school.

All year Anne had longingly watched the children at play at the village school, which was just across the Common, and had looked forward with eagerness to autumn when she would be old enough to join them.

We also looked forward to that time, but with misgivings deeper than those normal to parents when the time nears for their first-born to leave them for a teacher and a schoolroom.

Among the factors which had hastened our departure from California was that Anne was nearing school age and we did not want her to start learning the cruel realities of race and prejudice along with her ABC's as was inevitable even in Los Angeles. We still did not want that to happen and had been much relieved to learn our daughter was under Vermont school age when we settled in the village the previous autumn.

And now, after almost a year in the state, we were far from sure how Anne would fare in its schools. It wasn't that our children had not enjoyed a good relationship in playing with others of their ages during this time, for they had. But we feared it might be different when instead of a few playmates, children of friends, Anne's association would be with scores of strange children when she entered school.

It was not just that she might encounter the small persecutions normal to school experience, but rather the indiscriminate cruelty of childhood which unerringly discovers and attacks what is most vulnerable about its kind. And we knew our babe would be vulnerable in her racial difference from the others.

Now while Anne, with her fair skin, gray eyes and light hair, was not markedly different in appearance from the others, we assumed they would know there was another kind of difference, that many of them would have heard, or overheard, their parents discussing us, identifying us by race in such a way as to have created an unfavorable impression in their children's minds, even though that might not have been intended.

That was why during the last several weeks before school opened in the fall of 1947, Helen fretted constantly. I tried to reassure her, but I was far from sure that our child was going to be all right. And no matter how well Helen and I might fare, if our children were going to have to start their lives by bucking race prejudice, we would have no choice but to go where such was not the case.

My mother visited us in mid-August and as I strolled from the village store one morning, all I was thinking of was that she was making one of my favorite breakfasts: hot biscuits, fluffy egg omelet, fried apples, broiled ham, and that it would be ready by the time I reached home. That I liked my mother's cooking was no secret. Helen liked it too, and whenever Mother visited us, we feasted.

As I turned into our drive I noted the mail had come, for there was a package on the mailbox. As I passed, I tucked the package under my arm.

Delectable fragrances assailed me when I entered the kitchen, turning what had been but pleasant anticipation into ravening hunger and I cried, "Hey, Maw, how long before chow? I'm starving!" and she, pink-faced from the oven heat as she removed a pan of biscuit, turned and chided, "Don't call me 'Maw,' young man, or that's what the children will be calling Helen next."

Busy setting the table, Anne frisking in her wake, Helen laughed. "Don't let that worry you, Mother," she said. "They call me everything else."

I put down my bag of groceries and glanced at the package I'd brought in. It was from my publisher. My heart began to thud, for suddenly I knew what it contained.

I don't remember leaving the house and going to my workroom in the barn. Awareness returned as I stood before my desk, staring at the package, watching as though disembodied, as my hands made a maddeningly deliberate rite of opening it, plucking from the carton within enough of its excelsior packing to reveal its contents.

It was, of course, my book, or more exactly, six copies of it; and when I withdrew one and held it in my hands, my heart gave one great turn.

After a while I was able to examine the book, to see it as a thing of substance. Despite my foggy state I perceived how beautifully it was made, how expensively. And it bore my name. Mine!

I was vaguely surprised when, carrying two of the books as though they were fragile, I returned to the house and found breakfast over and the kitchen erased of its signs. Mother and Helen sat in the living room, and as I entered it, readying words of apology for what I supposed was my mysterious absence, Helen extended her hand and with gentle mockery said, "All right, Mr. Thomas. May we have a look at it—now?" and then I knew why I had been left undisturbed the past hour: Helen had known what was in my package and had understood something of why I had stalked out without a word just at breakfast time. Mutely I handed copies of my book to her and to my mother.

Neither spoke as they examined it. I looked at my wife's

rapt face and was stabbed with dismay because I had not thought to share with her my great moment, remembering that had it not been for her there most likely would not have been any such moment at all.

Later, when I tried to apologize and ask forgiveness, I could not, for my lips were sealed—by hers.

CHAPTER *eight*

WE TOOK POSSESSION OF OUR NEW
home in late August. Every day thereafter I drove up from
the village to work at cleaning up the accumulations of junk
in the basement and the attic, and to see what repairs were
needed. They were considerable.

Although eager to have the work completed so that we
could move in, I pondered for a while before doing anything
about it. Supposing Rene had been wrong about the local
artisans? Perhaps they still would not hire out to me. I could,
of course, have workmen from the city, but I didn't like that
idea. Neither did I relish the possibility of another rebuff
from my townsmen.

However, I decided I must risk it. Progress would only
come through meeting rather than evading situations.

And so: "Hey, Ollie, are you right busy now? Got some
plumbing to do at our new place. Think you could help?"

And Ollie: "Well, not right off, Bill. Kind of tied up just
now."

*Tied up just now, huh, Ollie? Don't you mean now and
always where I'm concerned?* Such was my thought. But I
said with a shrug, "Well, if you're tied up, you're tied up."

"Yeah, Bill. But tell you what. If you ain't in too much of
a rush, I could help you soon's I get through over to Don's

in a coupla days. He's gettin' water piped into his barn."
Ollie chuckled, adding, "Better he should leave be piping
water, and fix that barn before she caves in."

We both laughed. The state of Don's barn was a local joke.

Looking into Ollie's clear blue eyes crinkled with good-
humored amusement at his sally, guilt stirs. I have prejudged
him.

And he asks, "How soon you got to have me?"

"Whenever you can make it," I reply, glad he does not
suspect what had been in my mind. "Only reason for any
hurry, we want to move in the new place as soon as possible
so Ed can get into the village house."

"E-yah. An' so Roger can take over Ed's farm. Kind of
triple play, hey?"

"Yeah. You a baseball fan, Ollie?"

"Kinda sorta. Used to pitch a little myself. Well, tell you
what: I'll go up to your new place tonight, after work, and
look her over so's not to lose any time when I get through
at Don's. What you got in mind to do?"

I told him.

Thus, the plumber, and so with the carpenter, the elec-
trician and the mason.

While the work was being done, cars and trucks slowed
up when they passed; sometimes they halted. Had I not
known better I would have felt the same suspicions I'd experienced those first days in the village when people passing our
house had also paused to stare.

But I knew better now, knew there was nothing mean or
unkind behind such curiosity. Now, if I were in the yard,
those who passed always waved and often stopped to chat, to
inquire how the work was coming, to fill me in on bits of
history about the place, its original and subsequent owners,
and to accept my invitation to come in and have a look at the
way the work was shaping up.

Even then I'd not become used to that hand-waving custom. In the South, practically everyone speaks or nods upon meeting but I had not known that to be a characteristic of Vermont, where the people are reputed to be taciturn.

Perhaps I've just not happened to meet that kind. Around our section, no matter how many times a day one meets a townsman—any townsman—waves as well as greetings are usually exchanged.

That seemed a friendly, warming sort of thing. To me it meant something more than a mere regional custom.

Once there had been two big maples in the front yard. Now there was one. All that remained of the other was a stump made unsightly by the former owner's attempts to remove it. He had dug deep, had done plenty of chopping, but the stump was still firmly rooted.

I casually mentioned this to the town road commissioner at a church supper. A couple of days later he clattered up the hill in the town tractor, a brute of a thing which effortlessly nudged out the big stump and rolled it to the back of the house.

I learned later that the former owner had tried to buy that same service, but never got it. I could not help feeling pleased.

All summer Anne prattled happily of her impending debut as a schoolgirl, bragged of it to her brothers, lorded it over them because they were too young to accompany her.

Helen and I hadn't the heart to attempt to dampen our daughter's enthusiasm in any way. After all, the fears we felt for her might prove groundless and we certainly did not want to sow such seeds ourselves.

Still, when the day arrived in September, our hearts were heavy as we prepared Anne for what was so obviously the most joyous day of her life.

If only the child didn't look forward to school with such unadulterated happiness, or if she were only a little nervous or timid at the prospect of meeting so many children all at once!

But our daughter wasn't shy or timid. She was, instead, overflowing with eagerness the morning school opened. She danced about so excitedly that Helen had trouble getting her dressed.

"Mama! What time is it? What time is the school bus coming?"

"Mama! Is it time for the school bus yet?"

"Mama! *Is* it time?"

"Almost, darling. But I'm afraid you'll have to wait a few days before you ride the school bus."

Anne, anxiously: "Why? Is it going to be late? My very *first* day?"

"It isn't that, honey. You see, there is no school bus from the village to your school, so Daddy is going to take you until we move into our new house. Then the bus that carries the children of that district will pick you up every morning."

"Mama—*why* can't I go to the village school? Mama, *please* why can't I?"

"Now darling, Mother and Daddy have already explained that since we are going to live in another part of town you will be going to another school. You've seen it, remember? That pretty little yellow schoolhouse we pass on the way to our new place?"

"Yes," chimed in little Will, "and you can even see it right down the hill from our new house, too."

"You'll meet lots of nice children there," Helen assured our daughter. "Not so many as at the village school, perhaps. But you'll probably have loads more fun, because there's lots of nice play space there."

"Well—"

"After we move," I said, "you'll ride the school bus twice every day."

"Shuckins," little Will said, "she don't even need to ride

any ole bus. She could just cut across the meadows down back of the house."

"No I couldn't," Anne cried indignantly. "Down over those ole rough meadows with all those ole cows and barbed wire fences and—and—"

The first day after I'd returned from taking Anne to school, Helen and I were pretty glum, nor did our spirits lift until our child was home again and we heard her happy chatter as she told of the wonders of being a schoolgirl.

But the next afternoon Anne tearfully related that the other children would not play with her, and our hearts sank.

But we comforted her, assured her that within a few days everything would be fine, yet we were soul-sick, for we feared Anne's schoolmates had spurned her because she was not of their race.

Helen was so upset she spoiled the batch of tomatoes she was canning—her first; and while I tried not to show it, I was equally disturbed.

The next day's news was no better. The other kids still would not play with her, Anne sobbed. We asked if any of them called her names or anything like that and she replied no, they just would not allow her to play with them.

That evening after we'd put the children to bed, we sat down to talk about the situation, but before we got started little Will padded downstairs, his face twisted in a scowl.

"Hey, Mama," he demanded, "how come those other kids won't play with Anne?"

"Oh, probably because they don't know her very well yet," his mother told him as we exchanged glances of dismay.

Our son mulled that over for a few seconds then his face began to clear. "Yeah," he nodded, "on account of they won't play with a girl named Mickey, either, Anne said. She's new, too."

When he had returned to bed Helen asked wistfully, "Do you suppose that's really all that's wrong—that Anne is new?"

"It could be," I sighed. "I'd certainly be happy if it was."

The next day I was happy, and so was Helen. Because Anne came home bubbling joyously about her "new friends." The children had played with her, accepted her.

But on the last day of Anne's first week in school, we feared that our rejoicing had been premature.

"Mother," Anne asked, "why is your face brown?"

"What!" Helen exclaimed, or rather, gasped.

Anne repeated her question. Her mother looked flabbergasted.

"Why do you ask that, honey?" I inquired.

"Oh," Anne answered carelessly, "some of the kids just asked me."

Helen began breathing again. Then she explained, carefully, casually, that some people were of one color, others of another, and I threw in the business about the same being true of flowers, clothes, animals. And there the matter ended —for then.

However, it posed a question we did not want to meet yet: how to tell our children about race. We felt they were too young to grasp any explanation we could make. But now we had to make definite plans to handle it, although we'd hoped that would not be necessary for quite a while.

We moved into our new home September 23rd, pleased because we had such a warm feeling for it. It seemed to bid us welcome. The children sensed that even more than we, for they ran happily all over the old house, racing upstairs and down, patting the walls and shouting, "Big ole house, we like you, we sure do, big ole house!"

I thought what a happy contrast all this was to the way we felt when we first came to Vermont.

Later that morning there was a long-distance telephone call from my publisher who congratulated me on my "new baby." I suppose he thought me daft, for at first I had no idea what he meant. Then I realized that this was my book's publication day—that it was the new baby. When the conversation ended I remembered that I was supposed to have been in New York at that very moment.

Ruefully I told Helen of my lapse. She laughed, asked whether I'd rather be in New York or in Vermont, and then I knew I was where I wanted to be. Happily I went back to what I had been doing, plastering a section of ceiling in our children's playroom.

The happiness of that first day in our new home almost ended in tragedy. Millie, a neighbor's daughter who had helped us in the village when Jeanne wasn't available, had been with us from morning on, assisting to put our house in order.

After supper we were all in the kitchen and Bradley, prancing about in high spirits, stopped, leaned against the unhooked cellar door, and vanished down the steep steps.

Helen and Millie screamed. I somehow got from the far side of the kitchen and hit the landing at the bottom of the steps an instant after Bradley, Helen at my heels.

Our son lay in a twisted heap in front of the big iron drain pipes which protruded from the wall. Sick with the certainty he'd struck those pipes, I picked him up, carried him up the stairs.

None of us clearly remembers the next few moments. I had laid Bradley on the kitchen table and bent tensely over his still little figure. Suddenly he wriggled, started bawling, and so did his sister and brother. Helen and I exchanged glances of relief, for in his cries there was more fright than pain.

Even after we had gone over him inch by inch without finding evidence of injury beyond a small scraped place on his spine we were still very frightened. During the excitement one of us telephoned the doctor; she arrived very soon, made a quick examination, and in tones of personal relief said gruffly, "Brad's all right. More scared than anything else. Can't say I blame him."

Helen let out her heartfelt, "Thank God!"

So great was my own relief I almost echoed her words. Almost but not quite. I went out into the warm dusk, walked around the house. I could just see the dim, distant bulk of the mountains, black against the darkening sky, and after a while I was able to unclench my hands and gradually my muscles unlocked and as I began to breathe again I ached all over, but mostly in my heart, and what I was feeling was not entirely due to the reaction of my son's narrow escape from injury, or death.

When mountains and sky blended beneath the fall of night, I went back into the house burdened with a nostalgic sadness for what I had lost so long ago and now could not find, however much I wanted to.

I am still unclear as to how the idea started, but late in September plans were in the making for a housewarming, and a mid-October date had been chosen.

During the past month, having finished the more urgent projects, I'd been taking it easier. Modern plumbing had been installed. An electric pump and pressure tank provided water at the flick of a faucet. Paint, plaster board and wallpaper had transformed the interior of our house, but all of the exterior wood trim and window casings needed paint. Rickety pillars on the back porch wanted replacing and the grounds around the house were lush with weeds; the front lawn was a mess.

Before the housewarming, *Ebony*, the picture magazine, queried me about covering it, planned to send a photographer. I saw the publicity potential in relation to my book well enough, but I certainly had not planned the affair to gain publicity. Nor was I at all sure I wanted to take a chance on anything which might not set well with my fellow townsmen. Besides, all we had envisioned was a modest afternoon drop-in party for those of the town who wished to come.

It didn't work out like that at all.

The photographer arrived a couple of days early. He took pictures of everything, including some shots of me allegedly helping to tear down the big barn across the road from our house.

The barn was being removed because in a weak moment I had yielded to Helen's objection to it because she said it impeded the western view. The truth is, she just doesn't like barns.

Inscribed in our guest register when the housewarming was over were one hundred and fifty names, but more than that dropped by, for in what was sometimes a crush, many went unrecorded.

We had expected only folk from our township except for a few friends from Montpelier, Burlington and one or two other towns close by.

However, from three o'clock on, that crisp October day, there was a steady stream of callers.

Eight of Helen's friends of the *Nous Servons* Club served as hostesses; Millie and other friends all helped receive guests, saw that they were served punch and cakes and the other edibles of which, fortunately, there was an adequate supply.

For me the whole afternoon was miserable, for just as people started arriving I developed a knifelike pain in my stomach. Neither aspirin, bicarb, nor amytal tablets gave me any relief. So I spent most of the afternoon in a chair by my desk in my study, striving to repress my desire to writhe and groan, talking with those who sought me out.

Aside from my bellyache, we decided the affair had been a success. We were pleased and worn-out. The minute my head hit the pillow that night I slept. However, I dreamed endlessly of walking toward a city of golden towers and turrets whose glow I could just glimpse atop a faraway hill. I wanted very much to reach it.

Sometimes I trudged wearily over flat sere plains, or climbed rocky inclines, and sometimes it was day, sometimes night, but always I could see the beckoning golden shimmer of that distant city. Yet no matter how hard I tried, I could get no closer to it.

The next morning, judging by my exhausted feeling and my aching body, I either walked a heck of a way in my sleep, or else foot travel in the dream-world can create the same fatigue as it can in the world we regard as real.

A week or so later, Helen and I were sitting out back gazing at "our" mountains when she suddenly remarked, "You know, it's just now occurring to me that except for Nick, *all* those people at our shindig were—*white!*"

"So what?" I yawned. "That's the only kind of people there are in these parts, you know."

"It isn't that," my wife said. "What gets me is that I never even thought about anything like that. They were just friends, neighbors, people." She shook her head. "I never dreamed I'd see *that* day."

CHAPTER *nine*

I WAS STILL THINKING OF WHAT HELEN
had said, when she spoke again.

"A year," she mused. "A year . . ."

"It's hard to realize, isn't it?"

"How do you feel about it?"

As I watched, the mountain peaks briefly glimmered in a
farewell flare of pink-gold afterglow from the just vanished
sun, and I wondered how I did feel about it—about our first
year in Vermont.

"Well," I said, "it hasn't been too bad, has it?"

"It hasn't been bad at all, excepting those first few days."

"It just could be that Vermont really is an okay state."

"I don't know about the whole state. I still can't get over
the way those clerks in the Burlington stores act."

"Oh, *that.*"

"Oh *that,* my foot! It still burns me up."

"Me too. But not for the reason it did at first."

"Hmph."

"I've done some research."

"So?"

"I guess I forgot to tell you. I got to talking with Rene one
day. I didn't say we thought the clerks acted like they didn't
want to wait on us. I just griped about the time it took to get
waited on in some of the stores."

"And—"

"Well, Rene just laughed and said that aggravated everybody. But she couldn't blame the clerks because she said they didn't make much money and didn't care too much about giving good service."

"You bought that?"

"No, not right then. But since, I've checked. Rene was so right. In the places we thought we were being ignored because of our race, other customers not of our race get the very same treatment. Haven't you noticed?"

"No. I haven't been back to any of those stores where we got the cold shoulder."

"Well, go back. You'll see."

"Anyway, *our* town is all right." Helen paused and added, "And I really like some of these women here as well as any I ever knew."

Again there was wonder in her tone.

"Oh, so you can stand the palefaces now, hey? Until we came here you didn't like 'em at all."

"Well, you were not exactly in love with them yourself."

"Not all of them, that's for sure. But some. Like Nate and Belle."

Helen laid her hand on mine, said, "I'm sorry. They *were* nice. I knew it then, but—"

"Well, you sure had a poor way of showing it, dear heart."

"Well, I said I was sorry and I am, so don't keep holding it against me, please."

"Oh, I don't hold it against you," I said airily. "I'm used to prejudiced people."

That ignited a slightly heated discussion before Helen caught on that I was teasing her. Then she exclaimed, "Oh— *you!*"

"No fools, no fun."

"Just the same, I can't see where prejudice is anything to kid about."

"It isn't. But we do it all the time, don't we?"

"I don't."

"We: The Negro people. We do it."

"Correction: Many of us do."

"Okay, if you want to get technical, many of us do. We make a game of it—among ourselves. You know that. You've heard that kind of stuff all your life."

"Yes, but maybe it would be better if we didn't make a joke of it, even among ourselves."

"Then we'd die of it, like slow poison."

The screen door slammed and Anne called from the back porch, "Mama! Something's burning in the oven, Mama!"

"The pies!" Helen cried. "Oh dear!" She jumped up, hurried into the house and I settled back in my chair thinking how many such frenzied dashes she'd made for the same general reason. Helen would never be anybody's paragon as a housekeeper, nor had she any such ambition.

I recalled her recent observation that the great reputation of New England women as immaculate housekeepers wasn't entirely deserved, a conclusion which obviously made her feel better about her own shortcomings of that kind.

It seemed significant that during Helen's first few months of contact with her townswomen, she had frequently and tartly remarked that *white* women were just like women of any other color. She observed that they were also late to meetings, they fussed, gossiped, feuded, wore inappropriate clothes, and there were a few who were not so careful about their clothes as they ought to have been.

Meaning their clothes were dirty?

Not visibly. It was not the eyes which made the discovery. It was the nose.

So what did that prove?

Well, for heaven's sakes, it proved white people were no different than Negroes, that's what!

Did she have to have that rather obvious fact proved? Biologically—

"Biologically some stew!" she exploded. "You know darn
well what I'm talking about. You know as well as I that in the
white view we have a monopoly on all the undesirable characteristics of the human race. And what," she demanded, "is
wrong with their eyes—and their noses—that blinds them to
those same failings among their own kind? When a white
person is stupid, uncouth, unclean or has any of the unlovely
traits they look down on us for having, why is that different?
Why does that make them think they are automatically better than anybody with a dark skin? Where do they get that
better-than-thou stuff, anyway?"

"They get it," I told her, "from the good old getting place
and for gossakes let us forget them and talk about better
things, like hot biscuits for supper."

So we then spoke of better things which, however, did not
result in hot biscuits for supper.

My reason for having so crudely changed the subject had
nothing to do with biscuits, though. I did it because what my
wife had been saying was disturbing, so revealing of the
traumatic impact inherent in the subject she had so heatedly
expounded, and worse, of her unawareness of it.

It seemed to me the very fact she had found it necessary to
remark upon, except for its color, the sameness of the cloth
from which she and her white sisters were cut, indicated a
need to prove that such really *was* the case. It was the existence of that need which caused a flare-up of old hatreds for
those who had created it, who had so wrought that despite
her intelligence, her academic training, her otherwise well-
balanced outlook, Helen was still compelled emotionally to
refuse what intellectually she knew needed no refutation: the
libel of her race, of its humanity, and hers.

That, however, was nothing new, for countless times I had
heard the same angry observations as voiced by Helen, the

aim being to prove whites were *not* superior to Negroes.
When younger I'd done it too, exchanging with others discoveries of both white failings and Negro achievements.

In time, when I understood why we did so much of that,
I ceased doing it, for it meant that in varying degrees, we had
been unable to resist the crushing weight of the dicta which
asserted the innate inferiority of non-whites; and because of
the lengthy and rigid enforcement of such dicta by the over-
whelming power of those who out-numbered us at least ten
to one in our country, I also understood why many of us
could not completely accept even the most obvious evidence
to the contrary.

But now, I thought again, having associated with them for
a year, Helen had remarked critically upon the housekeeping
of *New England* women, and not, as she had referred to them
at the outset, as *white* women.

Did that indicate a slow healing of old, deep wounds of
mind and spirit?

I thought, thankfully, that it did.

Faint upon the cooling air I heard the muted buzzing of a
milking machine, and from the pasture just below, there
floated up the lazy tinkle of cowbells. And I wondered was
there healing for me, too?

I wasn't entirely sure. As I sat, still gazing at the mountains now wreathed in filmy purple, I could not remember
when I had enjoyed a greater feeling of well-being. There
was something very satisfying in living as we did now, beyond sound and sight of others, yet knowing that we were
not at all alone, that if there was need, help would come as
quickly as among our own kind. Yet, how could I really
know?

A hint of chill had crept into the air and dusk was swiftly
mantling the valley, obscuring the peaks beyond. From now

on the days would shorten, the weather sharpen, and soon winter would come.

There was pleasure in that prospect. We had a stout, thick-walled house, fuel, food; and now I felt capable of coping with such exigencies as might arise.

I heard Helen calling me to supper but for a few more minutes I watched the first stars emerging, had one final look toward the mountains, but now they were hidden in the black distance.

Stiffly I pushed up from my chair and walked toward the house idly wondering what was for supper but not really caring because there would be apple pie and Helen's pies were good.

The thought came that many other things might also be good, or at least not as bad as they had seemed. But an inner voice scornfully rejected that possibility and I growled disgustedly to have this pleasant moment spoiled by it.

I had meant to work that rainy autumn day but behind the closed study door I was, instead, with my jeweler's glass, exploring the mechanism of an old silver watch.

About watches I knew little, but the workings of the small machines had always fascinated me. Studying this one, product of oldtime Yankee craft, I reflected that in the creation of material things at least, man was indeed touched with genius.

Helen's tap on the door destroyed that line of thought. "Telephone," she called.

"I'm not to home," I mumbled.

"It's that lady again."

"Aw—tell her I'm milking the cows."

"Will!"

"Okay, okay."

"Well, stop muttering and come on. If you had answered her letter in the first place—"

"I meant to," I grumbled, emerging from my lair, "but it slipped my mind."

"Tell it to the lady," Helen bade.

I did, with apologies which, while graciously accepted, did not get me off the hook; the woman wanted me to speak to a churchwomen's group in a neighboring town.

As our talk ended, my caller said, "By the way, Mr. Thomas—we were wondering if you would mind leading us in singing a few spirituals?"

With specious regret I replied, "I'm sorry, but I'm afraid I cannot."

"Oh, Mr. Thomas—please! We had so counted on that!"

"I'm truly sorry," I lied, "but the fact is, I don't know any spirituals, and if I did I couldn't sing them because I can't sing."

A tingling, possibly incredulous few seconds of silence. The lady asked faintly, "Uh—you really can't sing?"

"I'm afraid not."

"Oh."

"Perhaps," I suggested hopefully, "we'd better call it off, don't you agree? I mean, if your group expects a singer—"

"Oh no, no! We just assumed—I mean—uh—well, anyway, we shall be pleased to have you *speak* to us. So we shall expect you Wednesday next, then?"

"I'll be there."

"At two. And thank you very much."

"The pleasure is mine."

On that cordial note our conversation terminated. And Helen jeered, "Pleasure, huh, Pappy?"

"Spirituals yet," I muttered.

"Why, Mr. Thomas! Are you implying dislike of spirituals?"

"Slave songs. Who wants to be reminded of that jive?"

"Don't you know, Mr. Thomas, that Negro spirituals are authentic Americana?"

"So say the Peckerwoods. But it seems to me if I were a Peck it sure wouldn't make me proud to exalt that type of Americana."

"Why?"

"Because our first so-called spirituals came into being among slaves as a means of conveying news of secret meetings whose objective was usually escape or something like that. That's why."

"You're a heretic, Mr. Thomas."

"That's better than being a Peckerwood."

"Don't try to change the subject. Just why did you tell that white lady you couldn't sing?"

"Because, as you well know, it's the ding-danged truth."

"But Mr. Thomas! All Negroes can sing!"

"Well I can't. But I can do a triple tap with my right foot, sometimes."

"Well, I suppose that's in your favor. How about chicken? You love fried chicken, of course?"

"Sure do."

"That's in your favor, also. Pork chops?"

"Yum-yum!"

"Now you're conforming! How about chitterlings?"

"Hawg guts? Ugh!"

"Don't be vulgar. But of course you do adore watermelon?"

"But of course I do not adore watermelon. But cantaloupe —ah me!"

"Cantaloupe," Helen admonished severely, "is not on the accredited list." She sighed, added, "Young man, I'm afraid you do not measure up."

"To what?"

"Oh come, now. You know quite well I'm referring to American Standards for Colored People. Why, your likes and dislikes are, shall I say—"

"Subversive?"

"Exactly! The very idea—not liking *watermelon!*"

"Naw, and I also do not like all these goldarned palefaces who believe all that rubbish about us."

"Well, as you have so often remarked," Helen said in her normal manner, "they just don't know any better."

"It's high time they were learning."

"Well, isn't that really why you make these speeches? To—er—enlighten them?"

"Such is my naive hope," I admitted.

"Then," Helen bade with a grin, "go you forth and spread your light, Mr. Thomas."

"I'd tell you right quick where to go to if you were not my dear and beloved wife."

"Am I really, truly, your dear and beloved wife?"

"Sometimes you are," I said as I stomped back into my study, "but this is not one of those times, dear heart." Then I closed the door right quick before she heard my chuckling, or maybe giggling. Because my wife had at last caught on to the game and she had laced me, but good. I said in a sonorous whisper, "Go you forth and spread your light, Mr. T. Your two-candle power light, Mr. T. Light up the world with it, Mr. T., since you're so doggone great."

But I didn't. Came the next Wednesday and I didn't even light up the small anteroom of the church where I was to speak. At least not enough for recognition by the lady who had called me and was the chairwoman of her group.

I'd arrived a few minutes early and, as directed, went in the side entrance of the church. Finding myself in a combination foyer-cloakroom, I knew I had chosen rightly because of the murmur of voices I heard beyond the door at the far end.

At two o'clock, I nervously adjusted my tie, smoothed my hair, started to light a cigarette but, remembering where I was, I stopped.

At five after two, I just *had* to have a drag and had started outside when the inner door opened, a woman emerged, gave me a fleeting glance, sailed by, went outside, looked around, returned, passed me with another cursory glance, vanished behind the inner door.

Had she been looking for me, for the speaker? Apparently not. I went outside, smoked, and had just crushed the butt beneath my heel when, at two-ten, the same woman came out again, eyed me briefly, looked up and down the street somewhat anxiously, frowned at the empty street, turned to re-enter the church.

"Pardon me," I murmured, "but would you be looking for Will Thomas?"

"Why—yes," the woman answered, her glance again worriedly sweeping the street. Then she looked into my face and anxiously asked, "Do you know him? Isn't he coming?"

"Well you see, I'm Thomas."

The woman made a faint, gasping sound. For a second or so she stared round-eyed, open-mouthed, and blushed from neckline to hairline.

I didn't mean to, but I couldn't help laughing. Then I made a bridge: "I don't suppose I look quite as you expected?"

"Well—uh—Well I—suppose not . . ."

"You were expecting a large, dark gentleman, perhaps?"

A mute, embarrassed nod.

"I'm sorry I don't meet expectations."

"Oh—uh—that's all right. I mean—uh— Well, won't you come in, Mr.—Thomas?"

Without awaiting my reply the flustered lady turned and hurried inside and I followed, my amusement at her revealing reaction receding before a weary anger, not at her, but at the millions of my countrymen of whom she was so accurate a reflection.

I didn't give a very good talk that day. I had no heart for it as I faced the blank white faces gathered in a neat semi-circle before the podium on which I stood. I had the feeling that nothing I might say would penetrate the minds behind the pale, staring masks. So I said my futile say and left as quickly as courtesy permitted. I vowed: never, never again!

CHAPTER ten

Our second autumn in Vermont was as lovely as our first. I wandered about our land, the browning meadows, our forest, a real one in whose dense mazes one might easily become lost both actually and in the imagination.

But it was the mountains which drew me most, particularly Mt. Mansfield's triple peaks which dominated our eastward view. Its likeness to the profile of a giant face was inescapable; it seemed to have a rough-hewn chin, a sloping, somewhat flat nose, and a long brow. Of all the hundreds of Green Mountain peaks it was the highest. It filled me with an impression of somber power, of lonely majesty.

Then, too, only a monarch could be so royally garbed in purple and ermine.

The children spoke of it proprietorially, referred to it with affection as "The Ole Man." Soon after awakening they would gather before the big windows in the boy's room to check on "him," and if he had altered his regal dress during the night, which generally he had, there was excited chatter which awakened and evoked irate squawkings from our room across the hall.

As the weather grew crisper, The Ole Man often wore a snow-white robe, and for his crown, if there was sun, a great

dazzling diamond. If not, it was a cap gleaming with crushed
pearls. And because the children did, I called him The Ole
Man too. But I thought of the rough profile as that of an Indian, brooding and with timeless patience waiting. For what?
An evening of the score, perhaps?

Once past the housewarming, which had delayed the re-
sumption of my writing, I began gradually to ease into the
strict regimen I meant to follow. But somehow as the golden
autumn sped by, that process was very gradual indeed, for
there·were apples to be gathered before the really killing
frosts; then weather stripping, puttying storm windows, burning trash—all had to be done during fine weather, and never
would there be a more wonderful time for wandering in the
woods, for long, exploratory drives.

But I didn't worry much, for winter would soon clamp
down, and *then* I'd have nothing to do except work at my
writing.

However, it was necessary to spend some time in my study
dutifully answering letters which began drifting in a few
weeks after the publication of my book.

Sometimes three or four letters came, then for days there
would be none. After a while the irregular flurry settled to
a small, steady stream. I hadn't expected anything like that.

There was another unexpected development: the requests
for me as a speaker increased. Then followed further complications, for usually after each speech, I received several letters. It was not bad when the writers merely expressed liking
for what I had said, for these required only "thank you"
replies.

What *was* bad was when they took issue with me, for I
felt I must try to give effective and, when possible, factual
answers.

I suppose I ought to have been flattered by these manifestations of interest, but I was not. However, I did realize that
through this sort of participation I might gain valuable in-

sights into heretofore puzzling mechanics, emotional and intellectual, by which the white brother continued so firmly to retain racial and religious concepts increasingly out of tune with the facts—and the times.

So in many respects our second winter in Vermont was much more eventful than I had expected or desired. By spring I felt I had gained much in knowledge of certain Vermont attitudes and reactions along the racial front. Through letters and countless personal conversations I came to the conclusion that, basically, Vermonters held almost identical beliefs with the rest of America's majority, with the difference that I had found no trace of animus in them, and that alone was unique.

Indeed, the very fact that many Vermonters seemed to believe the traditional racial stereotypes was what endeared them to me, for despite what I can best sum up as their old-line "darky" concept of us, they still freely extended friendship, fellowship, and hospitality.

Best of all, few Green Mountain folk, high or low, felt it necessary to even mention race unless I mentioned it first.

All of that was fine, but I didn't get much work done, especially on the major project I'd planned. I did some articles, a few stories, and so kept some income dribbling in, but aside from letters, that was all the writing I accomplished.

In Los Angeles I had belonged to an ancient fraternal order, and I had discovered many "brothers" among my Vermont townsmen.

But I made no effort to join the local lodge because our order, at least in the U.S.A., was as completely segregated as the vast majority of the nation's churches. And while I was learning that Vermont could not be judged by any other state, I did not know if its fraternal orders conformed to the general pattern, nor wished to court rebuff in case they did.

However, I wore my fraternal ring occasionally and as a result was invited to attend a meeting of our order in a nearby town. I accepted despite a feeling I ought not. But I thought perhaps in this matter, as in others, I had prejudged.

So, with several townsmen-brothers I attended the meeting, was introduced to officers of the lodge, many of its members, and I took part in an initiation ceremony.

In a cautious way I enjoyed it, for at no time was there the least sign that my race made the slightest difference to any-one. Even so, I was not fully at ease. I had the feeling of waiting, a premonition that something unpleasant was sure to happen.

After the formal ceremonies, there was a half-hour interval before the banquet which was to follow. During that period I met many more brothers and talked at length with one in particular, whom I shall call Mr. Roe, an extremely pleasant and well-informed man. We spoke of such things as the state of our nation, and the inadvisability of the rapidity with which we were disarming.

In due time we took places around the banquet table. Mr. Roe at its head as toastmaster, deftly set into motion an en-tertainment in which the brothers arose in turn to tell anec-dotes, mostly on the ribald side. The minute *that* started, I wished I'd not come.

Maybe some amusing yarns were told, for there was much laughter and applause. But I could not join in, and tension within me tightened as the joke-telling progressed around the table, because I knew—I just *knew*—that sooner or later some-body was bound to tell a "darky" story. However, the circle was finally completed except for Mr. Roe, and some of my dread began to fade. I was able to breathe again and was im-mensely relieved the ordeal was almost done, for surely Mr. Roe would not cast the shaft I so feared. I was even able to raise my eyes from my untouched plate and glance at him as he got up, a tall, well-groomed man, who smiled as he began *his* joke.

"This," he announced, "is about a couple of coons, Rastus

and Sambo. Now it seems that one dark night these two big
nigger bucks were walking through the woods and they came
to a graveyard—"

Laughter, anticipatory whoops and chuckles, for everyone
knew how terrified *niggers* were of graveyards, especially at
night.

"—and as I was saying," continued the speaker, his eyes
twinkling, "these two big nigger bucks got to this graveyard
and just as they were edging past it, ready to run at the drop
of a hat, of course—"

More laughter, louder whoops. *Of course!*

"—why, just about then an owl hooted in a tree right over
their kinky heads and—"

I don't know what happened to Rastus and Sambo after the
owl hooted, for I grew sick with humiliation.

In that moment I cursed the folly which had placed me in
a position where such a thing could happen when I was unable to fend it, to hit back, to do anything but sit frozenly
and take it.

Dimly I became aware again of my surroundings, of tense
muscles that shrieked for release, and of the sounds of sub-
siding applause and laughter. For a few seconds I dared not
move, nor lift my eyes. When I did steal a quick glance about
the table, it was poor comfort that no eyes were upon me. In
fact, the man next to me hunched me with his elbow and
chuckled, "Say, that was a good 'un, wunt it?" and I mumbled something he took for agreement and he said, "Hey
Brother, you ain't hardly touched your plate. Don't you like
turkey?"

I was glad to get home. Helen had retired, much to my relief, for she would have been interested in the meeting and I
would not have cared to talk about it.

But I kept thinking about it long after I'd gone to bed.

Had Mr. Roe told that awful joke with malice afore-
thought? We had conversed, face to face, and he must at

least have noticed my swarthiness. He knew I was a writer and he must have seen some of the recent newspaper stories about me, most of which mentioned my race.

Of course it was possible that he had not—*really* had not—known I was a Negro.

But supposing he had? Did his pleasant look hide a sharp racial animus? Did he tell the story to let me know I wasn't wanted in the group?

I didn't know. One minute I thought yes, the next, no. In strict justice I had to assume him innocent, for at the very least he was only following a traditional custom in relating a "darky" joke among a gathering of his kind.

But—supposing he *had* known?

Finally, I slept.

I still don't know if I would be permitted membership in a Vermont lodge of our order, even though I've learned that a Negro, a prominent orchardist, not only belonged to one, but several times served as its "Master." That I have not learned how I might fare is due to my determination never again to get in a spot where any Mr. Roe might come out with this type of "joke" in my presence.

I am glad of one thing: the experience did not make me think less of our fraternity, per se. As Helen once said of religion, the trouble was not with *it,* but with the *people* who professed it.

In any event, although I have not been in official association with those of the bond for the several years of my Vermont residence, I have enjoyed dozens of informal contacts with individuals of our illustrious order, who, unlike its national heads, have warmly recognized our brotherhood, both fraternal and human.

Just after Anne's birthday in November, the children began pestering me about a Christmas tree. We had just millions of them right over in our very own woods, didn't we? Well then!

I held out until a couple of weeks before Christmas and then, trailed by my small fry, I broke trail across the snowy meadow to the woods.

It took an hour for the kids to make a selection. But they wanted three trees, not one. There, I put my foot down, firmly. We did *not* need three trees for Christmas, and that was *that* and they had better hurry up and decide upon one because it was growing dark. The very idea—three Christmas trees. Why, there were lots of children who wouldn't have even *one* on Christmas day.

"Why not, Daddy?"

"Because their parents are too poor to buy them one, Anne."

"Not even a teensy-weensy one, Daddy?"

"No, Brad, sometimes not even a teensy-weensy one."

"Well, why not, Daddy?"

"Because, Will, not everyone is as fortunate as we, for we've a whole forest."

"Poor means when you haven't got any money, doesn't it, Daddy?"

"Something like that, Sister."

"Yes, and when you haven't got anything to eat, huh, Daddy?"

"That's right, Brad."

"Are there lots of poor people, Daddy?"

"I'm afraid there are, Will. Far, far too many for a great, rich country like ours."

"Well, we've got zillions of Christmas trees, why couldn't we give them to all the poor children?"

"I wish we could, Anne."

"Well, why can't we?" little Will demanded.

"Now look," I said, "this is not the time or place for such a discussion. Decide which tree you want and let's get going before Mother decides we're lost."

"I'd *like* to be lost in the woods, Daddy. I'd make a fire—"

"Well, *I* wouldn't, especially at night!"

"Yes, because it would be dark and the wild animals would get you and eat you up, huh, Daddy?"

And Daddy roared, "Quiet, you pickle-heads, and let's head for home!"

By then dusk was really falling. As we started back over the meadow the porch light of our house came on and Anne said, "Mother's afraid we will get lost, isn't she?"

"Yeah," little Will said, "that's why she just turned on the porch light, huh, Daddy?"

"Lost or not," Daddy panted as he waded through the knee-high snow, "that light sure looks good."

"Yessir, Mister Daddy," Brad asserted, "it sure as hell does!"

"Brad! That's a bad word!"

"What is a bad word, Daddy?"

"Why-why, *hell*. It's a word you shouldn't use."

"Well," Bradley said, "you use it all the time, Daddy."

"You sure do," little Will chimed in.

"Yeah, like when the car won't start, or something," Anne said.

"Less talk," I ordered, "or we'll never get home."

Christmas was a happy time, almost as we had imagined it would be before we became Vermonters, except that somehow I failed to picture our house cluttered with three lavishly decorated Christmas trees.

J ANUARY AND FEBRUARY TOOK FOREVER TO drag by; then, incredibly, it was March, the hinge-month be-tween winter and spring, and it was time to try my hand at sugaring.

In the village we hadn't had a single maple tree, but on our new property we had so many we couldn't count them. I had no intention of starting a full-scale operation and meant only to tap a few of the trees which lined the road.

I had built a little arch of bricks and stones just big enough to accommodate a sugaring-off pan, and one day when I made an experimental tap and sap flowed, I knew it was time to get busy.

With much advice from my children, I drilled three holes in each of six trees, and into those holes I hammered sap spouts, and on them hung my eighteen buckets. And smugly I thought, "Shucks, there's nothing to it."

I thought I was prepared to boil as soon as my buckets had filled. But the operation proved much less simple than I'd thought.

For one thing, the kids and I had gathered an enormous pile of wood for fuel, but it was damp and not at all the kind, even had it been dry, to make the quick, hot flames needed for good boiling. I learned that when, having loaded a fifteen-gallon crock—my storage tank—with clear sap, I filled the sugaring-off pan and made a fire in the arch.

Soon I decided it wasn't much of a fire, nor was it much of an arch, for most of the smoke rushed back into my face instead of going up the stove-pipe.

I figured more stove-pipe was needed to create a stronger draft, and found some after a couple of hours of rummaging in the dusty attic. By then the day had waned, supper was on the table, and I called it a day.

In the morning I added the additional lengths of pipe to my chimney and by the time I had devised ways and means of wiring it so it would not topple, it was noon.

After dinner I thought I was all set, so made another fire in the arch. This time the smoke didn't come back into my face. Neither did it go up the chimney. Furthermore, the feeble fire wasn't enough to warm my pan of sap.

Something had to be done, but just what I didn't know.

Finally I set a small electric fan at the mouth of my arch. This worked pretty well, at least well enough for me to ignore my wife's snide references to it as an anachronistic note in my primitive arrangement. When the fire finally showed real signs of life it wasn't long before the clear liquid in the sugaring-off pan began to steam and I started to calculate how much syrup I was going to make.

I'd heard twenty to thirty gallons of sap were required to make one gallon of syrup. So for the five to six gallons I hoped for I would have to boil down a minimum of—good gracious—one hundred and twenty gallons of sap. And I thought in dismay, "Oh, *no!*"

But, as the fellows say around here, "I stuck with her and even though she took a week, I done her." Or maybe she done me, for when she was finished, so was I. Because once my fire got going, that huge pile of wood I'd thought ample for weeks of boiling vanished in two days, and thereafter I

had to hustle and chop wood all day, and feed it into the
flames as tenderly as though it were a votive offering.

Anyway, the syrup was pretty good even if it was dark and
thick and not the fancy variety which is pale and thin.

There was a snow a couple of days later and we had sugar-
on-snow and enjoyed it the more because the "sugar," really
nothing but hot maple fudge solidified by sudden contact
with the snow, came from our trees and was made by us.

I began to feel like a real Vermonter and cautiously to
believe that some day I might really be one.

In April I was invited to be a speaker on the annual spring
tour of Vermont Forums, Inc. Subject: Race Relations. I
didn't want to accept even though I knew how worthwhile
that nonpartisan organization's work was. It sponsored discussion of pertinent and controversial subjects to the end that
Vermonters would be better prepared to study and decide
about current issues.

But I did accept. I had to. On a limited scale I had been
trying to do the same thing on my own. Besides, my friend,
the Reverend Richie Low, was going to be moderator.

Just the same, I looked forward to the tour as an ordeal.
However, after I had met its director, Bradford Smith, a
writer of Shaftsbury, Vermont, I began to have a much
better feeling. I liked him at once.

My dread completely faded after I met the other two
speakers. One was Palestine-born Alisa Klausner Eskol, behind whose vivid, young, dark beauty glowed love of her
native land and its people.

The other speaker was a native Californian, Sam Ishikawa,
a stocky young Japanese-American who, during the war, had
been evacuated from his home and confined in an American
concentration camp.

I had never been in more delightful, stimulating company,

nor among a group so dedicated to the crusade for freedom. I even began to look forward to our rostrum appearances.

Richie's droll commentary during his deft running of our "show" was really something, and nightly I anticipated the moment when Alisa spoke, for—even when she became so enthused her words blurred—what she wanted to convey was delightfully clear and everyone loved her.

Behind Sam's placid exterior, his grave mien, his solemn manner of speaking, there was a subtle humor which gave sharp point to some of the things he told his audience; and sometimes there was sadness in his words, a wistfulness which bespoke a deep yearning to be accepted as an American in his native land, to discover that America was, after all, the land of the free.

How well I understood that.

Behind the scenes it was Brad who made things run so smoothly, who arranged everything, thought of everything. Beyond his normal crisp competence I sensed his conviction of the importance of what we were trying to do.

My part was not easy despite the heartening responses of the always large audiences throughout the state. It was not the actual speaking which troubled me but what I would say.

From the various newspaper reports and by audience reaction, I judged that what was most wanted of me was to tell of my Vermont experience, and that Vermonters without realizing it were inclined to be just a little smug about their traditional racial liberality.

It seemed to me that when I spoke of unfavorable racial conditions elsewhere, particularly in the South, it was as though everyone in concert nodded in agreement.

As I well knew, there was substantial justification for such an attitude and I supposed it natural for people to like hearing their virtues extolled.

Yet, in southern Vermont I had seen signs outside of a

few inns and hostelries discreetly reading, "Gentiles." To know that was countenanced in Vermont was saddening.

When I was the house guest of a prominent local couple in one of the towns where such a sign was in evidence, I mentioned it and asked why the people tolerated it.

My host shrugged and commented that such things were bad, that all kinds of discrimination were bad.

"But, Will," he observed, "in the case of Jews it goes much deeper than race, you know. Besides, you are a Gentile. Why should you be disturbed?"

"Why shouldn't I be?" I countered. "Prejudice toward anyone, any race, any religion, is evil. Besides, isn't discrimination contrary to the basic tenets of both the law and religion in which American Christians claim to believe?"

"Oh, come now, Will," my host said indulgently, "isn't that a rather sweeping indictment? After all, would you deny anyone the right *not* to associate with those he dislikes?"

"Of course not," I replied. "The choice of friends and associates surely is an inalienable right. But I do not believe anyone has the right to refuse public accommodations to otherwise acceptable persons because of religion or race. Aside from the inherent wrongness, it's a contagious disease."

My host laughed and asked, "Well, what's been *your* experience in public accommodations, Will? In Vermont, of course. Have you been refused anywhere?"

"That's not the point," I replied.

"You're ducking, Will!" my host exclaimed. Eyeing me quizzically, he asked, "Why do you defend the Jews, anyway? What have they ever done for you? For your people? They discriminate against you, too. Isn't that true?"

"Oh, gosh," I said, "let's talk about the weather."

My host laughed triumphantly. "Aha!" he chortled. "Ducking again."

"Not at all," I denied, feeling suddenly bone-tired. "Of course some Jews discriminate against Negroes. But that has nothing to do with what you called my defense of them, because I am not defending them."

"Then what are you defending?" asked my host with a skeptical grin.

"Nothing, really," I sighed. "But it does seem to me there is something ridiculous about anti-Semitism in our country."

"Ridiculous, Will? *Hah!*"

"Yes! Ridiculous! A supreme example of the irrational nature of prejudice. Prejudice Americans feel towards Negroes, Mexicans, Indians, is somewhat understandable in terms of a perhaps natural antipathy to those markedly different in physical characteristics, such as color. But Jews are not different in that way. They are a white people."

"Says who?"

"Oh, for heaven's sake!" my hostess suddenly exploded, "that's just quibbling and you know it!" She had been sitting quietly beside her husband, apparently not too interested in our discussion until her outburst.

"Attacked from the rear," he groaned. "What are you trying to do, madam, sink me?"

"Sometimes," his wife said tartly, "I think you need sinking." Then to me, "You were saying, Will—?"

"Just that Jews are as white as any other so-called white people. But what gets me almost as much is that they are treated so badly when, despite their small numbers in our country, they have made such terrific contributions to our culture."

"I challenge that," my host said. "What contributions? They are like parasites: they take, not give."

"Challenge the record," I suggested. "In the arts, sciences, human relations, the record rates them high. How do you justify Gentile prejudice against a people who are both white *and* capable of such great good?"

"I don't justify it," my host said, for the first time in a really serious tone. "I merely face the facts, the realities, one of which is how most people feel about Jews." He made a decisive thumbs-down gesture, adding, "And it is like that not only in our country, but all over the world. It is one of those things we accept, take in stride, like the weather."

"The weather, indeed!" his wife sniffed.

"See there?" my host said in mock sadness. "My own wife . . ."

"Why," I demanded, "do we *have* to accept what is wrong according to the principles of both our religion and our law? There are punishments by law for practically every other crime, such as theft, murder—"

"Well now, I've heard everything!" my host exclaimed. "So all of us criminal Gentiles ought to be shot at sunrise, huh, Will?"

"What a wonderful idea," his wife remarked.

"Ah, you two," her husband growled. "So prejudice is a crime, eh? Now there's a great concept, Will."

"I think so," I replied, "even if we don't mean it the same way. When prejudice is used as a punitive weapon, it seems to me as criminal as a gun used to maim or murder, and not only against individuals, but against humanity itself. Don't forget that the human spirit is more important than the flesh, or so we are all taught to believe."

"Seems to me you're completely ignoring the larger issues," my host said impatiently, "the realities, the as-is and as-of-now. You've got it all wrong, Will."

"He has not," his wife said firmly. "You have."

Throwing up his hands, her husband groaned, "Okay, I'm licked. By the minorities. How about a drink?"

I was glad of a drink, even more of a change of subject. Yet it was still uppermost in my mind as we talked of other things, nor could I forget it during the remainder of our tour, for it was a shadow on my conscience each time I told audiences of the goodness of my experience in their Green Mountain State.

Still, was I to judge the whole state by the one serious flaw I had encountered in it? Obviously, I could not.

And yet . . .

The highlight of our tour was our final stand in Burlington, before the largest, most responsive audiences of our swing around the state. To me it was like coming home, for there were many who knew me.

I was greatly relieved to be done with it all, but sorry to end the fine association with Alisa, Sam and Brad. One consolation: Richie and I would continue to meet, for we lived in the same area.

So uniformly good was my experience with Vermont hospitality that had it not been for those "Gentile" signs, I would have felt almost ready to make a favorable judgment concerning our future as Americans. But when I came to it I found myself unable to do so.

I was happy to be with my family again, close to "our" mountain, and to dismiss all disturbing matters from my mind even though I knew it would not be for long, because, alas, like most troubles of importance, these were autogenous.

CHAPTER *twelve*

W<small>HEN WE DECIDED ON VERMONT AS A</small>
tentative alternative to emigration, I at least never thought of
locating anywhere but in a rural area, and preferably on a farm.

My reasons included the possibility of atomic disaster, and
my feeling that cities were less than ever desirable for rear-
ing children.

Perhaps the frightening possibility of atomic attack had
much weight in my preference for a farm, for if it came, I
had it figured the best chance for survival was to be not only
as far as possible from obvious target areas, but where food
could be raised, where there was wood for fuel and wells or
springs for water.

So now we had a farm I meant to have at least a garden,
perhaps some chickens and pigs, if not a cow. The latter I
had given up until such time as my sons would be old enough
to help tend it.

I had one pig a friend had given us and it required little
care except, of course, feeding, which the children could handle. I also had a garden or, as soon as it developed, it had me.

Had I been more perceptive I would have taken warning
from the neighbor who plowed our large garden plot. Because
he had remarked, "You can raise quite a lot of truck in a
space as big as this, Bill. *Quite* a lot."

There was admonition rather than comment, but I had not then lived in Vermont long enough to understand the nuances of what appeared to be commonplace remarks. Indeed, I read into what he had said just the opposite to what he meant, and so replied that I *meant* to have plenty of fresh vegetables—*plenty*.

My neighbor nodded in a way I assumed was approving, and just before he drove away on his tractor said, "Well— good weedin', Bill."

I laughed and waved as he departed, not realizing he had repeated the warning, which translated was, "That's too much garden for a man to work without power tools. And one thing sure, you'll have to hump it plenty to keep the weeds down."

I humped it plenty. Helen also wielded a vigorous hoe and once in a while we were able to bribe or bully the children into helping a little; but we did not keep the weeds down and it was not long before we abandoned half the plot to them.

Even so we did have lettuce, green onions, mustard greens, carrots, and in time, cucumbers, tomatoes, and even a few ears of corn which somehow had escaped a night raid by somebody's holidaying cow.

Helen canned a fair lot of stuff, including blackberries and applesauce when those fruits were ripe. We really worked.

Often, as I weeded the garden, or picked berries or apples in our tangled old orchard, it seemed a lot of effort for so negligible a return. But there was consolation in remembering that possibly on some future day, the more the experience of this kind the better the chance to keep alive.

But there was time to relax, too, and when on hot days I reclined in the shade of our big maple, or during the cool evenings lolled in the backyard watching the mountains fade into mystic shadow, I often thought: "This *is* the life."

One afternoon in late spring Anne came home from school in tears. Gorman, a schoolmate, had called her a "great big ole black nigger."

Our little girl didn't know what "nigger" meant except it was very bad because some of the other children had fussed so at Gorman for saying it and the teacher had warned him never to use any such name again. Besides, Anne wailed, she was neither black nor old.

The incident was a shock, for all had gone swimmingly for Anne since those first few days at school when the other children had barred her from their play; and our expectancy of further incidents had just about vanished.

And now, this!

My first impulse was to tear down to Gorman's house, which was not far, because I figured the child must have learned that racial epithet at home. I suppose my hope was that Gorman's father would sufficiently resent what I had to say to cause us to "lock horns."

Fortunately I cooled off quickly enough to abandon the idea, because I knew quite well that fighting with Gorman's father would not solve anything. But I still burned because there was no other way in which I could strike back.

The next day I was glad I had done nothing so foolish as I had thought of doing, for there came a note from Gorman's mother expressing sorrow "that it had to be *my* boy who did a mean thing like that," and saying that not only had she punished him, but that his father had also "lambasted him plenty."

In the end we felt sorry for Gorman, especially after the little boy at school who considered Anne "his girl" punched Gorman in the eye the morning following the occurrence.

And there was no more trouble of that kind.

Not long after the completion of the Vermont Forums Tour, which was the highlight of this eventful spring, we

had a visitor: Horace Cayton, then on leave from his post
as director of Chicago's Parkway Community House, to re-
cuperate from a severe illness ascribed to overwork.

Cayton, one-time research assistant in the sociology department of Chicago University and twice a Rosenwald Fellow, was co-author with St. Clair Drake of the book *Black
Metropolis,* 1945 winner of the Anisfield-Wolf Award. Cayton had traveled much at home and abroad, had won recognition as a sociologist and lecturer.

Mr. Cayton's particular field was the socio-psychologic aspects of American interrace relations. But what I most appreciated of his many abilities was the one which enabled him
to translate his findings into down-to-earth language in his
hard-hitting weekly column in the Pittsburgh *Courier.*

His visit with us was indeed an event, for beneath his impressive largeness of body and manner, his close-cropped red
beard, there was a complete absence of stuffiness. Yet there
was a dignity which he never lost, even when, as happened
while with us, he went crashing through the woods and over
the meadows after a horse he wished to ride.

I still chuckle, remembering the incident, although I can't
say I much blame the horse for fleeing, what with so large
and determined a human jogging in its wake.

Incidentally, Horace never did put leather on that horse,
because when he finally cornered him in a rocky meadow, the
animal made a sudden dash, sailed over the barbed-wire fence,
and drummed up the road to freedom.

"You know," Horace observed thoughtfully when he had
regained enough breath for speech, "I don't believe that
beastie wished to be ridden."

I agreed, not solemnly, that such appeared the case.

When he first came, Horace, while certainly no invalid,
was patently far from well. He looked tired, drawn, had
obviously lost much flesh; and just below the surface there

was a tenseness I recognized and believed I understood.

In the weeks following, we discovered that on certain important levels ours had been a similar experience. We each had early become aware that something was radically wrong with the picture of our country as we had been taught to see it, and in only slightly different ways we had rebelled, had engaged in adventurous enterprises, had reacted similarly to racial prejudice, and had suffered severe spiritual wounds because of it.

The point where our paths diverged was when, in Los Angeles, the cumulative effect of those wounds mounted to the danger point, I had managed to escape (and just in time, Horace thought): first, through the release of the decision to leave the "battleground" to emigrate; and secondly, by the healing effect of the compromise which had brought me to Vermont.

He had not been so fortunate as I, Horace said, for he had not escaped to Vermont to find, as it were, a "better 'ole," but had doggedly stayed and fought, not only for his own right to manhood, but for that of all depressed groups in his land.

Physical illness sufficiently severe to put him in a hospital had been the price he paid. It was, as both he and the noted specialist who attended him agreed, almost entirely psychosomatic in origin, a direct result of prolonged emotional disturbance.

Horace did not need to explain the cause of that emotional disturbance. I knew it well. We agreed that both its incidence and destructiveness were in direct ratio to the sensitivity and awareness of those it affected, and that in the case of Negroes, living as they did in a culture so bewilderingly contradictory, the toll must be fearful.

Never before had I explored such matters with anyone so well versed in their scientific aspects, who also had extensive personal experience of them. And I felt an even greater respect for the man when I realized he had deliberately made himself a laboratory of psychic experiment, even though he, better than most, realized how dangerous that was.

Why had he taken such a risk? When I asked that, we were walking in the woods. Horace stopped and for a few seconds stood staring at the exposed roots of a fallen tree as though to find an answer in them.

Then slowly he said, "What else could I have done?" and he raised his eyes and we stood regarding one another thoughtfully and at last I understood, and understanding, shook my head in wonder. For what he had done was beyond and above considerations of race, of the fierce personal thirst for full human status: it was, I thought, the selfless act of a true scientist.

But I grinned at him and said softly, "What a chump!"

Horace smiled, shrugged, quietly replied, "Well, it was a job no white person could have done because he could only work at it from the outside."

I nodded. "I can see that. I sure can. But me, I'm going to look out first for number one."

Horace laughed, said derisively, "Who do you think you're kidding, Will?"

Horace had other sides, including a wry sense of humor which took account of not only the foibles of the white folk, but of the dark, although each had its place in his understanding of psychological patterns; and when he chose he could send Helen and me into gales of laughter with his droll anecdotes.

With or without his Vandyke, Horace happens to be of rather a distinguished appearance, and that, plus his extreme ruddiness and lack of what are called Negroid features, causes his race more often than not to be unrecognized by whites—something I, too, had experienced.

That is, as he says, except for his hair, which he describes as "Sam moss;" although red, it is crinkly, of a texture unlike that of most white people.

Knowing that he could "pass" (so long as he kept his hat on), Horace took advantage of it to evade racial bars in public accommodations when convenience or necessity dictated.

On one occasion, in San Francisco to attend a meeting connected with his work, he registered at the downtown hotel most convenient to its sessions.

But just as he finished registering (this was in wartime), an orchestra on the mezzanine started playing our national anthem and everyone in the lobby at once uncovered.

Everyone, that is, but Horace, who hesitated only a few seconds, but long enough, as he put it, "for all those super-patriots, including the desk clerk, to start glaring at me." Then slowly he removed his hat.

All during the rendition of the Star Spangled Banner his "unwhite" hair was closely scrutinized by *all* the desk clerks. When the anthem ended, Horace asked, "Well, do I still get the room?" To his surprise the reply was, "Bigod, you do!"

When he departed from Vermont after three weeks, he looked a different man and said he felt one, too. We were very glad of that, but sorry to lose such wonderful company.

By July the weather was good and hot, but there had been rain enough and everything flourished except our pig, "Mister Wiggy." Mister Wiggy, named by the children, was not quite the runt he had been when we got him, but he was far from the size he ought to have been by then.

Besides, Mister Wiggy was a malcontent, ever full of complaining grunts and squeals; he was always trying to climb out of his pen or bite the hand that fed him—mine.

One blazing day he accomplished both.

Helen and I were dawdling at breakfast when from outside there came an alarming racket. We dashed out to see what caused it.

"Mister Wiggy got out!" Anne screamed.

"He climbed up to the top of his pen and fell out," little Will shouted.

"Well, where did he go?" I yelled.

"Thataway," Brad yelled back, pointing to the culvert just beyond our driveway.

I looked and there was Mister Wiggy rooting vigorously. I made frantic signals for the kids to retreat, to stop hollering, and I began sneaking toward him.

I was almost upon him when the children suddenly stopped their noise and as though warned by its abrupt cessation, Mister Wiggy glanced around just as I reached down to grab his tail. Then I leaped back, shaking a bitten hand, for where Mister Wiggy's tail had been, his snout, plus teeth, had suddenly materialized.

Helen cried anxiously, "Did he bite you?"

"A mere scratch," I said, glancing at my bleeding hand.

Meanwhile, Mister Wiggy had backed off a few feet and stood regarding me with pure malice. I called him something other than his name, lunged furiously at him, but he skittered into the road and took off, with me right behind him.

I hadn't known that pigs, even young, lean ones, could be so fleet, but I learned before I got close enough to Mister Wiggy to bring him down with a flying tackle which carried us both crashing into the culvert.

I was thankful then that Mister Wiggy wasn't much of a pig in size, for by the time I was able to lock my arms around his flat belly we had threshed about so vigorously a thick dust cloud hovered above us.

By then Helen had arrived on the scene, and just as I was trying to get to my feet without releasing my grip on the pig, she asked brightly, "Who is winning?"

I just glared and that set her to laughing, and the kids also suddenly found the proceedings excruciatingly amusing and abandoned themselves to screams of merriment.

Completely unamused and puffing mightily, I climbed
back to the road, tightly clutching the furiously protesting
Mister Wiggy, while trying to avoid his efforts to disembowel
me.

I fixed Mister Wiggy, though. After dumping him somewhat violently into his pen, I paddled him good with a lathe,
which he did not seem to mind. What he did mind was my
nailing a strip across the top of his pen, for while I was doing
it he directed a look of such utter evil at me with his cold
gray eyes that the hair at the nape of my neck stirred.

Mister Wiggy never did amount to much. And that fall
when we sent him off to be processed, we toted up the cost
of the grain we'd fed him and found he'd cost about a dollar
a pound: the price of store-bought pork had skidded to about
fifty cents at the time.

But I consoled myself by thinking that if and when it became necessary to raise our own meat, I'd grow the grain
myself to feed the animals. And in case of atomic war, if
there were no fuel tractors, well then, I'd get a couple of
horses.

Anyway, I'd manage.

CHAPTER *thirteen*

A LETTER FROM MRS. FISHER INFORMED us she would be in Burlington on a certain date and invited us to have dinner with her. We were delighted that at last we would actually meet her.

But we delayed our reply while we debated whether or not we should accept her invitation. Perhaps we could have the joy of meeting her without dining with her. For a couple of days Helen and I discussed the situation before finally making a decision.

With more sadness than bitterness I said, "It seems a shame that in such a simple matter, and in Vermont, too, we should have to beat our brains out trying to know the best course to follow."

"Maybe," Helen suggested, "we ought to inquire—to find out."

"Oh no," I declared. "None of *that* stuff. If we're going to do it, let's do it right and let the chips fall where they may."

"I'd die if anything came up in *her* presence," Helen said.

"I, too," I said. "But she is Vermont's most famous woman —Why, she *is* Vermont! Surely they wouldn't dare!"

"What I'm thinking of," Helen said troubledly, "is how *she* would feel if they did."

"Well, what do you suppose is worrying me?" I demanded. "I don't want to take a chance on our being humiliated and I certainly would hate it if anything like that happened in her presence. Besides, she believes *so* implicitly in the democracy of Vermont. Helen, if those people pull anything, I'll—"

"No you won't. That would only make it worse."

"You're a mind reader?"

"When you use that tone, I am. Anyway, we've decided to accept her invitation. Let's not keep worrying over something that may not happen."

"Well, it happened to Marian Anderson."

"So we've been told. Maybe it didn't, really."

"So okay, maybe it didn't. But it sure happened to Roland Hayes when *he* stayed there last fall. We *know* that. And both Miss Anderson and Mr. Hayes are famous people. And if that hotel would dare pull anything on *them*—"

"Maybe we'd better write Mrs. Fisher and beg off. Because—"

"No," I said with a sigh. "Maybe you're right. Maybe nothing will happen. Richie Low is always telling me not to anticipate that kind of thing. And to a certain extent, he's right. But just the same—"

Just the same we met Mrs. Fisher in the lobby of the Hotel Vermont, Burlington's best hostelry, and if, because of her many kindnesses, we already bore a great affection for her, we fell in love with her when we saw her. She was very lovely, and when we chatted with her we knew she was a great and good woman.

When we went in to dinner I, at least, had almost forgotten what had so perturbed us, for nothing untoward happened, nothing at all. I do not remember what we ate, for just to be in Mrs. Fisher's company, to listen to her wise, friendly talk, to hear her laughter, see her blue eyes twinkle—these were more than enough to cause forgetfulness of all else.

Only when we were driving home did Helen and I compare notes.

"All that stewing and fretting for nothing," she sighed.

"Yes, but how could we know? The hotel management asked Roland Hayes to have his meals in his room. That meant they didn't want him to use the public dining room because he was a Negro, didn't it? I mean, why should we expect to be treated any differently?"

"Well, Mr. Hayes *didn't* have his meals in his room," Helen said with a laugh, "and he *did* use the dining room. And so did we."

I laughed, too, remembering the part Reverend Low had played in that incident. Mr. Hayes had come to Burlington to do a concert for a local organization, and when the committee sponsoring it learned the famed singer had actually been asked not to use the dining room of the hotel whose guest he was, several of its members took swift action.

With Reverend Low as its spokesman, the irate group descended upon the hotel. What had tickled us so much was Reverend Low's method of handling the awkward situation. He had warmly thanked the hotel's manager for wishing to extend to Mr. Hayes the very special service of permitting him to dine in the privacy of his room, but assured him that even though Mr. Hayes *was* a very fine gentleman, he was content to use the public dining room just like anyone else.

Could it be that aside from a fear to offend so famous a Vermonter as Mrs. Fisher, the management had changed its attitude toward Negro patrons once it learned that even *some* white people wouldn't stand for it? Perhaps those who objected to discrimination should not remain silent about their convictions.

It was a lovely summer night, and I drove slowly as we talked. When we were within a few miles of home I exclaimed, "Good night! We're spoiling it. Let's talk about Mrs. Fisher. Wasn't she grand?"

We agreed that she certainly was.

Mostly the weather was fine that summer, although once in a while the skies suddenly would darken, rumble, explode with thunder blasts, and dazzling lightning and rain would fall in a deluge. These unpredictable thunderstorms seldom lasted long, but sometimes they were frighteningly fierce.

When the sun returned, it often made a shimmering rainbow over the valley below us. Our children liked the storms for the beautiful rainbows which followed.

Anne, the schoolgirl, spoke knowingly of the pot of gold at the end of the rainbow, and when asked by Will, Jr. at which end the gold was, she airily informed him "at both ends."

Helen and I also liked to watch as "our rainbow" materialized for it was truly lovely against the clean-washed green hills and the dark backdrop of the mountains. We didn't think of pots of gold, for to us the rainbows seemed to be omens of happiness.

Old Harve said casually, "She might not be such a good idee, Will."

It was a golden autumn afternoon. I looked up from my garden task and asked, "Why not?"

The sturdy, white-haired old man said flatly, "Because she's a-gonna rain, that's why."

"But just a few minutes ago I heard a weather broadcast and—"

"Poot. Gadgits."

"Well, how do *you* know?"

Harve jerked a thumb skyward. "Them clouds."

I glanced up at "them clouds," a few white filmy cirrus masses drifting slowly across the deep blue sky. "They look all right to me," I said.

"Them have got mares' tails."

"Oh?"

"Yeah." Harve speared a forefinger groundward. "Lookit that there chickweed. She's closed up tight, ain't she?"

"She sure is," I agreed.

"An' look yonder in your neighbor's pasture at how them horses is all bunched up in that corner an' how they're a-stretchin' their necks an' a-sniffin' th' air."

"Those are rain signs?"

"Yup. 'Sides, you mind they's been lots a bugs an' beetles a-flappin' around nights here of late? Well, there won't be none tonight. *They* know, too. An' if you see that big yeller tomcat a yourn a-lickin' hisself, come afternoon, well, she's a sign, too. Likewise any fresh mole diggin's."

So I did no fall planting that day since old Harve said she was a-gonna rain and she sure did, hard, all night.

Old Harve, a "bachelater" as he called himself, lived alone on a small farm in the eastern hills. We'd met that summer when wandering in them, I chanced upon his ramshackle place.

At first the old man hadn't much to say when I asked for a drink of water as he sat on his rickety porch, a cat on his lap, three dogs at his feet. He looked at me suspiciously, questioned me sharply before drawing me a drink from his mossy well. But when I praised the sweetness of the water he thawed a little, admitted it wasn't too bad, and then we got to talking.

Old Harve had heard of me, although I didn't suspect it until he casually remarked, "You don't look like no niggerman."

"I don't?"

"Nope. Heared there was a nigger fambly moved here. But I allus thought niggers was black. You ain't black."

If I correctly understand the meaning of the phrase "taken aback," I was so taken, to put it mildly.

"Well—uh—you see," I floundered, "all Negroes are not dark."

"Wun't speakin' of *Neegroes*, whatever they might be. I was speakin' of *niggers*. Are you a *nigger*?"

I told him that I was not, explained that *nigger* was a hated word for *Negro*, tried to keep my explanation simple, and he sat looking at me with a face like stone.

"Well, sir," said old Harve, "I didn't mean no offense, sure didn't, a-callin' you 'nigger.' Ain't nothin' wrong with 'em, I reckon, no more'n they is with them as ain't. Like a glass a cider?"

Old Harve never said "nigger" again in my hearing. And often I made the long walk up to his remote place to sit and listen to his pungent talk of times fifty or sixty years back, when he was a lad, and to cautiously sip his potent cider, a jug of which he always kept suspended on a rope in the well.

Once in a while he'd show up at our house, usually when I was embarking on some project about which I knew less than I supposed, and old Harve always knew more than I supposed. He didn't care much for my "store boughten" potables and gave his "receipt" for home-brewed beer, which he urged me to make in the interests of my "gizzards."

People of our locality couldn't understand our friendship. They said that as long as they could remember, Harve had never taken up with anyone before, would barely speak to his contemporaries. He was supposed to be something over eighty.

I suspected that Harve excepted me somewhat from the contempt he seemed to harbor for the entire human race because of the enormity of my ignorance of the multitude of useful things about which he knew all.

One day the old man stopped by while I was puttying storm windows; he said it wasn't no use puttin' 'em on afore th' middle of December, if then, because she was a-gonna be a warm 'un, kind of, and she was a-gonna be a dry 'un, too, an' peculiar-like, too.

As usual, Harve was dead right. It *was* a warm winter, at least for Vermont, and it was also a dry one, and in other ways it was also a peculiar winter. For there was no real cold and the little snow that fell in late December lasted long enough for the traditional cold white Christmas, and then it thawed.

And as to "her" being a peculiar winter, well, she sure was, because elsewhere in the nation the weather was reported as the most severe in our history. And I, the ex-Californian, came in for a lot of needling when snow fell and temperatures dropped below freezing in that sunny state.

Until late January, road scrapers, not snow plows, got all the play in Vermont. And even old Harve claimed he'd "seed nawthin' like her in all my borned days," for him an unusual admission.

"But," he told me with the kind of bragging pride which reminded me of Rene, "this here Vermont weather, well, you can be sure about one thing: she's a-gonna do just as she's a mind to, an' that's no lie. An' this ain't no lie, neither: whilst I was a lad I uset to hear th' old people tellin' about how it was so cold back in 'sixteen (he meant 1816!). All summer that year, lots of scary folks kilt themselves because they was afeared th' sun was coolin' down. An' snow fell on some part of th' state ever single month in that year. Yessir, that's a fact! An' they was killin' frosts nigh 'bout ever night. Why my gramma, on my Ma's side, why she kept a little book that she wrote down all kinds of stuff in, and she had it writ down that between May an' September—just about all summer—well, all that time th' temperature didn't get up over forty-five."

I listened, not sure old Harve wasn't pulling my leg, as he did sometimes, and then I said, "You right sure about all that?"

"Ding tootin' I'm sure," he exploded. "Them old folks wan't fibbin'. Why just four years afore I was born, in 'sixty-two think it was, nary a flake a snow fell for fifteen solid months."

I went to the records to check, and what Harve had related was true. So I hastily gathered information for an "un-usual weather" article, then extremely topical, wrote it, sent it off, and sold it the first time out.

That spring I started three hundred broilers, which strictly on my own I managed to raise so successfully that I lost but six; at ten weeks my birds averaged between five and six pounds, which was supposed to be very good.

I was pleased, and started figuring the neat little profit I would make when I sold them. But I didn't make any profit, for the day I sent those broilers off to market, the price dropped from 38¢ to 26¢ per pound. Still, I had enjoyed raising them, although I must say I agreed with little Will's opinion of them, which was that "they didn't have any sense at *all*."

Besides, I had learned enough to enable me to write and sell several articles on poultry-raising.

I also tried out Harve's "receipt" for beer during that time, except that I put a whole spoonful of brown sugar into each bottle before filling, whereas Harve's direction called for a half spoonful. My idea of the extra sugar was that it would give the stuff a better kick, and it certainly did, for one eve-ning as I dozed in my chair I came awake fast when grenades started exploding just beneath it. Only it really wasn't gre-nades, it was my beer. When the racket finally subsided, I went cautiously down to the cellar to investigate. The floor was foamily awash and littered with fragments of broken glass. I had bottled twenty quarts. All but four had exploded, and I covered the remaining ones with a heavy box.

Once over her alarm, Helen thought it all rather amusing. But the next day when she went to the basement to hang the wash, her amusement soured, for, she claimed, the place smelled worse than a brewery and she certainly wasn't going to expose her nice clean wash to such an awful atmosphere.

A month later I remembered the box and cautiously lifted

it to find all four bottles still intact. Gingerly removing one, I took it up to the kitchen, got an opener, used it, and a geyser of foam shot up and splashed the ceiling, me and practically everything else. I got out of there and went for a long, long walk.

I never did tell Harve what happened, either.

"I hear you got some mighty prime broilers out to your place," Vic remarked as he totaled my grocery bill. "That right?"

I admitted it was, asked how he had known.

"Your feed man," Vic explained, "was in the other day. Said he never saw finer birds."

"I guess they'll do," I said.

"You going to sell 'em?"

"Yep. Except a couple of dozen we're going to have dressed and frozen for future reference."

"How about a couple for me?"

"Aren't the chickens you sell any good?"

"All we stock is canned or frozen. Why don't you bring me a couple of broilers?"

I promised to, although I hadn't intended selling any to private buyers. But Vic and I had become friendly through my visits to the chain store he managed, and a few days later I brought him two six-pound birds in a burlap sack.

We went to the rear of the store to weigh them. I removed the birds from the sack and laid them on the scales, but although their legs were bound and I had placed them on their backs, they kept flapping around.

Vic stood grinning as I tried vainly to quiet the chickens long enough for weighing and soon he laughed and exclaimed, "Why, Will! You mean to tell me you don't know how to make a chicken play dead?"

"Well, my feed man told me to lay them on their backs, but that doesn't seem to work," I replied.

"Well I'll be darned," Vic chuckled. He put his hands on his hips and shook his head as though in amazement. "You mean you *really* don't know?"

A little irritated, and sensing what was coming, I said shortly, "Vic, all I know about chickens is what I've learned in Vermont."

"Well, doggone!" Vic chortled. "Here, let me show you." Quickly, deftly, he tucked the head of each bird under its wing. Instantly both relaxed into immobility and Vic looked at me with a smile and said cajolingly, "Now, Will, don't tell me you didn't know that little trick."

"Sorry, Vic, but I didn't know that little trick."

"What kind of a colored man are you, anyway?" he demanded in high good humor. "Why, I learned that from the colored boys down in Florida one time. I worked with a gang of 'em and they liked me because I treated 'em just like they was human. They'd do anything I said. Why, they practically worshiped 'Mist' Vic.' And they told me lots of things they wouldn't tell any other white man. Like how to remove chickens from somebody else's hen-house without them making a single peep! And *you're* going to tell me you didn't know——"

Vic went off into gales of laughter.

I stood there thinking, waiting wearily for this merriment to subside. When it did, I said, "Well, it is a neat trick. I'll be sure to remember it when next I go out on a chicken-stealing expedition."

Wiping his eyes with his apron, Vic gasped, "Oh, hell, Will! I know *you* don't steal chickens. But I thought *all* colored folks knew that trick."

"You *thought*," I reflected bitterly; but I contented myself by suggesting that many colored people, just as many white people, knew no more about chickens than that they made good eating. And for good measure I mentioned having recently read that the incidence of chicken-stealing was increasing in Vermont, so maybe a few other white people knew the trick of silencing chickens. Vic laughed, agreed and finished weighing the birds.

When I got home I went to the enclosure where my chickens were and seized one after another and tucked their heads under their wings until I had a long, neat row of motionless birds on their backs, their feet sticking stiffly upward. Helen came out and asked what in the world I thought I was doing and I told her I was practicing and she asked what for and I said to be a chicken-thief. She stared at me and said I'd better come in out of the sun and for heaven sakes to stop making those poor chickens look like they were dead and I said I wished bigod they damn well were, and all the white folks, too, and maybe all the colored. Helen shook her head and went away, and after a while I restored all the mesmerized chickens to their feet and went out back and stared at the mountains for a long, long time.

That was several years ago. Since, Vic and I have had many good conversations, but never again on the subject of chickens.

CHAPTER *fourteen*

I TOSSED THE FLOSSY MOVIE MAGAZINE TO
Helen. She glanced at it and asked, "Who gave you *that?*"

"Nobody. Look at it, will you?"

Helen looked, her eyes widened. "Well, for heaven's sake!"
she exclaimed.

"See?" I asked.

"The white folks must be going crazy!"

"Going, going—gone!"

"I never thought I'd see the day!"

"Nor I."

The lovely face on the magazine cover was that of Lena
Horne, and Lena Horne was colored.

So no wonder Helen thought the white folks were losing
their minds. White magazines simply did not feature colored
women on their covers. For that matter, women of color were
rarely even mentioned by them, except as maids or cooks.

Yet there was our little Lena, smack-dab on the magazine
cover. And in the featured article about her, Miss Horne was
referred to as "beautiful, lovely, charming," and her clothes
and hairdo were discussed without the least trace of patronage or condescension. Her race was mentioned, but simply
as a background fact, like nationality.

"You know," I mused, "there's been a lot of that in the

the past year or so, come to think of it. Not cover features on
white magazines. But mentions in places and ways that before the war—well, it just wasn't done."

"And that's the beautiful truth," Helen observed. "Burly
black brutes, Negresses, stuff like that, yes. But——"

"You know, I think Jack Benny had a lot to do with that
trend. I mean featuring a Negro comedian, not only on his
radio program but in some of his movies, too."

"Yes—Rochester. Mr. Benny certainly gave *him* a break."
Helen paused, then added thoughtfully, "But for *my* money,
Mrs. FDR really set the example. I mean, not only the things
she does and says which show where she stands, but her
willingness to be photographed with colored people. Like
Mary Bethune. Like that picture we saw in one of our papers
not long ago where she was being escorted by a Negro ROTC
honor guard while she was visiting Howard University."

"It means something. And for *my* dough, Mrs. Roosevelt
is still First Lady. I've often wondered if it ever occurs to
those who seem to hate her so that she, more than any public
figure of our time, personifies the democracy which our country professes. And she acts as she does knowing the widespread resentment she arouses among some whites, and not
just those of the South, either. That takes a rare kind of
conviction, an even rarer courage."

"It sure does," Helen said thoughtfully. She shook her
head and wonderingly said, "Putting Lena Horne's picture
on the front cover. *Well!*"

I nodded understandingly. Maybe times *were* changing for
the better. And I thought of the many clippings and marked
articles in magazines which Mrs. Dorothy Canfield Fisher
had sent me from time to time over the years which indicated
this. I had paid them little attention, for usually there was
too much of an opposite nature in the publications *I* read.
And suddenly I wondered if I had been so intent upon what
was wrong that I had been unable to notice and evaluate

what was right. Impulsively I picked up a copy of one of our major Negro newspapers, the Chicago *Defender*, which I had already read, and went through it again. Many of the stories I had not bothered to read, had skipped as old stuff, phony baloney, for they related the same type of thing as the clippings Mrs. Fisher so often sent me where white people had made some gesture intended to show progress in race relations, but which past experience indicated were merely gestures.

But now I carefully read the stories of that kind which I'd previously passed over, such as:

> LOUISVILLE COP WINS PROMOTION TO LIEUTENANT
> LOUISVILLE.—A 41-year-old Negro police sergeant here became the first man of his race below the Mason-Dixon line to become a law enforcement executive.
> A. Wilson Edwards, member of the local force for fourteen years was promoted . . .

Hmmm, I thought . . .

> FEPC ORDNANCE PASSED BY PHILADELPHIA COUNCIL
> PHILADELPHIA.—This city became the first in the state to have a Fair Employment Practices Law when the City Council approved the Measure Thursday without a dissenting vote . . .

Without a dissenting vote? What went there? Politics? An impending election? Or could it possibly be on the level? An expression of the majority will? When I'd been around Philly the majority hadn't gone in for such good works. Then I hadn't noticed much of the brotherly love for which that city is famed.

Yes, but that was long ago, remember? Change . . .

ST. LOUIS POST-DISPATCH HIRES NEGRO REPORTER

The brief story told how John Henry Hicks, University of Illinois journalism graduate, had been "added to the repor-

torial staff" of the famed daily paper. And in Missouri yet!
Why then was such an event not featured?

I remembered why: it really wasn't so momentous an event
after all. The *Post-Dispatch* was only doing again what it had
already done, for once it had employed Lester Walton as a
reporter—the same Walton who later became Minister to Li-
beria, a Negro minister for a Negro country.

Still . . .

CBS Program To Report Year's Advance in Race Relations

Well, there was something I didn't have to suspect, not if
the CBS news chief, Edward R. Murrow, had anything to
do with it, for he was a truly great reporter. I'd be listening
to *that* report.

And:

Threaten Mixed Student Group

I'd passed that one up, too, for it had seemed old stuff. But
now I read it:

> Columbia, N. C.—Latest effort to further goodwill here
> was halted this week when students of three races were
> forced by the threats of one hundred whites to abandon
> their experiment in group living and to quickly depart
> Tyrell County . . .

That was nothing new, either. Or was it? At least that
experiment in group living in the *South* was certainly new.
Naturally nothing of that kind would be tolerated down there
behind the sun. Yet the very fact that it had been attempted
meant something. Was it a tiny new thread of the pattern
that was really changing, that could only change thread by
thread?

The thought created a faint stir of excitement, a feeling
of discovery. Maybe more people than anyone knew were

starting to wonder, to look about with a clearing vision at
their country and what it was really like; and it just could be
many of them were not liking all they saw, and among these
might be more than a few Southerners, especially among the
young, but not excluding a few older ones.

After all, not all the Southern people were insensitive to
shame because of the more brutal exhibitions of race hate
some of their kind had for so long put on for all the world
to see. And maybe they were stirring toward a rejection of
much they had unquestioningly accepted from their earliest
years.

That experiment in group living—had no Southerners had
a hand in it? Surely no Northerners would embark on anything like that unless they had some reason to believe it *might*
be permitted. Perhaps some of those Chapel Hill folk. . . .

As such thoughts worked through my mind it came to me
with a shock that until that very moment I had never really
believed that anything short of unimaginable catastrophe
could bring about any real change in the American racial
picture; had long since decided that practically all white people in my land *wished* to maintain the status quo whether or
not they believed it wrong or right.

And I thought I'd better do a little checking, because just
possibly I'd been so busy looking exclusively from my own
point of observation that I might have missed seeing other
things of importance in other directions.

"What's the matter, Pappy? Something got you?"

I blinked, said, "Huh?" so blankly that Helen laughed.

"My goodness," she said, "where have *you* been the last
half hour you've been sitting there with that newspaper in
your hand and that faraway look in your eyes?"

"Who, me?"

"Yes, my love."

"I guess maybe I've been having pipe-dreams or something."

"Like what?"

"Oh, about a dame."

"Maybe you'd better not bring home any more magazines with Lena Horne's picture if she sends you like that. And besides, don't call her a dame."

"I wasn't thinking of Miss Horne, although she does send me, but not this time. The chick I was thinking of *is* a dame. I mean, she rates."

"Will, what in the world are you talking about?"

"A dame, like I told you."

"What old dame?"

"Why, Justitia, of course. You know, the lady with the big shiv in one hand, scales in the other and a blindfold over her eyes?"

Helen stared. "You mean the Goddess of Justice? The Blind Goddess?"

I nodded. "But she's not blind and that thing they've got tied around her eyes is slipping a little, maybe."

"Honey, do you feel all right?" my wife asked.

"I feel swell," I assured her. "But I was just thinking what she was going to do with that sword of hers when that blindfold sags enough for her to see that somebody has slipped a little extra weight on one side of her scales."

My wife came over, laid her hand on my forehead and said, "You've got a fever, boy."

"Oh no, I haven't," I denied. "Not any more, I haven't. At least, it's cooling off."

"Maybe you think you're kidding, but your skin is really hot, Will. I think you *have* got a fever. I'd better get you a couple of aspirins."

"Don't bother, Angel. I've had some."

"You have not! When?"

"I have so." I tapped the newspaper I'd been reading. "Out of this."

"Will, you *have* got a fever!"

"Well, if I have, Mother, I'm getting over it."

Then, as she sometimes did, my wife crossed me up for she nodded thoughtfully and said, "You just may, at that. How about me?"

"Oh," I said airily, "you'll be okay. You didn't have it as badly as I."

"No? Don't be too sure of that, man."

I looked at her and I wasn't sure of it any more and I said, "Who do I think I am—*anyway?*"

"Yes," Helen laughed, "but make it 'Mister Anyway,' please."

According to an old Arabian proverb, darkness is deepest at the candle's foot. I was pondering it even as a doe and two fawns delicately picked their way over the swampy stretch below, pausing often to nibble the ferns which flourished there.

My vantage was a sheltered spot atop a great rough upthrust of rock and mossy earth from which grew pine and hemlock so profusely as to create a cool twilight below.

Of late I had come frequently to this spot deep in our woods to sit in the shadowed cathedral silence above the lush green swale below; I had seen other forest creatures passing, unaware of human presence: a lean red fox drifting as a shadow along the swale's edge; a dowager porcupine waddling through the ferns followed by three plump, playful offspring.

Once such sights would have aroused a hunter's lust, but although I usually had one of the rifles I was always buying or trading, no such savage urge any longer awoke. Somewhere along the way I had changed sides, favored now the hunted, nor knew why except that this was somewhat consonant to the other, deeper change.

Was it thus for him who from the dark at the candle's foot crept painfully outward to where its light was cast? Or was that bright glimmer only for fox-fire ghostly on some imagined heath?

Many times as that summer waned, in the still gloom of woodland aerie, in solitary contemplation of the mountains, in lonely night-wanderings, I sought an answer, but vainly.

During this time I searched for evidence of real progress in American race relations and to this end scanned all kinds of newspapers, magazines, reports, and yet I was still unsure, for while there seemed a definite increase on the affirmative side, there also seemed a similar increase on the other. There were still two sides of the coin.

As witness:

2ND NEGRO ADMITTED TO UNIV. OF ARKANSAS

OKLA. U. PUTS A "FENCE" AROUND NEGRO STUDENTS

At historic St. John's College, in Maryland, by a 162-33 majority, students voted to admit Negroes while the United States Senate approved Texas' Tom Connally's amendment to the federal aid-for-education bill which would *prevent* denial of federal aid to states which segregate school children.

"CHRISTIAN DEMOCRACY" GOAL SET BY BAPTISTS

METHODISTS STUDY OWN SEGREGATION

Ought one to laugh? Or jeer? Or weep?
But:

BROOKLYN CATHOLICS GET A NEGRO PRIEST

And the Reverend Curtis Washington, Florida's first Negro priest, celebrated his initial Mass at the white church of the Little Flower, in Coral Gables, which was packed with white and Negro communicants, and when the service ended, *all* remained to receive his blessing.

In New Orleans, Archbishop Joseph Rummel cancelled the annual Holy Hour Observance in a local park when the park commissioners insisted that Negro and white Catholics be segregated during the ceremony. In St. Louis and Kansas City two famous Catholic girls' schools for the first time in their histories opened their doors to Negro girls, and Kansas City's Loretto Academy had already graduated one named Carmen Forte.

There were deeds, not words. But in contrast there was this headline from Kansas City:

EPISCOPAL CHURCH DRAWS COLOR LINE

Kansas City . . . The Episcopal Church . . . The Color Line . . . Nothing new there. For the rebuffed were members of St. Augustine's, the same church where I had been christened and confirmed, and where first my disillusion began when the rites were performed by a white bishop. Now the members of that church had been asked, said the dispatch, not to attend a reception honoring another bishop, white, of course, who was retiring after serving the diocese for two decades.

Nor was the following "news":

RACIAL BARS FOUND RIGID IN CHURCHES
BUCK HILLS, PA.—Politics, sports, education, trade unions and industry have been more successful than the Christian churches in breaking down racial barriers, Dr. Liston Pope, Dean of the Divinity School of Yale, declared here before a meeting of the National Council of Churches.

The theologian revealed that less than one percent of the Christian congregations in the United States were unsegregated.

In California when a Negro youth and a Mexican girl were denied a license to wed, their church swung into action —the Catholic Church—and beat the state law against interracial marriage.

Los Angeles.—There have been 80 mixed marriages in Los Angeles County since the State Supreme Court upset the law banning interracial marriage, according to the County Marriage License Bureau . . .

The breakdown: licenses for marriage between white women and men of other races: Negroes, 23; Filipinos, 20; Chinese, 9; Malayans, 7; Japanese, 4. Licenses were issued to 17 white men who married: Japanese, 8; Negroes, 5; Chinese, 2; Malayan, 1; Filipino, 1.

And inevitably, this:

Protestants Warned of Catholic Gains Among Negroes

Rock Island, Ill.—Alerted to mounting competition of the Roman Catholic Church in rural areas of the South, Protestants were warned to wipe out prejudice in their churches.

Seven hundred theological students were told by Kermit Elby, of Chicago University, that "as long as Protestants have one segregated church, we shall continue to lose our members."

And I thought what a strange commentary on the Christian scene that some Christian denominations were influenced but to *consider* the actual concept of brotherhood only when another practiced it, and apparently only *because* of that.

Yes, except for dynamic action of non-Protestants, the Christian Church lagged most of all the divisions of American life in breaking down racial barriers, whereas, according to the base upon which it was built, it ought to have been foremost.

But the educators, almost equally culpable, historically, were starting to move in the right direction. Nor was there in this vital field anything approaching the great smog of doubletalk arising from the other.

It was no longer uncommon, especially on higher educational levels, to utilize abilities of competent Negroes. Harvard had given impetus as well as sanction to this trend by appointing to its medical school as clinical professor of bacteriology, Dr. William A. Hinton, a Negro; and Columbia University had but recently appointed a Negro from Howard University's faculty as a visiting professor. Similar precedent-smashing appointments had also been made by many other educational institutions.

Now that I was trying to fairly evaluate the signs of the times in their relationship to the central problem of race relations, I could see that while education led the way, or perhaps because it did, other great divisions were following, slowly, but certainly.

When I checked the many sources from which I obtained my information, it appeared that however thin the distribution, the integration of Negro Americans into the nation's economic life seemed greater than in all other years of our history.

As never before, Negro skills were finding outlets. Chemists, engineers of various kinds, physicists, bacteriologists, electronics experts—all were represented now. Negro scientists were increasingly being included on research teams, and it was no longer particularly unusual for them, or for Negro schools, to receive research awards from industry or foundations of one kind or another.

All that and more, including Supreme Court decisions voiding residential restrictions against race, and those requiring admission of Negro students to white colleges in sections where such facilities were unequal, had meaning.

For it was really but yesterday that a young Negro student, Ralph Bunche, was by some regarded as visionary, unrealistic, because he was bent upon becoming an expert in political science. Why major in that field, many of us thought, since the only possible use for such training would be teaching in some Negro college?

Yet today, Dr. Ralph J. Bunche has won international fame in diplomacy, a field from which, more than almost any other, his race was debarred. It was he who had scored so resoundingly as mediator in Israel; who had become Director of the United Nations Trusteeship Division, with a Harvard professorship waiting.

Yet had he not been so well prepared he would not have been able to obtain the background experience provided as head of the Howard University Political Science Department nor from there to have become associate chief of the Division of Dependent Area Affairs of the State Department, the springboard to his UN affiliation.

With his example and with that of others who were now accomplishing much in other fields from which yesterday Negroes had been rigidly excluded, the effect upon our younger generations was bound to be very great whether or not they aspired to similar achievements.

For those who did so aspire, what with the pace education was setting in eliminating total exclusion by race, as well as racial and religious quotas, might now prepare for almost any profession with a reasonable expectation of finding employment in it.

Now these *were* favorable auguries of a most important kind, particularly the trend of the Supreme Court decisions, which could be expected to continue. And obviously the basic question of segregation itself would soon come before that high court, and it was hard to see how it could rule adversely upon it.

I wondered where I'd been during the few short years all this was developing. Where? Why, I'd been watching it, but with cynicism, ascribing change to various factors, such as a need for skilled artisans and professionals sufficient to override old racial taboos, and as a transparent effort to counteract damaging enemy propaganda based on American treatment of its minorities; and, in fine, as an intrinsically phony overall gesture.

And yet, how could I have viewed it otherwise? Previous to World War II, any advances permitted us (and how small, how few they had been) were grudging, sharply limited, of little real importance. Most of the gains resultant from the Roosevelt administration had to be forced from it; but even so, no pressures we could have created, even though led by the NAACP, would likely have accomplished much, as usual, except for the exigencies of the times.

Such a belief is soundly based, for in the past, politicians and their parties had promised much, but delivered little, not even a law against lynching. And who could doubt that if Northern Congressmen had sincerely wished such a law, a way would not long since have been found to overcome the use of the filibuster by Southerners to block it? There had been a heap of wind, but little dust.

So was there *really* any basic change for the better? Or did I now, for reasons too deeply embedded in my subconscious to understand, try to reverse my field, and stumble toward the opposition's goal post?

Morosely, I concluded, that that old Arabian proverb about the darkness at the foot of candle was certainly true.

But just how *did* one get out into the light? I thought I had made a good start; goodness knows I'd tried hard enough. Certainly there was enough surface evidence to justify a more hopeful outlook. Yet—there still was Yesterday, which I could see in bitter detail, while Tomorrow—well, both it and I were at the foot of that candle where it was dark indeed.

CHAPTER fifteen

"RICHIE," I ASKED, "HOW DOES A GUY GET down from a tree when there's a varmint waiting at the foot?"

Reverend Low grinned. "Well, Will, I'd suggest that he do what the fellow did who had the bear by the tail."

"What?"

Eyes twinkling, Reverend Low said, "Well, according to the story, or song, or whatever it was, the fellow prayed."

"Oh—that. Something about 'Oh, Lord, if you can't help me, just please don't help that bear.' You're a lot of help."

Richie chuckled, then asked quietly, "What's wrong, Will?"

"Maybe," I said, " 'I'm standing in the need of prayer.' "

"Well then, why not pray?"

"You know why, Rich."

The minister nodded, and for a while stood in silence, his gaze fixed on the mountains. He did know why, had known almost from our first meeting, but my disbelief had not interfered with our friendship, nor had he ever tried to alter it.

On this day he had dropped by for a visit, as he usually did whenever he was in our section, and had been coaxed into staying for supper, which Helen was preparing.

While we waited, Richie and I had gone out into the crisp autumn afternoon and, as usual, we soon gravitated around back where we stood drinking in the view.

I'd been more glad than usual to see him, and could not rid myself of the feeling that his coming on this particular day somehow had a special significance. But that, of course, was nonsense. He had just happened by when I chanced to be more beset than at any time since coming to Vermont.

But still, was it only chance which had brought him on this day, this hour? Was it merely my deep affection for the gentle little Welshman which had made his unexpected visit so welcome, so—opportune?

I shrugged that off. In any event, I was glad he had come, especially because he was one of the very few people who knew some of the things which most troubled me, and with whom I felt completely free to discuss them, as with a beloved brother.

Lost in such thoughts, I heard Richie's voice as if from afar, from the distant mountains, and it was saying, "Will, isn't it possible that the varmint at the foot of the tree and the one trapped in its branches just could be one and the same? If that is so, it seems to me it's up to the one who is trapped, or thinks he is, to take charge of the other, to send him about his business."

"But how, Richie? I've tried that."

"Have you ever tried climbing right down and giving that other varmint a good hard kick where it hurts most?"

"I'm afraid that would be murder, Rich. . . . Mine."

"Not necessarily, Will."

"Then what's the gimmick?"

"Faith, Will."

"Oh."

"Don't sound so let down."

"Well, I can't help it. If I haven't been able to believe in God before, how can I suddenly——"

"Will—did I mention God?"

"No. But you said faith——"

"I could have meant faith in men."

"But, Richie——"

"Think it over, Will."

That stopped me. Had I liked the man less, had I not respected him more than any other I'd ever known because he
lived his principles, even as had Christ and Ghandi, I would
instantly have rejected what he had said. Faith in men, indeed! How could that be, for men were more evil than good.
One had but to look to see how evil were their works. One
had——

"Hey," Helen called from the back porch, "would you two
prefer a bit of mundane fare to mountain-gazing? Soup's on!"

Richie took my arm, said, "Come on, let's eat," and I, a
little shakenly, replied, "Well, at least that's a substantial
idea."

"And the other?" my friend asked.

"I'll have a good look at it," I promised.

"Do that, Will. But not because I asked you to. Don't do
it on my account. You've got to do it because you really want
to, or you'll never see it."

"Okay, Rich," I said soberly. "I'll give it a spin."

"Make it a good one, Will. A real good one, do."

"Yeah. A real good one."

And I did. But all that happened was that I got dizzy. Because how was one to believe in his brothers who believed
not in him; who constantly made clear how completely they
rejected such fraternal relationship by trying to beat your
brains out? All the faith you could ever work up in them was
that they were going to keep on doing that until they either
finished you, or you got strong enough to lay them out, and
for keeps.

Besides, you'd been over that ground before, that battleground. The whites of the world stomping on the non-whites.

Well, it just didn't have to be like that much longer. We

were sick of that jive, all of us, in Asia, Africa, and the U.S.A. And one of these fine days——

Oh—to hell with all that! Besides, what difference did it make to anybody what *I* thought? Who cared?

That didn't click, not quite. Because I was somebody and *I* cared. But I didn't have to knock myself out with this eternal bickering with myself, did I? And besides, I was doing all right, wasn't I? At least in Vermont things were pretty much okay. In our town——

In whose town?

Ours. In our town, the people were solid, were strictly all right. If *all* white Americans were like our townsmen——

Yah! And if ifs and ands were pots and pans a lot of factories would be out of business. So snap out of this stupid kick, Willy, before you flip your lid like you almost did out there in California before I talked enough sense in your head to make you get farther, fast.

But still——

Oh for chrissakes, cut it out!

But still . . . were my townsmen, the native-born of this Green Mountain state, were these different from their kind elsewhere in our land?

Are you kidding? They're no damn different from those Dixie paddies. They are all from the same stock, aren't they? And they would be as lowdown mean to Sam as those Southern rednecks if they had happened to be born down in 'Bam. Why don't you stop asking such simple questions when you already know the answers?

"Oh shut your big fat mouth, Varmint!" I exclaimed as though to a palpable presence. "Forever belittling. Leave me alone."

If I do, pal, down the drain you'll slide!

"So I'll slide. Drop very dead, will you?"

Now looky, Willy: it's strictly your funeral you're asking

for. Because I can see that I don't count. You're an ingrate,
Willy, and a square to boot. So all right——

"So I'm an ingrate and a square and it's my funeral, so let
me bury myself in peace, will you?"

But——

"Shut up!"

. . . Now where was I? Oh yes, if Vermont people could
be as they were, under other circumstances could not other
Americans be as they? Maybe it was as Helen believed about
religion: it was the people who fouled it up—some people.

Some people?

Well—yes. Not all of them. Not Vermonters, not New
Englanders. Not a lot of people maybe, even down South.
Like Lillian Smith. Like that Judge Waring Waite. Like
those Chapel Hill folks, like that fellow at the University
of Miami, Malcolm Ross. Like so many others, including
many less well-known folk.

So what? Supposing there *were* some white Americans who
believed enough in democracy to practice it, or even to speak
out for it? They were only a few drops in a great big bucket.

Yes, but hadn't I been studying up on the deal, scouring
all the newspapers, magazine reports, and everything else I
could secure for pro and con evidence? And hadn't I found
plenty of pros, more than at any time previous? Hadn't I——

Right about then I had enough. That other part of me that
jeered just might have been right. And again I thought, to
hell with it, and determinedly began shagging out of my
mind all those perplexing pros and cons. A little peace and
quiet in that region would be nice, for a change.

Previous to the incident of Lena Horne's picture on a
magazine cover which had initiated what now, in weary disgust, I thought of as "soul-searching," I'd felt that my com-
munion with mountains and woodland, with the silence of
the nights, might be going to pay off.

Several times I'd had the feeling that somewhere in those subterranean areas from which so often rise inexplicable revelations, presentiments which prove true, understandings which conscious thought processes have failed to achieve, there was important activity. And now it occurred to me that had I perhaps waited for its result, instead of galloping off into a lot of material research, I might have had a better reward.

Maybe it wasn't too late for that. Many times when alone, when I was away from reminders of what and why, I'd managed a kind of detachment. As though freed of body I floated in another sea, soundless, unmoving, yet more than a mere nothingness.

I determined to recapture that state, to again enter those silences which are as space, where, suspended, I could watch, listen, await whatever might come.

I tried to do that, went again to my woodland aerie, walked in lonely places, attempted to lose myself in the mountain vistas, but nothing happened. My surroundings might be as hushed as dawn's witching hour, but within me there was movement, a restless stirring.

I persisted, perhaps out of stubbornness, and after awhile, although I was not at first conscious of it, strange oddments and fragments which were neither thoughts nor anything identifiable began to drift through my consciousness.

It was as though I watched them collect in a homogeneous agglomeration which finally I tried to expel as trivia. But failing in that, slowly I began to see how all the meaningless, unrelated scraps were as tiny, jumbled parts of a complex picture puzzle; gradually they came together in more orderly fashion, detaching themselves here and there from the central mass to join and fit with other parts, not enough to complete the main design, but sufficiently to indicate there was one.

I felt then the heart-lurch, the breathless thrill of exulta-
tion which surely the explorer, the prospecter, all men must
experience at the moment of great discovery. And even before the picture took definite form I sensed what it was going
to be like, knew somehow that soon I would discern the great,
shining thing which I'd glimpsed so many times just beyond
the shadows which seemed always to have rimmed my life.
I'd glimpsed, but so fleetingly, I had believed I only imagined it.

Of one thing only was I certain: it was going to make
quite a difference in my life.

The days that followed were another of those interludes
which poor Helen has come to accept as a part of being
married to a fellow who occasionally gets lost in abstractions,
and until they end, he were better absent also in the flesh.
But I think she understands, although there was a time when
my morose withdrawals, forgetfulness of meals, my complete
general blankness for days on end, must have been upsetting
to her.

This time, after a week, she finally asked, "Hey, Pappy,
what's biting you?"

Her timing was just about perfect, for I was just then
emerging from a grapple with the most profound experience
of my life.

"Well, I'll tell you," I said, still half bemused, "varmint's
been biting me, but I think I stomped him real good."

"Uh-uh," Helen sighed, "here we go again."

But it wasn't like that. I was not ready to talk about it.
Maybe I was not yet able to believe it, dared not speak of it
as though it were a golden bubble which the touch of words
might prick and burst.

Besides, I did not yet clearly understand what had happened to me, only that it had.

It did not occur to me for a while to wonder to whom or what I owed thanks for what I knew was a precious boon. Was it the mountains which finally spoke? Or was it some magic whisper from the woodland, the night skies? Or had I the key from Richie, or from some other?

No matter. I would know that too, in time.

But really, did I not already know? In my heart, didn't I?

Perhaps. But now somehow I sensed it was unwise to try and force answers of this kind. Suffice it that I no longer crouched in the darkness at the candle's foot, but moved slowly, surely outward into the light it cast, and this was not the time to press, to push, to hurry, to demand. Too much was at stake.

So now, if ever, I must have patience. I must not probe or push, but simply wait.

And believe.

CHAPTER SIXTEEN

MOST MORNINGS NOW THERE WAS FROST on the ground, snow on the mountains, warnings of how little time remained to prepare for winter, which everyone agreed would be severe because the previous one had been mild.

I managed to get the needful done around our place, but absentmindedly, for my thoughts were on other matters. I was seeing many things in a new light, from a new viewpoint; and often I experienced a sense of peace which was as balm to old wounds.

Again I looked forward to the long, frozen months ahead, and again planned to fill them productively. This time I was resolved to sternly restrict all outside activities in order to do more writing. I was committed to a few speaking engagements, but meant to take on no more, to allow nothing to interfere with my personal plans.

But there came an opportunity to do a series of radio broadcasts. I simply could not pass it up, for I would have the opportunity regularly to address a much greater audience than the total of those to whom I had spoken in the past. My feeling was that now, more than ever, the failures in understanding by one race of the other was the biggest block to the national unity I believed was not merely important, but urgent. And if I could, in however small a way, contribute to an increase in that understanding, I felt that I must, regardless of the cost to my private ambitions.

It seemed to me I was in a somewhat unique position to help in this matter. Of necessity, I was familiar with what it was like to be a Negro American, and I had learned at first hand how even well-intentioned white Americans who sincerely believed themselves racially unprejudiced, lacked the experience to realize that such a belief was only partially true; and that it could not be otherwise so long as they had no basis by which to judge whether or not all the stereotypes of race they had accepted as facts *were* facts.

So my plan was to try and explode those racial stereotypes with facts, with a presentation of how things really were in the dark world of which so little was known by those not of it.

Thus began a new experience which I hoped would be helpful to others, but which did prove helpful to me, because it vastly increased my knowledge of the really substantial gains being made on many levels of American life; for I had to search more widely than I ever had for evidence of those gains.

It was, of course, much easier to discover developments of an opposite kind, but I was becoming able to understand that is how it *had* to be; that the great, inert mass of ingrained race prejudice in our land would not be perceptibly moved at first; and that there was and would continue to be powerful resistance to any social advances by which Negroes might benefit.

At the time I began my broadcasts, a wealthy ex-Mississippian who had made a fortune in Texas oil, offered fifty million dollars to a military college in his home state on the condition that it teach white supremacy, and exclude the non-white and non-Christian as students or teachers.

The story hit the press and radio with a spectacular splash. Once such a story would have enraged me, would have been another proof that bigotry, not democracy, was really the American way.

But while the incident did not make me happy, I was able to take a clinical view of it. I saw it primarily as a gesture of defiance to those signs of change indicative of a greater integration of colored citizens into the real life of our country.

So that is how I spoke of the wealthy Southerner's fabulous offer; and in exploring the whole story, I suggested that it might have an even greater significance, so patly did it coincide with the visit to the United States of India's top man, brown-skinned Pandit Nehru. What better way, publicity-wise, could have been chosen to make a thumb-at-the-nose gesture at all Asia, at all colored peoples, and even at our government for receiving one of them with such fanfare?

I also suggested that the Mississippian had supplied deadly ammunition to enemy propagandists, and how effectively it would be used among the uncountable millions of Asia, the Near East, and Africa, who would not be permitted to hear anything of a contrary nature, and who would be unlikely to believe it if they were. For it was only yesterday that I, a native American, had found it difficult to believe anything good of my country.

But in my today's view, I saw the Mississippian's action as the furious lashing of a wounded monster's tail; and most important was what had caused its wound.

But my main and continuing theme in my broadcasts was that even as nations were choosing sides in the swiftly shaping battle for world leadership, so were the American people choosing sides in the battle for democracy within America.

The wealthy Mississippian's spectacular gesture symbolized those who opposed it, including Southern members of our Congress and other Americans of great prominence. Among the latter I mentioned one who was a former Secretary of State and a former Justice of the Supreme Court, and was

currently the Governor of South Carolina, who in that capacity had been reported in the newspapers and over the
radio to have threatened to close all publicly-owned educational institutions in his state before he would permit unsegregated attendance in them.

But other prominent citizens were outspokenly on the side
of democracy, for in the same Congress attended by Southerners elected on "white supremacy" platforms, were such
genuine advocates of the democratic way as Hubert H. Humphrey, Wayne Morse, Herbert Lehman, Paul Douglas and
others, among whom the Arkansan, Fulbright, had to be included. And in the White House a fellow Missourian named
Harry Truman had proved to many people that his greatest
concern was his country and its people, and he had made it
clear that these included *all* of them.

I had approached the broadcasting arrangement warily, for
while I meant to stress the good things about our country, I
did not intend to suggest that everything was fine, which
I feared might be what was really expected of me.

One reason for this feeling was that the owner of radio
station WCAX, the Vermont CBS affiliate, also a Missourian,
had been a newspaper publisher in the real South and was,
therefore, doubly suspect in my view, as had been Mr. Truman when he first became president.

I had been wrong about Mr. Truman. I was equally wrong
about the radio station owner, because he not only told me,
in effect, to "shoot the works," but urged me to do so.

And, as on other occasions and for similar reasons, I wished
I could kick myself where it hurt most, for I had again been
guilty of prejudgment, of that which was so unforgivable
when those on the other side of the racial fence were guilty
of it.

But then, how difficult to break old habits, particularly
when for so very long they have been shield and buckler.

Judging by the letters I received, my broadcasts may have

done some good. In my mail of this kind were letters not
only from Vermonters, but from listeners in other states and
quite a few from Canada. Mostly they were encouraging.
But I noted one thing: each time I mentioned any development through which was revealed progress of racial integration within the Catholic church, there would be quite a rash
of sometimes virulent protest. Didn't I see what the Catholics were up to? That they were trying to get control of the
U.S.A. for the Italian Pope? And, demanded these writers,
did I not know that in Franco Spain, aye, and in Rome,
Protestants were barely permitted to exist, were often as-
saulted, and that this was also true in South America and in
Quebec, Canada? Why the real danger to not only our country, but to the whole world, was Catholicism, not Commu-
nism.

I received only a few anti-Semitic letters and no anti-Negro
letters at all.

I did not touch the subject of Catholic-Protestant relations
in my air talks, but merely reported the news, just as it broke,
regardless of whose feelings might be ruffled, for what I
reported was fact, not opinion.

All in all, that broadcasting experience was interesting and
illuminating.

Thus passed that winter and spring.

In mid-summer I was summoned to Kansas City by the
sudden death of my mother. I was away for two weeks and
during that unhappy time I had frequent letters from Helen
assuring me that everything was fine at home. That was
comforting because, aside from my natural concern for her
and the children, I had started several hundred broilers that
spring and my abrupt departure left it up to my wife to take
care of them as well as everything else around our place.

Then, too, it had been hot and dry before I left and our
spring had shown signs of belying its reputation as "never
failing," but Helen wrote that all was well.

When I returned, I found that all was not well. Within hours of my departure, a windstorm had swept the state, shearing trees, felling telephone poles and creating general havoc; and our place had not escaped.

For days thereafter there was neither telephone service nor electric power, the lack of the latter making our "waterworks" inoperable; and for several hours practically all roads were blocked by fallen trees. Helen and the children had been badly frightened.

Soon after the storm ended, our nearest neighbor cut across the soggy fields to see how my family had fared. And within hours, other neighbors showed up, knowing, as such things are quickly known in a close-knit community like ours, that I was away. So they cleared the trees from the road and the debris from the premises and did everything else required by the situation, even to replacing a roof on a range shelter where we had a number of pullets. They also carried enough water from the trough across the road for immediate needs.

Later, other friends stopped by to check on how Helen was doing and to offer help. Until my return some of them saw to it that she got whatever she needed, including groceries daily from the village store.

Just about the time telephone and electricity were restored, our spring finally failed. Ordinarily that would have been sufficiently serious, but with hundreds of thirsty chickens to water, it created a real problem. However, our townsmen realized it as quickly as my wife and thereafter various of them kept her supplied with the precious and scarce fluid by bringing milk cans of it to her each day until my return.

The final blow was when coccidiosis, a dangerous poultry disease, broke out among our broilers, and although we easily might have lost all of them, Helen administered the sulfa medicine already on hand every four hours, night and day, and incredibly enough, we lost not one bird. But even with

such help as the children were able to give, that was an ordeal which still makes Helen shudder when she thinks of it.

I got home in mid-morning. After things had settled down
a bit, Helen and I sat talking, and I remarked gratefully about
the help and kindness extended her by our townsmen.

"These are really swell people, aren't they?" I asked.

"They sure are," Helen replied feelingly. "I don't know
what I could have done if they hadn't helped like they did."
She frowned, adding, "Maybe I shouldn't even mention it,
but they also kind of cross me up, too."

"How so?"

"Well, I guess it isn't anything, really."

"What's the score, Mama?"

"Oh, just that I read in the paper that a Grange chapter
had been started here."

"And——?"

"And some of those I thought were my friends were listed
as members, that's all."

"That's *all*?"

"Well—*we* were not asked to join."

"No? Well, maybe it's one of those things. Maybe the
National Grange charter has a racial exclusion clause or something. You wouldn't expect our townsmen to pass up having
a chapter here just on our account would you?"

"No. But still——"

"Ah, forget it, honey. We've more important things to gab
about."

"Yes, but it's the first time we've been left out of anything.
It spoils things, a little."

"Well, forget it," I urged again. "After all, when you
needed help you sure got it and——"

"I know, but——"

I managed a change of subject and although I had tried to
gloss over the matter of the Grange, it clung in my mind,

and for me, also, it was a small dark cloud in a sky heretofore wonderfully clear.

About an hour later, a neighbor stopped by.

"Heard you was back, Will," he said as we greeted him, "and I hate to bust in on you so quick, but I've got to go to town for some feed right off and Grange meetin' is tomorrow night and I reckoned I'd better come by now, while I had a chance."

"I'm glad you did," I said, not allowing the heartiness of my tone to be dampened by his reference to the Grange meeting.

"Do you suppose you folks won't be too wore out to come to Grange tomorrow night?" he asked.

"Well," I temporized, "I don't know. Are we supposed to?"

"I reckon so," my neighbor said. "We're just sort of gettin' started and we want all charter members to be there because we've got to elect officers, and all."

"Yes, but we're not charter members," Helen remarked a little stiffly. "At least not that *I've* heard of."

Our neighbor laughed. "Well, Helen, you and Will are down for charter members and somebody or t'other even paid your fees and dues so's to make certain it was all legallike. I reckon I just sort of waited until your man got back to mention it." He looked at me and asked a little anxiously, "I hope we wasn't maybe a mite too forehanded, joinin' you folks in like that before we even asked, was we?"

I let out a big breath and said, "I should say not! Where's the meeting to be and what time?"

"Town Hall, Will. Eight o'clock, or thereabouts. If you want, me and th' wife'll pick you up, seein' as this will be your first meetin'."

"Well, thanks," I said. "That'll be just fine."

"We'll be by around seven-thirty."

"And we'll be ready," I promised. "And—thanks a lot."

"Why, it ain't nothin' at all. See you folks tomorrow night, hey?"

As soon as he had gone I bent over and said, "Your turn first, Mama. And make it a good, hard kick."

But Helen just stared at me from tear-blurred eyes and mutely shook her head. Then muffledly she muttered, "These people!"

And, not quite so muffledly, I said, "Yeah. These darn wonderful, crazy people."

A couple of months later, Herb and Dot stopped by for a visit and I mentioned the Grange incident and both laughed.

"You've nothing on us, Will," Herb said. "We've also got a new Grange chapter in our town."

"Yes, and we thought *we* were being left out, too," Dot said. "Boy! Was I ever burned up!"

"Dot was all for telling off some of what she called our 'two-faced' friends," Herb chuckled.

"And I would have, too," his wife declared, "if you hadn't talked me out of it."

"Good thing I did," Herb said.

"What happened?" I asked.

"Oh, you know how it is up here," Herb shrugged. "Kind of slow doing things. We thought we were not going to be asked to join the Grange, but when we were, we found we were actually among the first."

"And that," I observed, "is good old Vermont for you."

"Yeah, but for a while," Dot remarked tartly, "I was ready to kick good old Vermont right square in the teeth!"

"Don't I know!" Helen exclaimed.

Then we talked of other things. But the experience of our friends started me thinking. Herb and Dot had not lived long in their town and if they had not been asked to join one of its organizations, it might well have been for that reason alone.

But Herb was a Jew, and he and Dot, who was a Gentile, out of past experience in other states, had been unable to believe they were not being passed up because of his religion, just as Helen and I had thought because of our race.

Herb was an architect, his wife a meteorologist, and both were of the clean-cut, pleasant type most communities would consider desirable had both been Christians.

Herb, of course, knew the score all along, but his wife had to learn it in bitter detail after they were married. But just as we, they were learning something different now: that they could not judge Vermont by what had happened elsewhere.

I pondered the matter, because among our friends in a nearby town were several Jewish families with some of whom we occasionally compared notes; and they, as we, had fared well, took part in all community activities, and in general, participated fully in town life.

On the other hand, the situation was not as good in Burlington, although some of its Jewish families were among its oldest, most prominent and best-regarded citizens. But beneath a surface cordiality there seemed not to be the complete acceptance of them which was apparently the case in smaller communities.

The same pattern, I had noted, existed in other larger towns, extending in the southern part of the state to openly discriminatory practices in public accommodations. Even in our section there were a number of inns and resorts which were anti-Semitic. I was sufficiently interested to check on the ownership of some of the places, both in our area and elsewhere, including some of our famed ski centers, and was somehow pleased to discover that in most cases, either ownership or management, or both, were by "foreigners," meaning *not* Vermonters.

That, of course, didn't mean that some Vermonters did not display prejudice against Jews, nor that many did not enter-tain the same stereotyped beliefs about them which were prevalent elsewhere.

What I thought it did mean was that anti-Semitism obtained mostly on the levels of public accommodation and that the *people* of Vermont were generally as ready to extend friendship to Jews, according to their individual qualities, as to anyone else, especially in the smaller towns, the more rural areas.

Too, I was aware that in many parts of the state there was more than a little prejudice against those of Canadian birth or descent, just as there was against those of Italian ancestry, perhaps because they were usually Catholics.

Even so, such prejudice was not of the vicious kind I had seen elsewhere and had, by reason of my race, myself experienced.

I remembered how I had resented a statement attributed to the late Sinclair Lewis, the famed writer, that there was as much native fascism in Vermont as anywhere in Europe.

Now I believed he was right, but that when Vermont's score was tallied, the degree of its democracy would still be high, higher perhaps than that of any other state in our land. Because Vermonters were, after all, human beings and it would be indeed strange if they lacked those fundamental traits universal among men which can and are and always have been used to subvert equally fundamental and universal traits of an opposite nature. For, while the seeds of evil are of man's heritage, so are the seeds of good.

Vermont, then, was no paradise, not even for white Christian natives, and it seemed to me that it was as dangerous to generalize about it as about any other state except that just as of the South one could say with truth that its ill-treatment of colored people by far outweighed the good, so with equal truth could Vermont be credited with an opposite tally, only for *all* kinds of people.

And so one day, without having consciously planned it,

I gathered certain papers heretofore carefully preserved, squeezed them into a big, loose ball, and took them out back and burned them.

Perhaps one day we would need another set of such documents, for we still planned to go to Haiti, also France, but for a visit only; and when that time came, they could be replaced.

CHAPTER *seventeen*

SINCE THAT DAY FOUR YEARS AGO WHEN it seemed to me my long quest was ended, nothing that has happened has made me think I was mistaken. The years since have been good, the best, if not the most prosperous, of my life. Yet there has always been enough money to keep my family comfortably housed, well fed and clothed; and while I would have liked more money in order to provide certain extras, such as a new car, or ponies for the children, it has been satisfying that I have at least earned enough exclusively as a writer to support us.

As many of our profession can testify, that is not exactly a minor feat, because success often depends upon much beyond our control, including not only the vagaries to which the publishing business is subject, but upon personal factors of considerable diversity that many of us are not always able to surmount.

In my case there were a number of such factors, of which the most damaging was my feeling that racial prejudice had seriously hampered my progress. And of course I was right, only the fault was more in me than in any arbitrary barriers set up by publishers. I know now that few, if any, such barriers really exist when one has a worthwhile story to tell and is able to tell it well, for it is this combination which publishers not only want, but for which they search widely.

Even after I was able to dismiss my conviction that my first book had made no great splash mainly because of what I had thought was inept editorial tinkering, I still believed its story might have done some good in interrace understanding had it only found a greater audience. And on that count I may have been correct. For after it was published in 1950 under another title and a new imprint, it sold more than four hundred thousand copies within a year, and I received scores of letters from all sorts of people in my own and other countries, including members of the United Nations forces in Korea. And so very many of these correspondents expressed a gain in their knowledge of how it was between the races in America.

That was gratifying, but even more so was the book's sale, for I had never dreamed anything I might write would ever sell like *that*.

Such was one highlight of these good years. Among many others was my election in the summer of 1952 to a fellowship at the famed Breadloaf Writer's Conference at Vermont's Middlebury College. There, through contact with topflight writers, noted editors and publishers, who were either on the staff or visitors, and in surroundings of utmost beauty and tradition, I found the stimulus and courage to break with the kind of writing I have done for so long and have been afraid to desert.

The returns of my "liberation" are, of course, not all in, nor will they be soon. However such as have been manifested are sufficiently encouraging to allow me to believe that if I work hard enough, I may really learn the true meaning of the writing craft some day.

I tell of this because it seems closely related to all that has happened since I set out in 1946 to seek the dignity and status as a human being which I was almost certain were not possible to me in my own land.

I consider that I have and am enjoying that status and

human dignity in Vermont. In a sense it may be that I have compromised in a way I was determined not to when my quest began. Many times after we settled in Vermont and even after it seemed that things might really work out well, I thought of Haiti, where I would not only have had the whole loaf, but where our funds, draining so swiftly because of high living costs in our own country, would have supported us for years even had I not earned a dollar. That factor alone was a great temptation, particularly when I was riding out another of the recurrent spells of the doubt and depression which made my life so miserable.

That I resisted was due to our liking for our town and its people, for it eventually became impossible to doubt that our acceptance was not sincere and without qualification. Participation in every aspect of town life was not merely permitted us, but urged upon us. That seemed the real test. It is not difficult for some people to profess racial tolerance, to subscribe in words to belief in human equality. But to practice such sentiments in day-to-day living is quite another thing.

We have a feeling of belonging, now. We have seen families move into our town, stay a year, two, or three, then move elsewhere. There have been many births, many deaths, enough of them for us to feel, as a pulse, the ebb and flow of our town's life; and because of it we have rejoiced, and we have grieved. And we have seen youths go off to war who were little boys when we first came; and some who were schoolgirls then, are now married and have children, or have gone out of the state to work. Helen has assisted at showers and weddings and other such events, in which I have had a part, too. And I have helped to bear to the grave one I loved.

I think of that, repeating the phrase: one I loved. Yes, I *did* love Mrs. Callen, else why was my heart so sorely wrung when she passed on? What had race to do with that, hers or mine? That she thought enough of me to want me for a pallbearer when she knew her course neared its end touched me deeply. For me there will never be a finer honor.

We have been asked, happily not too often, if we do not miss "our people" and our reply is that we don't. We have as many friends and as much social life here as we had elsewhere, and we could have more if we wished.

Helen and I have often discussed this, and only against the backdrop of the past does it seem in the least unusual. We have concluded that when law and custom permit a free mingling of people, differences of race, color or religion are apt to lose importance; and that when one may, in a normal, unhampered way, discover what another is really like as a person, an individual, prejudgments on each side are likely to fade away.

Friends of our pre-Vermont days have predicted that we will eventually tire of living among "white folks" and will return to our own kind. That is, of course, a possibility. But if we should, it will not be because we have tired of living among white people, for we no longer think of our townsmen and friends in that way; there is no reason that we should. Our relationships with them are not based on race, but on what we and they are like as human beings.

But if, for whatever reason, we should have to leave our town, our friends, and this state, which we cannot fail to love because it has given us so much, it would be with something deeper than regret. And should that happen, we believe that regardless of the attitude of others toward us, we will be able to judge them as individuals and not according to race, religion or sectional origin. We are teaching our children to do likewise, always.

One morning recently I stood at a window watching the sun rise behind the mountains and thinking about things like that, and I thought how much better the world would be if all its people made its judgments in that way. And I thought that perhaps in time, they would. I thought that perhaps it would be my country which would lead the way, because as none other it is fused of people of almost every race, nationality, color and creed, and as none other it was *conceived* and *dedicated* to liberty and justice when these so little existed in a world where tyranny was the rule.

It came to me that it was not strange that we of America have not yet realized those ideals, or in that flash of time since Plymouth Rock that we have run the full gamut of human failings, for how otherwise could we have learned their meanings and profited by them?

Surely, out of the ashes of those failures, those human mistakes, there will arise the phoenix of ancient prophecy, but it will not be some fabled creature of the air, but a new nation whose spirit would be as a wondrous beacon of hope to all who suffered and were oppressed, everywhere on the face of this earth.

For it cannot be wanton circumstance which has so precisely prepared us to accomplish this. It is, it must be there is design and purpose in the selection of our land from all others to be so vast a melting pot of humanity as to place within our hands, if we will but use it, the power to prove by our example that all men, of all kinds, can dwell together in peace, and as brothers.

That is what I was thinking as I watched that sunrise the other morning. It is also what I believe, and I pray to God, Who made us all, that it shall come to pass.

AFTERWORD TO THE NEW EDITION ❧

Dan Gediman

Y INTEREST IN THE LIFE STORY OF
Will Thomas began in bed, on a cold March day in 2003,
while recuperating from the worst case of the flu I had ever
experienced. I was bored after too many hours watching
bad TV and looking for something good to read. I found a
book on our bookshelf that I'd never seen before—an an-
thology of essays from Edward R. Murrow's 1950s radio series *This I Believe*. I was intrigued, mostly due to Murrow's
titanic status in my chosen field of radio, and quickly dug
into it. I found many impressive essays within the book, but
none caught my attention more than one by a completely
obscure African American author with a compelling tale to
tell. He wrote about how he came to renounce his American citizenship due to racial injustice and then, at the last
minute, decided to give this country one last chance.

My first thought after reading this essay, which can be
found later in this book as an appendix, was that I wanted
to find the children of this man and learn the rest of the
story—what happened after their initial years in Vermont,
which are covered so vividly in *The Seeking*? My second
thought was that the radio series that spawned the essay
was a pretty nifty idea that I might want to consider bringing back to life—a cause I did, indeed, pursue over the next

decade, founding a nonprofit organization, This I Believe, Inc., in order to do so.

But my fascination with the Will Thomas story never really left me, even as the focus of my attention drifted toward nurturing this new venture. I brought up Will's story over and over again to anyone who seemed vaguely interested (and many that weren't, I'm sure), trying to get others as excited as I was by this amazing saga. Then, a few years ago, my dear wife Mary Jo gave me a wonderful birthday gift, used copies of both *The Seeking* and *God Is for White Folks,* Will's two published books. I immediately devoured them, especially savoring details about Will's life in *The Seeking* that were only hinted at in his brief *This I Believe* essay.

I was once again inspired to find Will's children, and now that I actually knew their names, I had some solid leads to go on. Unfortunately, Will's last name during this period was Smith, not Thomas, which made any research into his children quite challenging. It turns out that Will was born William Thomas, Jr., but at some point he took the last name of his stepfather Howard Smith, who likely adopted him, though I've not been able to find any official records of the adoption. He reverted to Will Thomas, however, for any serious writing he attempted—as opposed to the hated pulp magazine articles he wrote to feed his family, for which he used unknown pseudonyms.

Since Smith was such a popular name, I figured that finding Anne, William Jr., or Bradley Smith in phone books and other databases without knowing their whereabouts would be tough. So I decided to begin my search in the last place I knew for a fact that they had all lived—Westford, Vermont, where the second half of *The Seeking* takes place. I started by contacting a librarian at the little town's only library. She hadn't lived in Westford during the 1950s and only knew the Smith family story through word of mouth. However, she was able to connect me to some of the oldest people in town, who I hoped would have memories of the Smiths. I began talking to several of them by phone, and the picture started getting a little clearer.

I learned that the family had moved away from Vermont in the mid-fifties after Will and his wife Helen divorced, and that Helen and the kids had settled in a Long Island suburb of New York City. I got some other good background information about the Smiths from speaking to these people, but I was no closer to finding Will's kids. Then, through re-reading *The Seeking*, I found some new clues. There is a section of the book where Will talks about the birth of his children, and he mentions the years in which they were born. Since William Smith was such a common name, and I had no way of knowing if Anne Smith had married and taken someone else's name, I decided to focus my attention on Bradley Smith, since I figured there would be fewer of them born in the year 1945. I turned to an online people-finding database and, thankfully, there were very few Bradley Smiths in the United States that had been born in the year 1945. After several years spent hoping to speak to Will's children, I finally narrowed it down to the right Bradley Smith, found a phone number in Florida, and called him.

Brad Smith was quite surprised to hear from me, but pleasantly so. I learned that both his siblings were still alive, though his brother William (Bill) was very ill with Parkinson's disease. Brad shared with me as many memories as he could about his father, though it was clear that there was much he didn't know. He gladly gave me his sister's contact information and encouraged me to speak with her as well. As the oldest sibling, he thought she might possess additional information that would interest me.

I then called Anne Smith, who had never married after all. She knew of the *This I Believe* series, had a vague memory that her father had participated in it, and expressed a willingness to let me interview her about her family's life in Vermont and, especially, to fill in the blanks about what had happened afterwards. Luckily, she had a trip planned back East to visit her invalid brother Bill along with younger brother Brad, and proposed that I interview her and Brad at the same time (after explaining that her brother Bill was so sick that he wouldn't be able to participate). We spoke a few weeks later and, to the best of their ability, they filled in some of the missing pieces of their father's story. I say to the best of their ability, because for most of the fifteen years between their parents divorce in 1955 and Will's death in 1970, they saw their dad rarely and had very little knowledge of where he went and what he did.

Here is the gist of what we know about the remainder of Will Thomas Smith's life after the publication of *The Seeking*.

In addition to Chester Himes, who was very close with Will and Helen (and was Brad's godfather), the Smiths had many prominent visitors to their Vermont home. Among those that Anne and Brad recall meeting were Ralph Ellison (author), R. L. Prattis (publisher of *Pittsburgh Courier*), Era Bell Thompson (author), and Ralph Bunche (United Nations diplomat). Will was also close with writers Richard Wright, James Baldwin, and Zora Neale Hurston, who was Anne's godmother.

Brad recalled rescuing the sole manuscript of *The Seeking*, which somehow fell out of the family's car. Brad and his siblings searched for it along the road where they lived in Westford, and Brad finally found it on side of road.

Their parents' divorce stemmed from an adulterous affair of Will's that Helen learned about. Their fifteen-year marriage had not been Will's first. Anne believes that he had been married three or four times, with one of his wives dying during their marriage, leaving him a widower, though neither Anne nor Brad could recall any of these past wives'

names, and I've been so far unable to find any marriage records for Will. This research is complicated by uncertainty
as to which name Will was using (Thomas or Smith) and
which of the many states (and countries) Will lived in that
might have been his residence at the time of a wedding.
The only census record I can find for Will that is definitive
is from 1910, when he was a boy in Kansas City living with
Anna and Howard Smith.

Helen moved with the three kids to Brentwood, New
York, a Long Island suburb, in the summer of 1955. She had
been recruited by a Vermonter, Dr. Eugene Hoyt, to work at
Brentwood High School as both a guidance counselor and
a journalism teacher. The divorce was finalized later that
year in November 1955. However, as a single woman with
three children, Helen could not qualify for a mortgage, so
she and Will remarried in late 1957 so that Helen could buy
a house in Brentwood. Will stayed there for a few years
but then moved out of the house for good in 1960 or 1961
and rented a room at either a hotel or rooming house in
the same area of Long Island. Helen got a Mexican divorce
in late 1962 or early 1963, and Will and Helen never lived
together again.

To make a living, Will worked at Pilgrim State Hospital
in Brentwood, first as an orderly, then as a librarian after,
according to Anne, he took some library science courses
at a local college. Pilgrim State was a huge facility. At the
time it opened it was the largest hospital of any kind in the
world.

Sometime after 1963, Will contracted a serious bone in-
fection (osteomyelitis) while working at Pilgrim State. It
spread to his body, and he had a long period of recovery,
requiring him to live in a nursing home in Bay Shore, New
York. He had a hard time writing after that, due to the effects of his illness. His daughter Anne had to send him
money to help him get by. He eventually sued his employer

for compensation and won the court case, receiving payments that provided some financial stability for him.

Prior to getting sick, Will wrote a long manuscript on living conditions and treatment of patients at Pilgrim State Hospital. Brad saw the manuscript during a visit with his father and has referred to it as an "exposé." Brad says his father worked on the book for about ten years, but he has no idea what happened to the manuscript.

One of the many mysteries of Will's later life is why he never published another book after two back-to-back successes in the early 1950s. His daughter Anne surmises that it was probably a combination of two factors. His bout with osteomyelitis, which lasted several years, definitely made it painful for him to pick up either pen or typewriter. But Anne also thinks his deep shame for the adultery that broke up his marriage and led to his family's dissolution was a millstone he found difficult to cast off.

The last time either Anne or Brad saw their father was during the 1963/64 period. After that, they never heard from him and, apparently, made no attempts to contact him either. The last family members to see Will alive were Brad's daughter and first wife, when they visited him in an area nursing home in 1967.

What happened in the next three years is complete conjecture. Brad has said that his father often talked about going back to Mexico, where he had lived briefly earlier in this life, and where he had felt at home as a man of color. But all that is known for sure is that Will Thomas Smith died on April 12, 1970, in Wyandanch, New York, one town over from Brentwood, where he had lived and worked for the previous decade. He was buried in Pine Lawn Memorial Park in Farmingdale, New York. The cause of death as listed on his death certificate, which was only recently unearthed by Anne, was coronary occlusion. No family members attended the funeral. Indeed, until I did this research, his children didn't even know what year he had died. I have tried to track down the man who was identified on the death certificate as the one who called the authorities when Will died. That man passed away in the early 1970s, and his only child died in 2010. The address they lived in at the time of Will's death is now a vacant lot. I also tried to track down who paid for the funeral and burial expenses, but the funeral home that handled the arrangements is out of business.

Will was survived by his ex-wife Helen, who continued to pursue her education credentials, eventually earning a doctorate in education from Columbia University in the mid-1960s. According to Anne, Helen never approved of the way the family was portrayed in *The Seeking*. She had been a published writer herself, on the staff of the *California Eagle* newspaper when she met Will, and later in life she published several poems. It would have been intriguing to see what kind of book she and Will would have written together had they collaborated on *The Seeking*, as Will had originally intended.

Helen died of complications from colon cancer in October 1974. William Smith, Jr. (Bill) died in August 2010 after a long bout with Parkinson's. He was a retired high school guidance counselor, a career his mother had also followed after the family moved from Vermont. Bill is survived by his son Jesse (a journalist) and daughter Asha (a 2012 college graduate). Anne and Brad Smith remain alive and well. Anne is a retired professor at Golden Gate University in San Francisco, where for many years she taught arts administration. Brad owns a health food store in Orlando, Florida, and has three daughters: Dagny, Deena, and Paula. Paula had not yet been born when Will died.

Though Will Thomas Smith is long gone and largely forgotten, I remain haunted by his story. As a white man who came of age in Massachusetts in the late sixties and early seventies, Jim Crow America was a distant, abstract phenomenon, encountered here and there in memoirs, history textbooks, and documentary films. Although I had read many of the classics of mid-twentieth century African American literature—books by Wright, Ellison, Hurston, and even Smith's close friend Chester Himes—I never really felt that period come alive in any sort of visceral way until I read *The Seeking*. While I agree with my colleague Mark Madigan that it may not be a literary masterpiece, I believe it is an important testament to the soul-sucking brutality of that era, and that it should be required reading for Americans of all ages and races, but especially those too young to have any memories of this shameful period in our history, when thoughtful African Americans believed it better to escape to another country than to continue living in the land of their birth.

ACKNOWLEDGMENTS

Mark J. Madigan wishes to thank Lawrence Christon, Gerrie Denison, Prudence Doherty, Dan Gediman, J. Kevin Graffagnino, Stephen Hull, Amanda Madigan, Ned Madigan, Jeffrey Marshall, Christine Sisak, Bradley Smith, Anne Smith, and Richard Yarborough. He is grateful for a grant from the Center for Teaching Excellence and for reassigned time from the Dean of the College of Arts and Sciences at Nazareth College.

Dan Gediman wishes to thank Larry Chandler, Janet Franz, Frank Howrigan, Mark Madigan, Roland Pigeon, Anne Smith, Bradley Smith, and Jesse Smith for all their help in researching the life of Will Thomas. He would also like to thank his wife, Mary Jo, who gave him copies of *The Seeking* and *God Is for White Folks* and encouraged this entire pursuit, and his children Ben and Maggie, who tolerated years of dinnertime conversation about Will Thomas with great patience and love.

APPENDIX

The Birthright of Human Dignity
Will Thomas

as heard on Edward R. Murrow's *This I Believe* radio series, 1953

In 1946 I decided I did not wish to live in my native land any longer; and that I would take my wife and children to Haiti, where as Negroes in a Negro republic, we would be free of racial prejudice and our opportunities would be limited only by our ability to use them.

I do not believe I need detail the reasons behind this unhappy decision, except to say that being considered and treated as an inferior on every level of life can become intolerable, especially when it is by one's race rather than his individual worth, or lack of it, that he is pre-judged—and condemned.

When I reached this point, I had become an unbeliever in both God and country, for it seemed to me that racial segregation and all that it implied was as rigid on the spiritual as on the temporal plane. And so finally I made the decision to leave my native land—permanently.

However, I did not do it. Love of country, I found, can be very deep, very strong. So I thought to make one final try in my motherland for the equality of status which I considered I had been denied; and I chose Vermont for the experiment. I reasoned that because of its great traditions of personal freedom there was at least a chance that I and my family might find there what we so yearned for, and we did. In the small farming community where we settled, we were accepted on a basis of individuality unqualified by race.

301

However, it is not that which now seems most important to me. It is, rather, that in such a friendly atmosphere, and amid the quiet of a beautiful countryside, it was possible to think calmly, and gradually to gain understandings by which I believe I can live in peace with other men, and with myself, for the rest of my life.

One of these understandings is that unless one seeks sincerely for whatever it is he most wants, he surely will not find it, and that what I really had been seeking most of my life was not what I wanted but instead was justification for the resentments I felt. This is not to say there was not cause for those resentments, but rather that I had so concentrated upon them I could not see that the picture was not all bad—that in fact, there was considerable good in it.

I had condemned my country and my religion because I viewed only what seemed wrong in both. But when I was able to remove the blinds of my own prejudice, it became clear that these failures, these flaws in church and state, were human failures, human flaws, and not mere self-willed bigotry; and that within each there were, and there always had been, many who had worked and fought for what was right.

I think the core of my earlier bitterness had been the conviction that I had been denied my birthright of human dignity. But I know now that is something which cannot be given or taken away by man.

It has been written that he who seeks shall find, and that to him who asks, it shall be given. And I can only testify that when I did seek, I did find; and that when I asked, it was given to me. And I know that only the God I once denied could bestow such precious gifts.

BIBLIOGRAPHY OF WILL THOMAS

Compiled by Mark J. Madigan

This bibliography lists the known publications of Will Thomas and selected journalism published under variations of the name he used in private life, Bill Smith. Many of his shorter works were published in magazines under pseudonyms yet to be identified. This bibliography also includes all known articles about the author and his work.

Books

God Is for White Folks. New York: Creative Age Press, 1947.
Love Knows No Barriers. New York: New American Library, 1950. Revised version of *God Is for White Folks*.
The Seeking. New York: A. A. Wyn, 1953.

Shorter Works

"Hill to Climb." *The Crisis* 53 (June 1946): 173–174.
"God Is for White Folks" (novel excerpt). *Negro Digest* 6.1 (November 1947): 89–96.
"Negro Writers of Pulp Fiction." *Negro Digest* 8.9 (July 1950): 81–84.
"Vermont Man of God." *Negro Digest* 8.9 (July 1950): 14–18.
"Fighting Family of Vermont." *Negro Digest* 8.12 (October 1950): 27–30.
"The Birthright of Human Dignity." *This I Believe*, CBS, July 30, 1953. Published in *Edward R. Murrow's This I Believe: Selections from the 1950s Radio Series*, ed. Dan Gediman with John Gregory and Mary Jo Gediman. BookSurge Publishing, 2009: 156–158.

Selected Journalism in the *Chicago Defender*

Smith, Billy. "Critic Says 'Blackbirds' is Best of Musical Shows." (December 7, 1929): 6.

———. "George Moore Back in Ring Game in West." (December 21, 1940): 23.

———. "'Hallelujah' Draws Praise, Criticism, Condemnation; but Most People Admire It." (February 22, 1930): 7.

Smith, Billy K.C. "It's Sad, But It's True." (February 1, 1941): 8.

———. "Bar Carpenter in Wake Island Defense Work." (February 22, 1941): 7.

———. "Folk Incensed by Race Angle in Vice Raids." (March 1, 1941): 12.

———. "California State Guard Holds Its Initial Drill." (April 5, 1941): 13.

———. "Hollywood Turf Club Cannot Bar Negroes." (October 11, 1941): 22.

Smith, William T. "Roland Hayes Wins Belated Praise from South After World Calls Him 'Great.'" (March 15, 1930): 6.

Smith, William Thomas. "Joe Dunning Aircraft Engineer." (September 21, 1940): 13.

Reviews of *God Is for White Folks*

Anonymous. *Burlington Free Press* (November 1, 1947): 7.

———. *New Yorker* 23 (September 27, 1947): 112.

———. "Racial Novel by a Former Kansas Citian." *Kansas City Star* (December 6, 1947): 6.

Bolman, H. P. *Library Journal* 72 (August 1947): 1110.

Borland, Hal. *New York Times* (October 5, 1947): 32.

C. G. W. "Westford Resident Writes Moving Novel of Those Born Part-White, Part-Black," *Burlington Daily News* (October 14, 1947): B6.

Feld, Rose. *New York Herald Tribune Weekly Book Review* (October 19, 1947): 24.

P.S. *San Francisco Chronicle* (January 11, 1948): 16.

Reeves, Elizabeth W. *Journal of Negro Education* 17.2 (1948): 167–168.

Rothman, Nathan L. "Invisible Man." *Saturday Review of Literature* 30 (October 4, 1947): 20.

Reviews of *The Seeking*

Anonymous. "Book of the Week." *Jet* 4.5 (June 11, 1953): 38.

———. *Kirkus* 21 (April 15, 1953): 281.

Dodson, Owen. "But Not Transformed." 129.12 *New Republic* (July 27, 1953): 21.

E. B. *San Francisco Chronicle* (August 23, 1953): 17.

Fuller, Edmund. *Chicago Sunday Tribune* (June 21, 1953): 12.

Gebo, Dora Reynolds. *Journal of Negro History* 38.3 (July 1953): 353–355.

Smith, Bradford. "Experiment in Democracy in a Northern Vermont Town." *New York Herald Tribune Book Review* (June 7, 1953): 3.

Walbridge, Earle F. *Library Journal* 78 (May 1, 1953): 809.

Yates, Elizabeth. "To the Honor of Vermont." *Christian Science Monitor* (June 11, 1953): 11.